The Limits of Transnationalism

The Limits of Transnationalism

Collective Identities and EU Integration

Markus Thiel

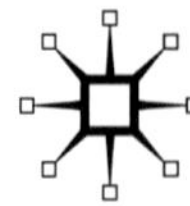

THE LIMITS OF TRANSNATIONALISM

First published in 2011 by
PALGRAVE MACMILLAN®
in the United States—a division of St. Martin's Press LLC,
175 Fifth Avenue, New York, NY 10010.

Where this book is distributed in the UK, Europe and the rest of the world, this is by Palgrave Macmillan, a division of Macmillan Publishers Limited, registered in England, company number 785998, of Houndmills, Basingstoke, Hampshire RG21 6XS.

Palgrave Macmillan is the global academic imprint of the above companies and has companies and representatives throughout the world.

Palgrave® and Macmillan® are registered trademarks in the United States, the United Kingdom, Europe and other countries.

ISBN: 978–0–230–11136–3

Library of Congress Cataloging-in-Publication Data

Thiel, Markus, 1973–
The Limits of Transnationalism : Collective Identities and EU Integration / Markus Thiel.
p. cm.
Includes bibliographical references.
ISBN 978–0–230–11136–3 (hardback)
1. European federation—Public opinion. 2. Group identity—European Union countries—Public opinion. 3. European Union—Public opinion. 4. Public opinion—European Union countries. I. Title.

JN15.T47 2011
341.242′2—dc22 2010044605

A catalogue record of the book is available from the British Library.

Design by Newgen Imaging Systems (P) Ltd., Chennai, India.

First edition: May 2011

10 9 8 7 6 5 4 3 2 1

Printed in the United States of America.

Contents

Illustrations

Tables

Figures

Preface

This book's cover, showing a stele commemorating the Maastricht Treaty, could in many ways be interpreted as a gravestone as much as a celebratory marker; despite the treaty's wide-ranging political implications, the effects on transnational identity creation were limited and its three pillar structure has been laid to rest with the superseding Lisbon Treaty. Based on post-Maastricht integration, this book has been the result of a long-term interest in issues of identity, transnational politics, and, resulting from my German background, an ambiguous fascination with nationalism. Recognizing that there is more to politics than what is expressed at the polling stations, through governmental decision making or purely domestic considerations, this book is an attempt at deciphering the complex interrelationships between domestic societies, national political cultures, and EU integration policies. The chosen observation span covers the years 1993–2005, which experienced the completion of the single market, the implementation of the euro currency, the establishment of the Common Foreign & Security Policy, and a constitutional debate that ultimately fell with the its public rejection in France and the Netherlands in 2005. The repercussions of these measures on the larger European public are the central focus of this work. Collective political identities are a complex subject, so this work attempts to provide approximate determinants through the application of multiple methods in specific domestic contexts. Despite the somewhat sobering results, it is my hope that EU leaders and the wider public will utilize the unique transnational opportunities that evolve through policy integration, critical junctures, and structural shifts, rather than to regress into an isolated form of Eurocentrism.

This publication would not have been possible without the help of so many friends and colleagues. A special thanks goes to Lisa Prügl, Roger Kanet, Joaquin Roy, Martin Schain, and Louise Davidson-Schmich. The Florida-Miami EU Center of Excellence at both the University of Miami and Florida International University (FIU) thankfully provided financial and institutional support, in addition to the departmental support received through colleagues and coworkers at FIU's Department of Politics and International Relations. My gratitude goes also to the dedicated editors at Palgrave, Robyn Curtis and Farideh Koohi-Kamali, and the supplier for the cover image, Alberto Tobias.

Lastly, I'd like to dedicate this book to my father, who passed away too early.

Chapter 1

Introduction

The consolidation of the European Union (EU), a deliberate attempt to integrate European states—among them many former enemies—into an intricate network of common trade, social, cultural, and other policies, represents one of the most important geopolitical events of the twentieth century. Starting out as a predominantly economic organization resulting from the aftermath of the Second World War, over the years the Union's institutions received significant political powers from its member states and in turn created a supranational model of governance for Europeans. As a result, EU citizens today have many commonalities: a political economy in which state and market closely interact, a cultural tradition that acknowledges common historical determinants, border-crossing governance institutions, a broad humanist philosophy, and a tradition of generally accepted welfare politics.

Constructed upon these cooperative features, the emergence of transnational cohesiveness and solidarity in the form of some sort of a common European identity is often postulated in public spheres and academic circles (Delanty, 1996; Habermas, 2001; Hermann et al., 2004; Katzenstein and Checkel, 2009). However, despite ongoing deepening of joint policies, widening in membership, and convergence in institutions, a remarkable dichotomy has become visible between the acceleration of European integrative measures, most notably through the Maastricht Treaty provisions creating a political Union in 1993, and a contradictory resurgence of nationalist and outright Euro-skeptic attitudes. While the EU attempts to push ahead with economic and political integration, developments such as the derailing of the Union's constitutionalization process, the heated discussion over the accession of Turkey, the disunity during the Iraq war, or the blame shifting resulting from the eurozone crisis are evidence of the volatile political standing of the Union in the member states. Thus, the question arises, what effects have European integration had on the collective identities of Europeans?

Much of the literature in the social sciences calls the object of this inquiry, for lack of a better term, "European identity." While research about the existence of some form of pan-European identity, based on historical, political, and other commonalities, exists in abundance, there is no consensus about its meaning or content, with some viewing it as a culturally based attachment and others allowing for an instrumental or civic component as well (see Chapter 2). I propose using the term "transnational" identity instead, as it is more exact in its description of an identity extension involving boundary-crossing relations and actors (Keohane and Nye, 1971) to a certain degree, rather than the suggestive completeness of European integration implied in the term "European identity." Supranationality, in contrast, implies the existence of hierarchical relationships among social actors. Transnational relations also involve various types of nonstate actors and discourses (Hurrelmann, 2009, Thiel, 2009, Risse, 1995), which are reflected here in the examination of the press discourse (see Chapter 6) as well as other nonstate agents (Chapter 3). Transnational agents are, according to most definitions, nongovernmental actors, which thus are distinct from the government-steered integration institutions in the EU. Yet, the EU created, by way of its policies, a transnational political space in the Union (Kaiser and Starie, 2005), and the acquisition of such a complementary identity can be traced to the realms of elite and mass publics, influenced by a variety of societal agents such as media outlets, nongovernmental organizations, and other civil society actors (Wessler et al., 2008). Transnationalism, then, can be distinguished according to its agent-based procedural character as well as its constituent characteristics, and thus the term provides us with a more succinct description of the research object in terms of process and shape. While this book concentrates on the social representations of transnationalism in identitive terms, it adds to the underresearched topic of the EU as a transnational polity as well.

In its attempt to qualify such developments among the European citizenry, this work draws heavily on responses toward EU policy implementation of the 1990s. Based on the coinciding realization of the single market in 1992, further common policies agreed upon in the Maastricht Intergovernmental Conferences (IGC) include, among others, the European Monetary Union with the euro as currency, the introduction of a common foreign and security policy, and the creation of a political union, which eventually led to the development of a draft constitution (Duff, 1994). Formally known as the Treaty on European Union, the Maastricht Treaty was designed as a realization of an "ever closer Union among the peoples of Europe" (TEU 2006, Preamble) and replaced the European Economic Community with the three-pillar structure separating economic, foreign, and home affairs in the EU. Thus, the treaty not only fundamentally changed the configuration of political cooperation of the member states, but also added significant integration goals for years to come, thereby in effect establishing a critical juncture in the development of European integration from a customs union toward a political one (Ross, 1995). Newer research has picked up on such junctures as particularly pronounced challenges to existing identities (Risse, 2010). The completion of the single market, the implementation of the economic and monetary union, and the addition of a common defense identity stood beside other goals such as the strengthening of a largely nominal European citizenship; voluntary collaboration in the newly created homeland security sector, "Justice and Home Affairs"; and additional objectives intended to forge a more strongly integrated political Europe.

Reminiscent of the recent constitutional period, a treaty with so many wide-reaching implications evoked a substantial level of discussion across Europe and, in some cases, considerable protest in the early 1990s. Not only traditionally Euro-skeptic countries worried about their national autonomy, as the difficult treaty ratification process, including the close French referendum and the Danish rejection in 1992, has shown. Politicians and academics alike noted the increasingly popular discontent and the drop in support for European integration, aptly titled "post-Maastricht blues" (Eichenberg, 2003). Previously, policy making in the EU had limited impact on the daily lives of the citizens, therefore no real debate about Brussels politics in public spheres and media discourses occurred. But through the politicization of EU policies and treaties in the past decade and a half, this permissive consensus has given way to a "constraining dissensus" (Hooghe and Marks, 2006), indicating a more contentious form of national as well as transnational engagement by multiple actors in the Union.

The debacle surrounding the Maastricht Treaty's implications and ratifications led to a rapid decline in public trust immediately thereafter, and was viewed by some theorists as a sign of continuously augmented disenchantment with the EU more generally, however without noticing that in a long-term perspective, public opinion values in the late 1990s recovered again. Aggregate data, then, supply us with a range of attitudinal values, which in this work will be further discerned through qualitative explorations of individual views and surrounding media discourses so as to be differentiated according to the compatibility of national political cultures with the goals of overall EU integration.

While some scholars explain populist and nationalist reactions as resulting from the perceived loss of sovereignty (Smith, 1992), others contest this view, pointing to globalization and specifically, Europeanization, of the EU member states and its citizens' identities (Risse, 2010; Cowles et al., 2001). Such transformations, in turn, produced an increasing demand for legitimacy of European integration policies (DeBardeleben and Hurrelmann, 2007). Following this paradoxical logic, several questions arise: Has the at times conflicting integration process advanced transnational identification with the EU, in addition to existing national, regional, and local identities, or has it led to increased protective nationalism? Can a transnational political identity be located in the realms of public opinion and mass media of EU member states? Is there an "identity spillover" evolving that can be attributed to a combination of neofunctionalist processes of integration, based on cultural commonalities and informed by path-dependent consensus of citizens to EU policies? Finally, is the future of the Union dependent on a certain degree of cohesiveness to retain common reference points as well as popular support?

The case studies of the United Kingdom (UK), Ireland, and Germany show how integrative politics, their communication, and reception have not only produced popular counterreactions in some member states, but more important, have also contributed significantly to a debate about European integration, thereby changing the sociopolitical identitive positioning of citizens toward their nation and extending it toward the EU. This process, in turn, necessitates a reflection on the extent to which the EU polity can branch out without being torn apart by conflicting interests and identities.

The research conducted for this book bears evidence that significant parts of the population of some states have indeed developed a form of protective nationalism, as in the case of the UK, while others have strengthened their transnational identification—however, only to the extent that national political cultures are compatible with EU integration and fellow citizens are considered "European"—as occurred in Germany and Ireland. To clarify, in addition to instrumental support aiming predominantly at the material benefits of membership, a transnational identification with the EU based on a pan-European cultural identity reflects the tension with preexisting national identities, as applied in the theoretical framework of this book (see Chapter 2). The remaining sections of this chapter present four research statements addressing the complex relationship between collective identities and EU integration, then conceptualize the measured variables and qualify the case studies. Lastly, the political and academic relevance of this endeavor is highlighted and the following chapters are previewed.

Four Hypotheses Regarding Europe's Transnationalism

Early studies of the impact of European integration on its citizens followed initially a neofunctional or intergovernmental line of investigation favoring either a projected incremental gain in supranational power of the EU or a static, government-steered rejection of such repercussions. More recently these assumptions matured to constructivist explorations recognizing the social structure and role of ideas, interests, and identities. Such constructivist research developed into a continuously expanding field over the past decade, consisting of three major avenues: counting identities, exploring the impact of identity politics, and analyzing the EU's "selling" of identities (Trenz, 2009). The hypotheses spelled out below touch on all three of these implications and thus produce more robust knowledge advancing the research on transnational European identities beyond simply attesting or contesting its existence. While the first three locate the current status quo of transnational identities in the case countries through empirical methods, the last hypothesis spells out important ramifications for the future configuration of EU policies:

H1: For the majority of EU citizens, EU integration is not perceived as a threat to national identity.

Public disaffection with the EU often leads to a viewpoint claiming national identities under threat from European integration—a suggestion coming mainly from opponents of the project. The first hypothesis thus postulates that EU integration is not perceived as a threat to the majority of EU citizens. While there may be parts of the population in various member states who feel that the augmented interference in domestic politics is detrimental to national culture and identity, in particular where fundamental policies such as currency or the military are concerned, the majority of EU citizens do not suspect that Brussels endangers the existence of their national identity.

In the following analyses, I therefore assume that in the EU's survey instrument, Eurobarometer, which reports on the meaning of the EU for its citizens, the "fear of losing national identity" will not be an important issue, nor will there be a significant increase in people perceiving their national identity as under threat. Furthermore, in the interview chapter, no indication is given that national identity is perceived as under siege by European integration. This should also be reflected in the media discourse of the case countries, with the likely exception of the UK, included as an outlier case in this study. Citizens in the EU naturally relate more closely to their national identity than to their supranational European one. However, this fact should not be conflated with an emerging reactive nationalism sweeping through Europe.

H2: Post-Maastricht measures, however, did not contribute significantly to a transnational identity in the EU, as EU policy implementation interacts varyingly with and is conditioned upon national political cultures and domestic discourses, resulting in either bounded transnationalism or protective nationalism.

This research statement holds that recent European integration, while having had an identity-altering effect on the collective identities of most EU citizens, did not produce a significantly increased degree of transnational identification with the EU. The Union's augmented political and regulatory activity, depending on the domestic reception in each case, resulted either in extended transnationalism or protective nationalism. The research design, based on time series observation, interviews, and print media analyses, enables one to explore how integrative measures in the Union changed the way people feel about their civic-political identity and how they connect it with the wider European cultural one. Few researchers have actually analyzed this process in a comprehensive manner, combining mixed analysis methods (Díez-Medrano, 2003).

The empirics employed here intend to show that functional integration, which is deemed to be as important for influencing collective transnational identification as endogenous cultural and/or external structural factors, has not produced a cohesive, unifying identity. The following chapters present evidence of the existence of varying degrees of transnational identification, colored by national sociocultural lenses. The variance in the results, then, does not allow for a conclusive statement about the congruent evolution of a pan-European identity based on integration policies. With regard to this hypothesis, I therefore expect dissimilar results in the three case countries displaying divergent support levels for policies as well as for European transnationalism. The former represent the independent policy variables, while the latter stands for the dependent, evolving one. The assumption put forth is that in countries such as Germany or Ireland, the data will show a limited degree of transnational attitudes as expressed in Eurobarometer data, the interviews, or the print coverage (what I term "bounded transnationalism"), while the British sample will not contain such favorable results ("protective nationalism").

More specifically, I propose that the support values and the extent of feeling European do not necessarily converge in all three case countries; rather, each individual state reacts to the introduction of integration policies primarily in line with its "sticky" national identity as well as its publicly deliberated expectations, norms, and attitudes—the domestic political culture—and only partially overlaps with other EU member states to the extent that the goals of integration are compatible with said culture and identity. Research has shown that questions of identity and legitimacy are essential in assessing political cultures of political systems (Majone, 2009), that a public culture discursively resonates with shared inclinations and sensibilities (Wessler, 2008), and that identification with Europe is in large part dependent on the national context as an extension of its historically and domestically assumed role, and thus not one European, but many national European identities exist in EU member states (Diez-Medrano, 2003; Caporaso, Cowles, and Risse, 2001). The covariational relationship is changing, however, in that the EU as a policy actor gained importance in relation to the citizens over the past years. As a result, domestic discourse in national public spheres, most visibly in the mass media, increasingly becomes Europeanized and thus, depending on the context in which the EU is perceived, either becomes less colored by previously existing viewpoints or, as a counterreaction, intensifies its projection of protective nationalist ambitions.

A further examination will focus on the question of how much identification with the EU is dependent on the constituent national characteristics expressed by history, elites, and nonstate actors, etc. Chapter 3 details the national experiences of the sample countries as they play out in the historical processes of national-identity formation and European integration. Less rigid than national culture, domestic media discourse across EU member states tends to converge slowly as a result of EU structural activity and other leveling factors, such as interdependence or common threat assessments in the international system. Evidence of this change in media portrayal can be found in the print analysis chapter, which observes the changing discourse of the press over the observation period 1993 to 2005.

H3: (Print) media influences public opinion and thus reflects as well as constructs people's identification with the EU—to the extent that national culture and discourse allow it.

Of all the instruments of nation building available, such as education, military conscription, or the use of different media, print media traditionally had the most significant impact upon the domestic development of public opinion (Anderson, 1991), along with television and radio programs joining in at a later time. The latter catalysts are conspicuously absent in European integration affairs, thus leaving EU portrayal largely to the member-state governments and the publishing houses. Public opinion is constituted by and manipulated through the information that is conveyed to the public. The way in which major newspapers frame and instrumentalize the EU shapes the attitudes of opinion makers and ordinary citizens alike, and thus contributes to a positive or rather negative stance toward belonging to the EU. In view of the extensive publishing markets in Europe, scholars have stated that "we find our information, and form our opinions, by consulting, using and interacting with one of the most sophisticated systems of communications in the world" (Anderson and Weymouth, 1999: 2). Those information channels represented through the mass media not only reflect public thought, but also set new agendas and may change the thematic frame from nationally restricted identities to expansive transnational perceptions (Bruter, 2005).

Tied to the communication model described above and expanded in the print analysis in Chapter 6 is the argument that a rudimentary European public sphere is emerging, whose salience in EU matters increases on a domestic level while simultaneously establishing a common frame of reference on a transnational level (Risse, 2010). Systems theory, a useful tool in the field of communication research, calls the process of action and reaction, of sending and receiving the "feedback loop," referring to the reactions of the mass public to framed political events, which then influence the orientations of the acting elites and, if passed on, of the general public. Therefore, the inclusion of print media content analysis is deemed sensible and feasible for the research of identity-formation processes, particularly as market-dominating newspapers that are widely read and discussed in the case countries are chosen.

A comparison of the themes mentioned as EU priorities in the in-depth interviews with the ones articulated in the press and the Eurobarometer data makes the reciprocity and congruence of this discourse apparent, as asserted by Díez-Medrano: "The existence of a permanent dialogue between journalists and the rest of the population with respect to European integration is reflected in the strong similarity between their images of European integration and European institutions" (Díez-Medrano, 2003: 110). Specific national perceptions will be taken into account, but instead of examining how an individual's characteristics correspond to a view on European integration—this aspect has been researched sufficiently in the field—I will concentrate on the importance that collectives and discourses in different domestic cultures attribute to post-Maastricht policies. Exploring how societies frame European integration and how "Europe" is represented through social agents, such as politicians or the media, provides researchers with a new understanding for international differences, e.g., why relatively similar countries like Germany and the UK, with respect to size and socioeconomic structure, show significantly different levels of support (Díez-Medrano, 2003). In the print media analysis, the treatment of EU issues as represented in the four integration variables in national press organs is examined, and then similarities and differences in timing and content of these affairs are noted. If the hypothesis is true that a convergence of views about the EU plays out differently in the member states based upon national culture and media discourse, I expect different degrees of transnational identity reflected in the treatment of the EU. Conclusively, qualitatively improved or deteriorated coverage of the EU parallel to the development of public opinion in the individual member states should be detectable, as well as a possible synchronicity of topic treatments across countries.

H4: In the post-Maastricht era, many EU citizens support a particularistic and possibly exclusionary conception of European transnationalism as compared to a universalistic, inclusive one.

In parts of the academic literature and in actual EU policy implementation, a rather particularistic notion of being European is advanced based on common policies, joint legal instruments, and particular socioeconomic as well as historical circumstances. At the same time, as described in the next chapter, many social theorists call for a more inclusive and universalistic, cosmopolitan conception of Europeanness to avoid a hypernationalistic "Fortress Europe." This hypothesis supports the view that a potentially exclusionary form of transnational identity is evolving in line with sociopsychological explanations and an EU identity construction of a particularistic European kind based on common political and cultural references.

The results of the analyses contain evidence that, in fact, the concept of a European identity evolves from the EU's cultural references to Europe and the homogenizing effects of EU integration policies. Thus, I anticipate respondents in the interviews to express particularistic ethnocentric statements when asked about the relationship among Europeans and between Europeans and non-Europeans that point to common (cultural) characteristics rather than to a belonging based upon attainment of civic values or adherence to common policies. In addition, a validation of this hypothesis should be reflected in the press coverage of the case countries, ranging from topics such as immigration to the discussion of enlargement candidates and, more generally, the treatment of EU affairs in a unitary manner. Depending on the extent of civic identity existing in the three countries, the treatment of these issues will indicate an exclusionary conception of European identity. The concluding chapter, then, notes the repercussions stemming from these results and cautions against idealistic expectations for European transnational identification.

How to Measure Identities? The Main Variables Operationalized

The Dependent Variable

As the overall aim of this work is to explore the emergence of various forms of transnational collective identification, this referent object will be the dependent variable. Studies on the existence of a common sociohistorical heritage and a corresponding cultural pan-European identity have been conducted exhaustively, often with an interdisciplinary and static focus. The next chapter makes evident the need for further research into the relatively novel procedural aspects of transnational identification as initiated by EU integration policies. Until now only few researchers, such as Richard Herrmann, Thomas Risse, and Michael Bruter (Herrmann et al., 2005; Bruter, 2003), have advanced research on the civic component of such an identity. Considering the complex characteristics of identitive constructs and the ambiguous part that the EU as transmitter of this collective identity plays—in creating a pan-European one as well as fostering national (counter)narratives—the relatively short existence of the Union compared to the long history of European nation states makes this research topic challenging but timely.

As defined more specifically in the following theoretical chapter, civic aspects as part of a transnational European identification are based upon the citizen's allegiance to democratic institutions and a system of rights and rules provided through EU as well as national governance. It should be distinguished from a cultural pan-European identity, which is largely based on historical-cultural commonalities and a shared heritage of common experiences and contacts. For the purpose of this project, then, a European transnational identity as a dependent variable needs to be purposefully operationalized in the research design. In the Eurobarometer analyses, it will be measured quantitatively as the percentage of people claiming to feel European to some extent (in the so-called Moreno scale question juxtaposing it to national allegiance), hence reflecting diffuse support and identification with the EU. Coming from a secondary data source, the chosen indicator is investigated by the EU's Eurobarometer survey, thereby establishing a fundamental cognitive link between the Union and the citizen's perception of a "European" identity. It is also the best possible indicator among various Eurobarometer questions pertaining to this topic, as others, for instance, simply probe the utility of membership. In the qualitative interview chapter, the dependent variable is operationalized as an open-ended response to a question about the participant's transnational identity and how this identity relates to their domestic one, reflecting the affective support patterns of the sample. Furthermore, respondents are asked about the meaning of specific integration policies for their national and regional identity (see the methodological overview below).

In the print media analyses, the topic of European transnationalism will be circumscribed by a quantitative classification of the analyzed press articles, as well as through descriptive content analysis. The positive, negative, or balanced treatment of the concept of "European" identity is used as reflective evidence, in particular where it relates to issues of EU governance and integration policies. In addition, the relative occurrence of this issue in annual coverage serves as quantitative indicator for the existence of such an identity in the national public spheres.

The Four Independent Variables

In the search for the most decisive integrative features of the recent past, I found that the following four measures were not only the most prominent ones with respect to the findings, but they are also anchored in the preeminent Treaty on European Union. The constitutional draft, even though not directly related to the treaty itself, was nevertheless initiated by the establishment of the political Union at Maastricht, and the discussion in the literature about the need for such a constitutional project increased tremendously during the years following the completion of the market.

Single Market

In the past, economic integration was not connected to questions of identity formation. Interestingly, though, it is generally assumed that citizen support for the Union is partially based on instrumentalist approval, which in turn has its origins in the structural conditions created by EU institutions. In this respect, economic and monetary policies are indeed identity-building factors.

The common or single market was enacted on paper in 1986 with the ratification of the Single European Act, but it took until 1992 to remove major political, economic, and logistical barriers. The harmonization of the diverse nationally protected markets of the member states presented an additional challenge. Since its establishment, the single market has increased the exchange of goods, services, capital, and people, stimulating free trade within the EU and shielding member states from the pressures of globalization (European Commission, 2005). Seen from a national point of view by looking at the opening of the service markets, the harmonization of trade laws or from the standpoint of the consumer, who is provided with cheaper products and a wider choice, the single market has proven effective under an externally protectionist EU economic policy.

This major integration step is in line with the expectations of the European public. "Nowadays, however, while the citizenry of the EU may disagree with some of the political aspects of European unification, it is almost unanimous in believing in this basic tenet of economic liberalism" (Díez-Medrano, 2003: 27). This statement, as positive as it seemed at the time, neglects the fact that especially with the removal of national trade barriers and the enlargement to Central and Eastern Europe, increased labor and product competition has led to a more critical view of common market policies, compounded by the recent global recession—and in certain cases to intra-EU protectionist labor movement laws, as installed, for example, in Germany. In contrast, Ireland and the UK did not restrict the movement of workers from the new member states and experienced a sizeable influx of migrants from those states. In sum, the single market started out as a nonpolitical project, but has become more contentious over time.

The Euro

Since its inception, the euro as a transmitter of identity has been hotly debated in the academic landscape and has received lots of media attention. As a bearer of pecuniary identity, the introduction of a common currency was without doubt one of the most daunting projects from a theoretical, political, and logistical perspective. The replacement of national currencies with a common European one was unthought of since currencies were an important part of a country's national identity. In all three cases, the national currencies were regarded in high esteem, and particularly cherished in Germany and the UK, the latter still remaining outside the common currency scheme.

In addition, the introduction of a currency had historically followed the creation of a state. The EU for the first time reversed this process by introducing a single currency for its members before establishing a state-like overarching structure, as was planned with the failed constitutional treaty. It was able to do this mainly because of its emphasis on the economic necessity to remove transaction costs and price differences among the member states. The euro as the single currency of currently in sixteen of the EU member states represents perhaps the most important factor for the unification of Europe and is increasingly recognized by political scientists as a major step toward transnational identity formation (Risse, 2003; Kaelberer, 2004). Sharing a common currency constituted one of the defining factors establishing modern national states, and as such, the euro might be the most decisive and tangible instrument in achieving more commonality among citizens of the EU. "The Euro could serve as a (cognitive) equalizer that enhances the feeling of unity, enabling people across Europe to compare wages and prices, pensions and savings, thus promoting intra-regional conversations about the basic elements of everyday life. Money alone will certainly not establish a European identity, but it will foster its development" (Cerruti, 2001: 13). Under rules established at Maastricht, a country must demonstrate price stability, keep its government finances sustainable in terms of both low public deficit and debt, and maintain a stable exchange rate and convergence in long-term interest rates in order for it to qualify for eurozone membership. Current eurozone member-state governments, including Germany, Ireland, and, most infamously, Greece, however, do not always keep in line with the fiscal conditions set upon them. The response to the euro as an integrative instrument will be of particular interest when focusing on the UK as a non-euro country, but with some domestic discussions about its introduction. Since the introduction of the European Monetary System and, in particular, the adoption of a common currency starting in 1999, the UK, along with other member states such as Denmark and Sweden, displays continued resistance to the idea of relinquishing the national currency. A considerable amount of domestic debate about the euro has led to the British government researching the feasibility of adopting the euro, with the preliminary result that the five tests set out for adoption of the single currency are not yet fully accomplished. At the time of the interviews in the summer of 2004, the level of public debate of this question was quite palpable. The inclusion of the UK in this analysis thus serves as a test case to explore the significance of identity-shaping factors such as currency. In the justification for the chosen case studies below, this aspect of the dissimilar design will be expanded upon.

The Common Foreign and Security Policy (CFSP)

The ongoing construction of the CFSP as well as the constitutionalization process present the challenge of evaluating policies that are not quite as tangible as the former ones. For one, both constitute policies that are further removed from the daily experience of the ordinary citizen than are currency and market policies, and secondly, both are still in the process of being calibrated to fit an increasingly diverse polity. However, like pecuniary affairs, measures affecting defense and constitutional matters are highly sensitive to and influential in creating national identity (Tilly, 1975).

The institutionalized foreign policy of the EU under the CFSP experienced dramatic changes since its inception in the Maastricht Treaty. Before, a loose European Political Cooperation served as a weak instrument for exclusively European action in security and defense matters. To foster the Union's external capabilities, the CFSP encompasses the Common Security and Defense Policy (CSDP) – the former European Security and Defense Policy (ESDP) – including common positions, actions, plans for an independent military force, etc. (Duff, 1994). Despite these provisions, this policy sector was notoriously underfunded and lacked a cohesive common strategy, as well as effective decision-making less reliant on unanimity—something the Lisbon Treaty aims to ameliorate. On the other hand, just as the Gulf War in 1991 changed European perceptions in search for more unity and, thus, a common foreign policy, the terrorist attacks of September 11, 2001, and the U.S.-led invasion of Iraq, together with the rise of nonstate terrorist threats, have initiated a stronger commitment to shared decision making in such matters in the intergovernmental second pillar. The call for a common foreign minister in the constitutional treaty was only one example of the perceived need to strengthen the external identity of the Union, and even the substitute Lisbon Treaty, now ratified, expands the role of the CFSP High Representative, creating a de facto EU foreign minister position currently occupied by Catherine Ashton from the UK. Without the groundwork laid in Maastricht's second pillar, the current institutionalization of the EU's foreign policy would have been impossible.

The Constitution for Europe

In contrast to the CFSP, a different picture emerges for the EU's constitutionalization process. During the constitutional convention of 2001–2003, the disagreement among major member-state governments regarding the rules and the allocation of votes in the Council, as well as other issues, significantly slowed down progress on the concluding negotiations of the draft constitution and produced irritations among a number of member-state governments. To make matters worse, the ratification process has been stopped indeterminately after its popular rejection in France and the Netherlands in 2005, and thus the constitutional project has been abolished for now. In its place, the refashioned Lisbon Treaty is poised to stimulate discussion in the public spheres even more as it created leadership positions and a more defined external profile for the EU. Plans for a post-national constitution had been contemplated for a while by political theorists and philosophers such as Habermas (2001), but only in the late 1990s was the need to reform and frame the existing institutions and policies under one legal document officially recognized. The Laeken Declaration of the European Council in December 2001 was borne out of acknowledgment that with all of the established integration measures and the enhanced involvement of the EU in national politics, a more democratically legitimate as well as accountable Union was required. The relevance of constitutionalism in view of the future of European integration is particularly obvious in cases where single states still act outside a common EU position or where disagreement over a common position leads to serious polarizations within the EU. After the reference to a federal Union disappeared in the draft, which was eventually rejected, and provisions for national autonomy in many areas still exist in the Lisbon Treaty, the discussion among political scientists about the progress and finality in either intergovernmental or supranational fashion will continue, as the concluding chapter points out. This bifurcation is somewhat reflected in the countries' transnational stances, as I'll point out in Chapter 7.

One of the concepts introduced at Maastricht, but left out as a determining variable, is "EU citizenship." While a conceptualization of citizenship is theoretically connected to issues of identity (InTune Project, 2007), for a variety of reasons the variable is problematic for an empirical investigation. First, as a "complementary" citizenship, it is based on a priori possession of national citizenship and thus it cannot be explored as an independent variable, nor did it add substantially to policy initiation or polity building. Secondly, it did not influence public opinion formation and identity formation (Kraus, 2008), aside from debates among a few academic and political elites, so there is little use in including it as such at this time. In fact, when the topic of citizenship appeared tangentially in the interviews, respondents were not aware of the concept, nor did it appear in significant numbers in the topical print analysis (see Chapter 6). This may, however, change once the privileges of transnational citizenship become more relevant to EU citizens and accessible to noncitizens.

Justification for the Case Studies Chosen

The countries chosen represent various stages of EU integration in the post-Maastricht period and thus mirror the impact of the EU on its citizens' identities over time. While this procedure should account for validity in the interviews and the press analysis, it will be accompanied by analyzed Eurobarometer data to ensure some degree of generalizability.

To receive a variety of responses, in a dissimilar design I conducted one-third of those interviews in one large founding constituent state (Germany, member since 1951), one-third in a small member state (Ireland, member since 1973), and one-third in a state with only partial implementation of major EU policies (UK, member since 1973). Those countries also display a significant variation in public support for European integration and transnationalism: While Germany has been a staunch supporter of ongoing integration and levels of mass support are comparatively high, the UK contrasts in that it is a rather Euro-skeptic state with levels of knowledge and support among the population being relatively low, and Ireland finding itself somewhere in between. Member states from Central and Eastern Europe were not included, as their accession in 2004 and 2007 precluded them from experiencing the Maastricht provisions over a prolonged period of time. In using a most-different system design, the case should be made that the same independent variables provided by European integration will have a varying impact on the civic European identity, thereby constraining the explanatory impact of integration policies. The choice for those countries might also serve to refute the so-called Euro-skeptic mentality generally assumed of non-continental nations by presenting differing perceptions of the EU in the UK as well as in Ireland. The following section presents some country-specific arguments in the choice of case studies. More information on the three states will be provided in Chapter 3, which explores these cases from a historical-institutionalist perspective.

Germany is an exceptional case in many ways; its historical development is unique, from its imperialist-nationalist ambitions in the latter half of the nineteenth century and the first half of the twentieth century to the staunchly pro-European state of today. Following reunification, Germany is only slowly coming to terms with its responsibility and international role as well as its own national identity. In addition, the country contains a diverse and important media landscape. The print media market is especially active and public discourse is influenced significantly by it, compared to the less saturated cases of Ireland and the UK.

On the other hand, the UK "excels" through its continued resistance to any attempts of further supranational integration. It is also one of the countries with the lowest knowledge and support levels in the citizenry, as reported by Eurobarometer and other sources. Its historical role of a world empire in the second half of the last millennium as well as its geopolitical setting as an island nation explain some of the Euro-skepticism that is prevalent there. One of the most interesting tasks of this chapter will be to show that in this problematic environment, traits of the transnational impact of EU policies have actually increased negative connotations to the Union. There are links to both other cases, in that it is geopolitically seen as an island on the edge of Europe, like Ireland, and as one of the few big and politically decisive EU member states, just as Germany is.

The Republic of Ireland differs from other comparable nations for many reasons: It is the only small case sample among the chosen cases, and it shows a remarkable and unique balance of strong national identity as well as attachment to the EU. It also has a special relationship with the UK, which makes for an interesting comparison considering the common history both countries possess. After becoming a member state of the EU, Ireland succeeded in using EU structural development funds to modernize and subsequently attract large foreign investment. The Republic of Ireland possesses a well-developed democracy marked by popular referenda, which have become a hindrance in the ratification process of EU treaties and served as volatile catalysts for (trans)national discussions. These aspects explain identification with the EU to some degree, but could just as much result in increased national chauvinism, which is why the interview analysis is important here. Finally, throughout Ireland's history, there has been a continued strong presence of the Catholic Church, which was fundamental in establishing its current societal and governmental structure, providing Ireland with a special outlook, in comparison to the secularized cases of the UK and Germany.

Methodological Tools

A treatment of multifaceted macrolevel variables, such as national and transnational identities, necessitates a comprehensive methodological approach. Therefore, the research strategy applies quantitative and qualitative data analysis in a mixed methodology, using both analytical techniques and interpreting the results in an integrated manner (Tashakkori and Charles, 1998). Here, the aggregate data used in the temporal analysis of Eurobarometer prepare the background for the qualitative, ethnographic interviews and the content analysis, which provide in-depth information on the specific identitive changes and the surrounding discourses. This methodology mix is proposed in order to pay sufficient attention to the cultural context of the individual experience as explored in the interviews, as well as to collective representations of identity formation provided by aggregate numbers and mass media analyses. In the following section, three different approaches operationalize the proposed research design.

Eurobarometer Analysis

For research on individuals on a nationwide level, it is very difficult to come up with self-collected data. For a variety of socioeconomic and other variables, there are suitable secondary sources readily available in the EU member states. Therefore, the research incorporates Eurobarometer statistics, cross-nationally collected data by the European Commission conducted several times a year along a broad range of topics, such as the institutions or policies of the European Union. The Eurobarometer surveys, first collected in 1973, were established as an instrument to monitor public attitudes toward the community, and integration more generally. Eurobarometer not only serves as a "barometer" for the attitudes and beliefs of the European public spheres, but also is considered a means to justify policy making. This secondary source has been frequently utilized for the analysis of European public opinion discourse, either by further researching citizen's attitudes with the data available or by justifying theoretical arguments with data retrieved from the Commission. In addition, its credibility in the social sciences has been verified by a number of scholars (Gabel, 1998; Panebianco, 1996).

From an empirical viewpoint, it is established that support and identification with the EU has increased unevenly but consistently. But while some quantitative evidence for this period suggests that the development of a generalizable European identity may be a matter of time, other research conducted on this question concludes that one cannot deduct transnational identification simply from length of membership. A short review of the past development of aggregate EU public opinion on support for the Union illustrates this point: There was not too much enthusiasm visible in the early days of Eurobarometer in the 1970s, with support values hovering below 50 percent. It grew in the 1980s following the announcement of the single-market plans in 1985, and remained regularly well above the halfway mark; economic recovery and the expected benefits of the single market are attributed as main factors for this Euro-optimism. At the beginning of the 1990s, then, a significant initial downturn in public opinion was registered, which was explained with sovereignty issues surrounding the ratification of the Maastricht Treaty, and the Treaty's expected outcomes more generally (Niedermayer and Sinnott, 1995). However, this downward trend recovered in the later part of the observation period as the time series in this chapter will show. The up-and-down movement over the period of only twenty years preceding Maastricht raises questions about the solidity of assumed patterns of support, which should be at least partly addressed by examining the environment in which these policies resonate.

In the initial descriptive stage of the Eurobarometer analysis, by comparing specific values through the use of time-series sequences, e.g., the percentage of people identifying themselves as Europeans versus nationals during the post-Maastricht decade, I look for a subsequent convergence of identification with the EU in the member states. This procedure is replicated for the individual variables, such as approval for the four integrative measures—the euro, single market, CFSP, and constitutional draft—in a cross-national comparison. The exploration of approval for the individual four measures occurs according to the observation through Eurobarometer, which means that the time-series analyses are not always established for the whole observation period, but as the data is being made available; for instance, in the case of the single market only for the first six years of the time frame. By doing so, the first hypothesis is taken into account and should be validated.

The data on the three case countries will then be isolated to find out how far they represent wider trends in the EU. In addition, I consult Eurobarometer Special Surveys that deal with particular topics, for example, the report about information on the EU and support for European integration. These secondary statistics supply issue-related, comprehensive information about attitudes and values in the sphere of EU public opinion.

In-Depth Interviews

The interviews with sixteen citizens in each of the three EU member states ascertain qualitative, in-depth information about civic attitudes and opinions regarding European integration and identities. These "ethnographic" interviews reflect on the commonalities of belonging to the EU while being residents of distinctively different national, regional, and local cultures.

A sampling matrix incorporating various demographic and spatial indicators was established and combined with a simple random sampling strategy to obtain a broad range of opinions in all three countries. In the field, I talked to people who were most readily available, and only after collecting the initial half of the sample did I search for participants demographically still missing in the sampling matrix. As a qualitative tool, statistical representativeness for these samples is irrelevant. However, to obtain a balanced view, the four-by-four categorical sampling matrix included a balance of cases containing both gender categories, different age groups, varying occupational statuses, and regions with differing population densities. Those individualizing distinctions are noticeable as far as they reveal characteristic differences in identification with the EU (Liebert, 1997).

The interviews lasted from about forty-five to ninety minutes each, depending on the availability and knowledge of the participant. Intended to obtain the participants' attitudes and identifications, the questions were as open-ended as possible. Only if the interviewee seemed to have difficulty or asked for an explanation did I assist with more information. In a few cases, such as when the response to the question about the euro was expressed very quickly and solely positively, I probed participants about possible alternatives. Also, if a participant seemed extremely willing and knowledgeable, I delved deeper into the research theme, asking additional questions about EU citizenship, enlargement in general, the case of Turkey as accession country, etc.

Beginning with the initial collection of biographic background data, the semistructured interviews contained few open-ended Eurobarometer questions, asking respondents to elaborate on their understanding of their identities within the EU (e.g., to what degree they identify as Europeans, or how they feel about the different integrative measures—euro, constitution, etc.) and how EU policies have changed their way of living in and perceiving the EU (see appendix for the interview protocol). The demographic information collected provides information about the socioeconomic status of the individual and makes it possible to establish a few descriptive statistics about the sample population. Questions 2 through 5 are taken from the last years' Eurobarometer to enable a direct comparison. By adding an open-ended, probing "why" to questions 2 and 3, more qualitative information about identification and support for the EU is pursued. The following nine questions are open-ended and deal with the respondent's cognitive and emotional response to the four integrative indicators (nos. 10–13) and with more challenging questions about national sovereignty (no. 9), as well as making national concessions for supranational goals (no. 14). Finally, the interviewees are asked about the existence of a transnational identity (no. 15).

Print Media Content Analysis

To complement the aggregate data and qualitative interview analyses, media sources were evaluated through Internet-based quantitative and interpretative-qualitative content analysis. The goal here is to examine selected European print media, using the two major newspapers of each of the three countries whose archives are accessible online. As with all media, one has to be mindful of the framing of issues, because "the information media in particular have to maintain a balance between the 'three

M's': pure factual research and reporting (mere facts), social-political evaluation and message (mission) and the economic requirements (market), which are often accompanied by a stronger emotionalization and personalization of events" (DeVreese, 2001: 288).

There are limitations to this technique as well. First of all, the selection of a limited number of print resources within a more educated market segment gives only a partial view of the discourse observed, which is why I also opted to contrast elitist broadsheets to outlets with higher tabloid content. Secondly, regarded from a meta-perspective, one has to be careful in directly linking intermediate information delivery to the identities that it is supposed to influence. Conclusions drawn from such an analysis need to be confirmed by accompanying changes in public opinion so as to be validated through triangulation, as is done in Chapter 7. The media markets in the chosen case countries are relatively similar in their market structure, although Ireland is an outlier with regard to the size of the markets. Both Ireland and the UK possess a more nationalistic press with regard to the general direction of political opinion. For example, experts conceive of the British press as portraying the EU "as primarily a foreign-dominated forum for fish-wars and sausage spats, and as a launching platform for those who wish to 'drag sovereignty away from the mother of parliaments' and to subject Britain to a 'mercilessly centralizing' bombardment of rule by Euro-money and Euro-directive" (Anderson and Weymouth, 1999: 23). The print media in Germany is very extensive, the market is widely diversified, and the tone is decidedly nonnationalistic. In 1990, West Germany was Europe's biggest producer of newspapers with 356 dailies, compared to 105 in the UK and only eight in the small Irish market. Interestingly, British citizens read the most: Of the twenty-five European newspapers with the largest distribution, fifteen are British (ibid.).

The selected papers for this analysis are national dailies and stand for slightly contrasting political views for each country, e.g., in Germany, the *Frankfurter Allgemeine Zeitung*, representing the more liberal-conservative view, and the *Süddeutsche Zeitung*, the more leftist-progressive one. Accordingly, in the UK, *The Daily Mail* and *The Guardian* are chosen to represent the diverging opinions, and in Ireland the more balanced *Irish Times* and *The Irish Independent* are examined.

By looking at recurring statements and patterns of the obvious semantic usage of keywords (e.g., "European identity," "single market," "euro," "European Constitution," etc.) and their context during the period 1993–2005, this content analysis provides a mixed methodology tool for the way identification with the EU is conceived and ideologically employed, for they deliver a range of texts with diverse usage of these keywords. The citations and interpretations regarding the EU in general and European versus national identity in particular present ideal material for an interpretive analysis of the current media discourse. They are expressions of certain political directions expressed by the political elites and contribute to shaping the consciousness of the EU's population (Zaller, 1992). At this point, a parallel media content analysis about particular national identities as opposed to their supranational content is neither organizationally feasible nor suitable since the print media chosen have a national focus from the outset.

A methodological triangulation, consisting of ethnographic interviews, media content analysis, and Eurobarometer statistical analysis is conducted in Chapter 7 to enhance the reliability and validity of my results in that three different research strategies control for the same outcome. These contribute to an actual description of current identification processes in the three case studies. In the same vein, the triangulation of data sources from countries with different experiences within the EU (Germany, Ireland, and the UK) is intended to ensure the consistency of the conclusions and to reflect international differences and commonalities.

Political and Academic Relevance of This Study

The world today is in the midst of a resurgence of cultural pluralism, despite the transnational economic and political trends exerted through the multifaceted processes of globalization. In a counterposition to the latter, these localizing cultural expressions of self-realization have profound effects on the political identity of citizens all over the world (Thiel and Coate, 2010), but in particular in the case of European states experiencing EU integration as a substantial refashioning of political, social, cultural, and economical structures.

Since 1992, the EU has increasingly taken over policy areas previously under sovereign state control. Although national governments initiated this transfer of power, in most cases citizens of the member states (except in states with popular referenda about EU treaties, such as Ireland or Denmark) did not have direct control over those changes. At the same time the current configuration of the Union touches people's daily lives and interferes with existing national procedures, laws, and institutions in more and more ways. In light of these developments, questions of public support and identity construction and formation as a vehicle for legitimacy appear. The debate over the future of the Union and its lack of legitimization has only augmented the perceived need to bring the Union closer to its citizen. This work shows that with the augmented salience of the EU and thereby the increased level of contestation, the realization of integration has become a divisive issue for the citizenry of the EU, with structural issues such as continued enlargement, aging, and immigration compounding problems of identity extension based on harmonizing policies and supposed common "European" characteristics.

The idea of European unification remains valued by the majority of citizens in the EU. However, rising nationalism for fear of losing national identity has also increased, with populist and right-wing parties articulating the fears of some Europeans. Xenophobic parties grew particularly in the 1990s and are still influential in many European countries, e.g., in France, Austria, Belgium, and the UK, as well as in the European Parliament (EP). Coincidentally, it is argued that the fear of losing national identity does not necessarily translate into outright opposition, but into a sort of ambiguity about the effects of European integration (McLaren, 2004).

Large centrist parties struggle with issues of multiculturalism and immigration, with neither national governments nor the Union's institutions being able to act against emerging populist tendencies by extremist parties from the right, who favor traditional identity protectionism, or from the left, who perceive of integration as the dictate of neoliberal market strategists. The unease about EU policies impeding national sovereignty is at times used as a scapegoat for unpopular decision making or policy implementation by domestic politicians, which leads to additional reservations against European transnational institutions. Even though the occurrence of right-wing extremism will not be the primary concern of this project, the a priori existence of national identities and nationalism provides the theoretical background detailed in the next chapter, which will then investigate the extent of transnational identification with the EU and Europe in the member states of Ireland, Germany, and the UK.

In particular, the rejection in 2005 of the constitutional draft in two important member states, the Netherlands and France, has been a blow to any attempts for deeper integration of the EU. In terms of prospects for collective identity formation, one could certainly draw parallels to the Maastricht Treaty creating supranational and intergovernmental policy pillars and the Lisbon Treaty advancing integration by collapsing and merging those structures. With regard to the latter, the short-lived creation of the Commission post for institutional relations and communications in August 2004 was in part intended to aid institutional self-representation, but has not been able to influence the outcome of the referenda or public opinion about the EU in any significant way. With the Union's increased presence in national public spheres and the mixed track record of its ambitious goals, it now comes under strong pressure to answer to public demands for accountability and transparency. If it does not improve in these matters, it faces mounting protests by citizens and their elected leaders. Part of this work thus illustrates the linkage between EU policies and public discourse in member states. One of the main outcomes of this research consists in the recommendation to involve national press and other media organs in the evolving communication strategy of the Commission more strongly since they possess an important relay function. On the other hand, the explanatory framework arrives at the conclusion that the maintenance and promotion of national identities ought to be recognized as valid goals by the Union, and that these regional and national identities ought to be explicitly supported and protected by the Union.

Despite the abundant literature about a European cultural identity (Delanty, 1995; Wintle, 2002; Passerini, 2000), empirical research about the impact of deliberate integrative EU policies on national sentiments and cultural identity and the resulting competing formation of a transnational political identification within the EU has received only limited attention (Katzenstein and Checkel, 2009; Risse, 2010). This book contributes to this agenda and, moreover, links the empirically gained results of the impact of agency-based integration to larger structural questions of future challenges such as immigration, continued enlargement, or the integration uncertainty regarding the EU's final status. Studies have been conducted to analyze national attitudes toward European integration over time, but few have related the subject to wider questions of nationalism, communication, and the structural conditions by which European integration finds itself constrained.

By supplying key indicators for common identification and distinguishing between the existing cultural allegiance to the state and the emerging transnational identity formation in the EU, an empirically tested and comprehensively analyzed report on the actual identifications in contemporary Europe is delivered, which contrasts with many lay explanations and normative expectations about future identity developments in the EU. Based on these findings, I caution against ill-conceived notions of cosmopolitanism in lieu of a more critical yet realistic view of the effects of European integration. This book does not argue for a particularistic account of Europe, but its empirical evidence highlights the need to take nationalistic externalities of EU integration and homogenization seriously, as only a few others have argued (Calhoun, 2007).

My interest in researching these changes in identities arose from the realization that individual and collective identity-formation processes are essential to any kind of democratic political development, yet are often neglected in institution-heavy EU studies. Nevertheless, identity and legitimacy play an important role for the future of European integration: politicization and democratization of EU-institutions are connected with taking the legitimacy problem seriously, with clarifying and promoting the debate on a wider than just national identity (Risse, 2010; De Bardeleben and Hurrelmann, 2007). Although both identity and legitimacy are interrelated in the integration process, they need to be differentiated with regard to their teleology. Whereas (trans)national identity strives for the self-realization of a collective, legitimacy exists as a basic problem of democratic representation. In the past, most research about European integration concentrated on elitist-institutional analyses of the decision-making processes in Brussels, and this emphasis still exists (Burgess, 2002; Hix and Goetz, 2001). In contrast, this book highlights the repercussions of those policies on the general public and collective national identities, thereby focusing on EU citizens instead of political elites. Together with the emerging sense of democratization of the Union, this work provides valuable information about current identity changes in the under-researched area of the European Union as a polity. It emphasizes that "a concern for identity, status, and cultural change rather than a concern for power and plain economic interest are the key to explaining international variation in identification with the EU" (Diez-Medrano, 2003: 18). In doing so, it provides an approximation of key indicators for support of European integration, but also delimits the chances for transnational identification, in particular with respect to the mass media and the ambiguous efforts in tackling future challenges of the Union.

Chapter Overview

The following chapters successively lead the reader through the stages of problem definition, exploration, analysis, and deduction. Chapter 2 establishes the theoretical foundations behind the often generalizing and confusing usage of the term "transnational European identity" and describes in more detail the processes of collective identity formation, national and European identity construction, and the theorized impact of recent European integration on these as they relate to neofunctionalist and constructivist theories.

The topic at hand, European transnational identification, necessitates a closer look at the historical developments of individual national identities in the case countries and the EU's impact upon those countries to fully comprehend national identity constructions. Therefore, Chapter 3 details the past and present of the chosen case countries as well as their experience with the Union, separated by levels of governance and public spheres.

In Chapter 4, I will focus on the qualitative interviews held in the three case countries, and I will analyze their contents quantitatively and qualitatively with regard to the attitudes and the identity positions of these participants to gain a more detailed and immediate understanding about the processes of identity construction and transformation.

Chapter 5 concentrates on findings from Eurobarometer, the statistical public opinion instrument of the European Commission, with the intention to discover broader identity changes and to look at temporal trends and key indicators of support in the three case countries of Germany, the UK, and Ireland, as well as for the EU-15/25. A qualitative survey of the "meaning of the EU" complements the aggregate time-series sequences.

Chapter 6 examines the press coverage of European integration through mixed methodology tools using descriptive quantitative approaches as well as qualitative content analysis, thereby disclosing the interrelated effects between media portrayal and public attitudes. As with the previous chapter, this investigation provides a temporal view of transnational developments.

The following section summarizes the results found in the individual analyses, evaluates the hypotheses, and sets the findings about the changing yet sticky and possibly exclusionary nature of transnational European identification in the context of current developments in the EU. Lastly, recommendations for future EU integration policies in the cultural and communication fields, as well as for future research in this study area, are given.

Finally, Chapter 8 addresses, based on the outcomes of the analyses, political implications that relate the results of agency-based EU integration to the structural challenges of regional integration. I conclude that the slow-changing nature of collective identities serves as a "reality check" for normative expectations of many social scientists and politicians regarding the development of transnationalism in the EU, particularly in view of future demographic as well integration-related challenges. I argue that a recognition of cohesiveness emphasizing national cultures, communication, and a concern for the final outcome of European integration is essential for the future development of sustainable transnationalism in Europe.

In an increasingly unsafe world in which seemingly accelerated changes in technology, trade, and communications impact all countries similarly, questions of social cohesion, cultural unity, and political solidarity become more important. The EU, in its function as a stable transnational polity, serves already as proof for the achievements of democratic peace and regional integration. The fostering of a transnational identification therefore remains essential, although common reference points may be harder to attain under conditions of enlargement and immigration. And while the majority of European citizens continue to stand behind the goals of European integration, the complexity of EU governance has increased, and so has the diversity among EU member states. This results in ambiguity and nationally differentiated support patterns. A concern for more socio-political cohesiveness, then, proves to be an often overlooked prerequisite to achieving a politically sustainable Union.

Chapter 2

A Primer on (Trans)National Identities

In the social sciences, identity-based theories relating to (trans)nationalism and its sociopolitical expression gained in importance with the end of the Cold War, the popularity of postmodernist thinking, and the accelerated processes of globalization evoking identity politics. One major problematic issue, however, remains the diverse and often generalizing, undifferentiated use of such theoretical constructs. In the following chapter a specification of the terms *collective identities* and *(trans)nationalism* and an overview of EU-related integration-based theories enable a closer look at the links between these concepts. Sociopsychological studies on identity formation and sociological writings on nationalism provide guidance in assessing the fundamental question about the sometimes antagonistic coexistence of national and transnational identities in Europe, while the political science literature on integration guides the hypotheses developed with respect to transnational identification with the EU.

Identities as a Social Science Concept

The interest in issues of identity emerged in the 1950s and 1960s as part of the sociological and psychoanalytical efforts to conceptualize identity (Kohli, 2000). Initially limited to the exploration of the individual and personal, the term now includes collective and group identities, and the variable identity is researched as both dependent and independent variable (Abdelal et al., 2009). The word itself stems from the Latin notion of "sameness," signifying already an emphasis on commonalities. In the social sciences, some scholars have linked the concept of identity to an immanent political meaning: if identity equates sameness, then there is automatically a distinction from the other, the dissimilar, and thus a categorization of inclusion and exclusion (Spencer and Wollman, 2002: 58). Thus, any ensuing social categorizations are initiated by socialization processes and then continued through communicative interaction with others throughout our lifetime.

The idea of a constructed nature of identity rather than an inherent unalterable state of mind possesses more credibility if regarded this way. For postmodern sociologist Hall, identities are "the unstable points of identification or suture, which are made within the discourses of history and culture. Not an essence, but a positioning" (Hall, 1990: 226). Yet, according to some theorists who emphasize its stability, identity possesses three major functions: it helps express a sociopolitical community's autonomy, it makes relations with other members of the group possible, and it provides strength and resilience (Guibernau, 1996). This does not mean that national identity should be regarded as fixed or as only transmitted and constructed by agents of the dominant in-group. Most contemporary Western societies, with their relative political transparency and observation through mass media and nonstate actors, offer a variety of messages concerning their collective identity to the respective public spheres. The latter domains, defined as discursive spaces of communication and deliberation, although still predominantly confined to the national level, co-constitute a transnational identity by shaping the image of Europe and the EU.

However, from a sociopsychological point of view, "there is no psychological theory which precisely explains how to argue coherently from the individual to aggregate group or mass behavior, which explains political integration and mobilization" (Bloom, 1999: 59). The cause of these theoretical blind spots lies in the complexity of identity construction, so in order to illuminate transnational identification processes, this inquiry begins with individual interviews, then looks at the aggregate data collected through the Eurobarometer dataset, and finally, researches the public discourse as represented in the press. Even though the proposed examination includes an examination of transnational attitudes in individuals through interviews, the subjects of this research are inextricably bound to collective identity, which will be the focus in the Eurobarometer surveys and print analyses. Sociologists and psychologists call this dialectical process the "bargaining" or "negotiating" of identities in social interaction (Bloom, 1987), no matter if it occurs on an individual or state level. It is through socialization forces that our identity is shaped and derived in a social context, be it in everyday encounters or in elite interactions. Those agents range according to their impact, from the parental unit to larger collectives such as schools and the socioeconomic milieu, up to the nation.

In addition to differentiation from others and continual negotiation, many scholars mention continuity over time and the politics of memory as constituting criteria of identity. They perceive of a nation as a historically developed entity that shares a common past. This gives members a reference point and an identification basis to act in distinctive manners and pursue traditional goals. Yet, in the same way as they can be constructed, identities can be deconstructed and reconstructed. With reference to the changing character of identity and its repercussions for polities, some have proposed that "it also means that identity and the process of identification are fundamentally political in character and we can then try and explore the politics involved in the construction of identity" (Renwick, 1996: 155). The intention here is to specifically research how supranational integration policies have influenced identification processes of EU citizens in either direction on the global-local identity continuum. The idea of a collective identity as a way in which self-understandings are expressed within the general public sphere can be conceptually anchored in locale (the place where people live), networks (the ways in which people interact), and memory (the understandings that are sustained and recreated over time) (Preston, 1997). Thus, the ambiguous coexistence of both fluid process quality and continuity over time is evident in the acquisition of identity, in particular through its expression in recurring practice, its institutionalization, and its normative spread among the population through social agents.

While identities as an object of inquiry have received more scholarly attention in recent years, there are also voices that criticize the "unscientific" use of the term in contemporary social sciences. Brubaker and Cooper, for instance, argue that identity as a concept has been used without really exploring the implications of the term, and often as a cover-up for other nonpolitical forms of self-realization. They call for—and partly deliver—a more specific understanding of identity and the process of identification as a category of practice (e.g., as in identity politics) and one of analysis (e.g., self-ascribed identity vs. prescribed identity vs. identification). In addition, they highlight the dichotomy between the use of identity as an expression of sameness and its function to suggest individuality. The authors seek more differentiated explanations and consequently define identification as an active process of seeking to achieve an identity (Brubaker and Cooper, 2000). These ascribing processes can be executed by oneself or other socialization agents, either by positioning in a relational web (for example, kinship or professional hierarchical relationships) or in a categorical one (such as language, religion, or nationality). While relational aspects are important, processes of identification can be also accomplished by discourse, thus without the need for specific external agents. Both analysts demand a better conceptualization of an object as complex as "identity," but all too easily dismiss the whole research agenda behind it. Rather, a specific formulation of the sort of identity under examination (collective, transnational, national, etc.) is called for, which the remainder of this chapter addresses.

Collective Identities

The concept of collective identities argues that, besides having a repertoire of shared ideas, values, and expectations, social groups are in need of distinguishing themselves from other collectives. They assemble and hold multiple individual identities and act according to the needs of the group or the situation. Yet, collective identity entails a core of shared attitudes, which members have in common, mentally and behavior-wise. As the collective self transforms through changes in membership, so its identity is in a continuous process of reconstruction. All defining identity aspects such as history, geography, language, conditions of life, and other cultural particularities are not objectively assigned to the collective, but have to be renegotiated as a common factor by the group (Münch, 2001; Kriesi, 1999).

In this respect, Bloom proposes an "identification theory," which states that "in order to achieve psychological security, every individual possesses an inherent drive to internalize—to identify with—the behavior, mores and attitudes of significant figures in her/his social environment [...] i.e. people actively seek to enhance and protect identity" (Bloom, 1990: 23). This, he argues, has significant implications for national identity as well as "supra-nation-building," which both develop along the same lines of protection and benefits for its members. The latter argument is of particular importance in this work, as national and EU identity construction could be viewed as such a protective and possibly exclusive construct.

As can be seen from the many components inherent in identity formation, the conceptualization of identities has been a major challenge for the social sciences. A research project at Harvard University recently developed a theoretical guide for treating this variable in social science research (Abdelal et al., 2009). In it, experts distinguish collective identities as a "social category that varies along two dimensions—content and contestation. The content of the shared category may take the form of four non-mutually exclusive types: constitutive norms; relational comparisons with other social categories; cognitive models and social purposes. Contestation refers to the degree of agreement within a group over the content of the shared category" (18), thereby confirming the above mentioned aspects.

With regard to the content, "constitutive norms" correspond to the normative strength of the identity, while relational comparisons make differences to other groups. Lastly, cognitive models explain to the collective how cause-effect relationships work and "why the world is as it is," whereas the social purpose of a group gives it meaning and specific goals. In the case of transnational identities in the EU, the content of the pan-European group identity based upon cultural distinctions is furthered through supranational policies, while the degree of contestation varies from state to state, as the empirical evidence will show.

Adding a political component to this basic characterization, Melucci describes collective identity as "an interactive and shared definition produced by several interacting individuals who are concerned with the orientations of their actions as well as the field of opportunities and constraints in which their actions take place" (Melucci, 1996: 75). This definition raises questions about equal rights for all members of a transnational society such as exists in the EU, in which competing collectives claim their rights, especially the right to exist autonomously and the right to be recognized as such. The former point needs to be taken seriously because collectivities are theorized to possess a so-called in-group bias, which puts members of their own group above others (Tajfel, 1982). It also emphasizes the co-constitutive character of both individual and collective identity. A transnational civic identity of Europeans, as proposed in this work, is still in the process of being developed, and as such, remains a thin or weak identity compared to the traditional national ones. However, while many analysts therefore do not perceive this societal change as significant, I argue that this relatively new development has major implications for national and EU policymakers, who need to more clearly define the political space given to the EU and communicate this intention accordingly. In opposition to current nationalistic tendencies, there are scholars who see transnationalism as already existing. Weiler, among others, pointed to the fact that by being able to accept treaties that are not only formulated by one's own nation but also by distinctly different communities, a kind of civic tolerance is actually already effected in the Union (Weiler, 2001). And Risse (2010) finds evidence of transnational identities in a variety of European public spheres where EU affairs already constitute part of domestic politics.

Historically, collective national identities became important in the realm of politics, aside from the Greek polis, only with the emergence of the territorially sovereign state after the Treaty of Westphalia in 1648. Previously, individuals were mainly subjects of power-holding, often transnational authorities such as royal or clerical dynasties. Belonging to a national body was irrelevant because no such institutionalized collective identity structure existed. The evolving territorial-sovereign state system in nineteenth-century Europe enabled modes of resource extraction, control, and protection that led to strong national identities (Tilly, 1975), which, while not unitary themselves, still reign preeminent across Europe.

Aiming to include all constitutive social and historic-political aspects, a useful operational definition of a collective national political identity is thus best described as: "i) the entirety of relations between citizens and institutions, such as the behavior and method of participation in political procedures, criteria for resources-and-costs allocation, and the implementation of them; ii) the values and symbols (rational or non-rational) on which collective narration and latent consensus have been built, as well as the justifications for the allocation of risks, costs, and benefits; iii) the reflexive combination of these two components" (Henry, in Cerruti and Rudolph, 2001: 49). This explanation encompasses behavioral, attitudinal, instrumental, civic, and, to some extent, cultural-historic aspects, and therefore seems appropriate for the application in the book's framework.

To add to this definition, any collective identity can be differentiated into two composite aspects, an internal and external identity. This book concentrates on internal identity formation, the one that evolves from within the collective, as compared to the external, which stems from the outside recognition of the EU as a political entity (Witte, 1987) or any other form of external attribution. To sum up, social and political science literature still has not yet adequately explored the implications of collective civic-political identities under the reshaping of the national states through integration processes, in particular under consideration of the accelerated processes of European unification.

National Identities and Transnationalism

A short review of nationalism theories aids in understanding the conceptual framework in which the postulated changes and extensions in identities progress. In many cases, the development of transnational identities in Europe has been constructed in much the same way as previous national ones. National identities are seriously confronted and at the same time reinforced by contemporary globalization and regional integration processes. The discourse on globalization represents more generally exogenous and structural pressures for adjustment (Held, 2000). Hence, economic, political, and cultural globalization prompts a revival of populist and neo-nationalist demands. In "globalized" societies, individual and collective political representations are often positioned in cosmopolitan opposition to the dominance of national identities. At first sight, a bilateral inverse relationship, it seems, exists between globalization and local, regional, or national identities: on the one hand, globalization gradually erodes national identity; on the other hand, strong counter-identities seem to form to protect the threatened culture.

Referring to the securitization of identities, Ole Waever (1996) sees identities as never being totally secure and in a constant state of fear, thus he recognizes the pressure to come up with new forms of identity defense. In the absence of massive external security threats on the European landscape, it is argued, internal others such as immigrants or minorities take the place of previous foreign enemies for purposes of collective differentiation. Although there may be some truth to this inward-looking distinction, externalization as a solidarity-inducing process exists as well, for example, in the ambivalent polarization toward the United States or even toward parts of Eastern Europe, Turkey, or Russia. What, then, makes the identity pressures and threats from European integration different from the ones experienced through globalization more generally? In the latter, there is no overarching international authority governing the globalization process, and thus, aside from a weak cosmopolitan ideal, there exists no intrinsic basis for the creation of an available cosmopolitan identity. In the case of the EU, identity formation can build upon a variety of factors, such as historical and socioeconomical linkages, as well as current governance, to establish a transnational identification, reinforced by the unitary "identity engineering" of the EU through treaties, policies, and symbolic means.

To return to the concept of nationalism, Anthony Smith, a leading contemporary scholar in this field uses "nationalism" as a term for "a consciousness of belonging to the nation [...], a language and symbolism of the 'nation' and its role, an ideology, including a cultural doctrine [...] and a social and political movement to achieve the goals of the nation" (Smith, 1991: 72). This causal categorization, despite its essentialist ontology, also espouses a procedural notion when talking about the political mobilization of a nation. His definition is also useful because in many instances, chronological or regional classifications are unable to encompass outliers, whereas causal ones are more comprehensive. On the other hand, because of the multidimensionality of nationalism, it proves difficult to categorize a particular nationalist movement in one constitutive category only. Research into forms of (trans)nationalism needs to be historically and situationally specific. Accordingly, the core of this work will be limited to the post-Maastricht period of European integration and to context-specific case countries.

Current international relations (IR) literature challenges the orthodoxy of the nation-state as the primary focus for political identity—as proliferated by the orthodox theories of neorealism and neoliberalism—and thus put the political subject at the center of analysis. Some (mostly constructivist) scholars call this (re)discovery the return of identity in IR, dismissing rationalists for not being able to adequately account for identity-driven political changes (Lapid and Kratochwil, 1996; Katzenstein, 1996). By (their) definition, then, being a national is an intersubjective classification. Expanding on this debate, the following division aids in the building of a theoretical framework that distinguishes between two basic camps regarding the general logic of collective identity formation: essentialism and constructivism. Others describe the same dichotomy, using the terms eastern/western, political/cultural, civic/ethnic, rational/emotional, or constitutional/authoritarian nationalism (Özkirimli, 2000; Cederman, 2001).

The essentialist approach to identity formation emphasizes ethnic-cultural variables, such as ethnic descent or the existence of an ethnic core, common history, language, and religion. Essentialist literature on nationalism exists in abundance but fails to clearly define what it entails. Anthony Smith, as one of the representatives of this school, defines a nation as "a named human population sharing an historic territory, common myths and historical memories, a mass, public [political] culture, a common economy and common legal rights and duties for all members." (Smith, 1996: 14). This description already makes the multidimensional nature of such a complex phenomenon apparent, from territorial delineation to the sociopolitical underpinnings of a national state. For the purpose of this project, the research of the underlying psychological and social functions is of primary interest, since these correlate to the wider categories of identity formation and self-definition, be it religion, gender, etc. In the literature pertaining to the essentialist field, scholars are divided between modernists who theorize civic nationalism as an elite-driven project for nation building (such as Gellner or Anderson) and primordialists who view ethnic nationalism as an expression of the eternal and essential constituents of collective identities (such as Connor or Smith). Even though few academics can be identified as pure primordialists, the latter group sees civic nationalism as not being able to exclude ethno-national and primordial sentiments. Smith, for example, identified himself in recent works as "ethno- or historical symbolist," a school of thought seeking to uncover the symbolic legacy of premodern ethnic identities and their meaning for the creation of modern nations. Ethno-symbolism supposedly constitutes a "third way" between essentialism and modernism or constructivism, taking into account aspects of both argumentations, but as the name emphasizes, essentialist components such as customs or ethnicity continue to feature heavily in this theory.

The modernist perspective, in contrast, emphasizes mass-based instruments of collective identity formation, such as education, army conscription, or media. Linking this view with the constructed nature of political culture and the emergence of print media to produce allegiance to the new states of the nineteenth century, the notion of nationalism as an expression of an "imagined community" achieved widespread acceptance and constitutes another base for this work. Benedict Anderson postulates that the spread of print capitalism has enabled citizens to imagine a commonality and find it reflected in the media. According to him, a nation "is imagined because the members of even the smallest nation will never know most of their fellow members, meet them or even hear of them, yet in the mind of each lives the image of their communion" (Anderson, 1991: 6). He was the first to point out that nations and nationalism are not quite as tangible or fixed as previously assumed, and thus strengthened the modernist argument and the importance of narrative culture laid down in print within the context of a nascent nation. However, his work has been criticized as underemphasizing the influence of historically developed culture, and some of his examples lack a convincing argument with respect to other imagined communities such as the church or a social class (Özkirimli, 2000: 49). For the purpose of my analysis of the print media's impact on (trans)national consciousness, his basic theories remain nevertheless valid. Modernists have been reprimanded for not being able to explain the existence of premodern ethnic groups and the fanatic passion aroused by nationalism, as well as overexaggerating the influence of elites in the nation- or state-building process (Özkirimli, 2000: 121). Notwithstanding these impediments, the concept of civic nationalism has been emphasized by Ikenberry as being more apt to accommodate global political, social, and economic changes because of its internal capacity to sustain those changes and to produce a wider conception of shared identity, which in turn generates stability (Ikenberry and Hall, 2003). While European integration could in theory construct such a civic pan-European allegiance, the research presented below will show that the appeal of long-standing cultural characteristics still takes precedence at this point in time. Before coming up with his previously mentioned critique of the use of "identity," Brubaker posited that nationalism exists as a heterogeneous ensemble of "nation"-oriented idioms and practices that are continuously available or "endemic" in modern cultural and political identity. While the basic tenets of this perspective are plausible, one has to critically view his conclusion that, because of its persistence, it would make little sense to look for any receding or advancing movement of nationalism (Brubaker, 1996). This reasoning lacks validity with regard to the fluidity of identities, which makes an examination of the identity changes brought about by current globalization and integration processes a timely endeavor.

In this regard, the argumentation of constructivists and instrumentalists who perceive of identities as changeable seems to have more explanatory power than the dogmatic persistence of the primacy of static national identities. Constructivists question the ethnic-cultural attachment to the nation, or, at the least, treat ethnicity only as a side effect in the process of identity formation (Cederman, 2001). According to them, active processes of social learning, mobilization, and manipulation shape collective identification. While some concentrate on the effects of norms and learning on institutions or elites, others seek to include larger collectives such as nations (Checkel, 2001; Wendt, 1999). Assuming that constructivist scholarship in EU studies concentrates on three different categories—the first dealing with the nature of a potential "European identity," the second analyzing the reconstruction of national identities upon integration, and the third theorizing the possibilities of a convergence of politically different cultures (Christiansen et al., 2001)—as an empirically oriented analysis, this work attempts to combine all three directions. Taking these analytical venues as reference points, in the last two chapters I venture into predictions about the future constraints of transnational identity formation. In yet another theoretical conceptualization of nationalism, instrumentalists highlight the variety of roles inherent in any given identity. Related to constructivists in that they advocate the existence of multiple identities, instrumentalists argue that people have always had a variety of identities and exchanges with other groups depending on their needs (Conversi, 2002)—a proposition that falls in line with the treated topic: the development of coexisting political identities suited to pertain to each level of the multilevel governance, from regional to national to European. Taking into account the context and the necessity of the situation as well as the role repertoire that a mature individual possesses, multiple identities are used as instruments for adaptation and, in the case of European integration, for collective power. A dichotomy that distinguishes between the more essentialist-statist and the constructivist-instrumentalist nature of collective identities might seem far removed from the current problems that affect European citizens today, but it has important consequences for the potential of EU transnationalism, as the following case shows:

> If we look into the ongoing debate on the future of the EU, we come across a claim that the absence of European demos, no matter if desired or undesired, prevents the European Parliament from providing a higher legitimacy to European integration and that the only place where it can be properly legitimized is in the national parliaments. Indeed from the positivist perspective, this is the only logical solution; if identities are pre-given then the

> institutional set up should reflect them. On the other hand, the constructivist perspective could show that a strengthening of the European Parliament is likely to contribute to the development of a European demos and European identity, regardless of whether it is desired or not. (Drulak, 1999: 13)

A recent research report about the use of identity in political analysis has indeed confirmed that most scholars prefer a constructed conceptualization of identity, corresponding with the modernist model (Bruland and Horowitz, 2003). This has major repercussions for the linkage between nations, collective identities, and politics, as pointed out in the next section.

The Relationship between Politics, the Nation, and Identity

In this study the interconnectedness and interaction of factors such as the nation, politics, and identity are essential and interrelated components. In the literature, at least two different models of interaction are available. One is a sequencing, causal chain whereas the other possesses an intersubjective, co-constitutive character. As will be shown below, the interactive model is best able to capture the relationships between the major components applied in this analysis.

The sequence model theorized by Hall attempts to explore the causal relationship between changes in political systems and collective identities (Hall, 1998). With an eye on the larger embeddedness of countries in the international system, he constructs a two-way sequential chain explaining transformational system changes: Collective identity forms legitimizing principles, which in turn through collective reproduction of those principles develop into domestic and/or international institutions and rules, and thereby constitute and change the political domestic or, in our case, European system. According to the author, those constituting sequences were found in the industrialized nation-states of the late nineteenth century. A reverse sequence is proposed for less powerful collectives. Here, the larger system influences domestic and/or international changes in institutions and their principles. As a response, a specific national collective identity evolves. An adaptation of Hall's sequential diagram conceptualizes his model:

1: collective identity → legitimizing principles → domestic institutions → political system

2: political system → change in domestic and international institutions → collective identity

Though the sequential model tries to connect causally responsible elements in the political domestic or international system, this one-way classification ascribed to states is not able to capture the interactive complexity of transformational changes within states, since states as actors and non-state agents themselves can change from powerful and active to powerless and defensive—and the other way around as well. The interrelated model developed by Pfetsch (2001) has more explanatory power, in that major constituting elements such as culture, politics, and identity impact and transform the nation, and thus co-constitute each other rather than undergo change through causally responsible agents.

In Pfetsch's national model, the three factors of politics, culture, and identity are influencing each other as well as the product, the nation, in multiple ways. While politics, with its utilitarian-material premises, sets the framework for cultural differentiation and the creation of collective identity, at the same time the political culture determines the values and intersubjective identity of the polity. Collective identity, in turn, directs and legitimizes politics, while simultaneously identity politics utilize identitive positions as a means for political action. In his model, the nation is located in the center, exposed to and influenced by all three factors. Pfetsch's model, unlike Hall's linear sequence, recognizes the simultaneous interaction between the three major factors impacting the nation and distinguishes between culture as the content of identitive knowledge and

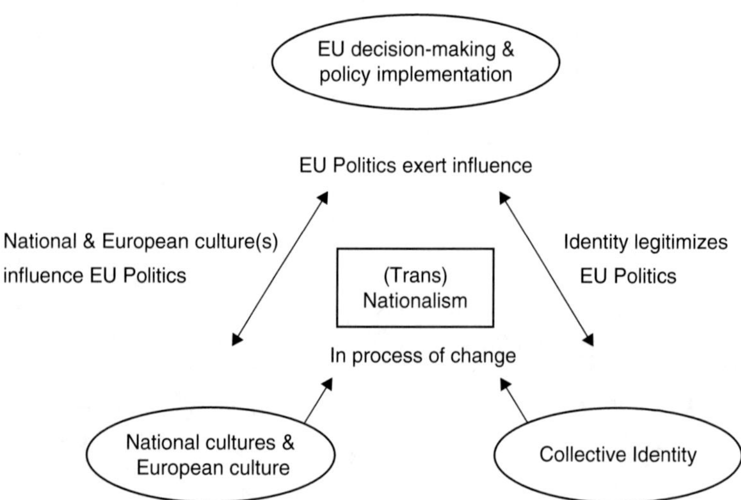

Figure 2.1 Interactive Model of (Trans)Nationalism

collective identity as mobilizing agent. Thus, it provides a more differentiated model to explain (trans)national identity formation.

In my adaptation, intended to tailor his model to the EU, EU decision making and policy implementation influence and are in turn affected by both culture and collective identity (see above). The factor culture refers to a mix of historical-customary representations, as well as political orientations of the public, and encompasses national culture(s) and a European one. A collective identity consisting of various societal groups that intersubjectively constitutes the nation provides the base for a transnational European identity. All factors exert considerable forming power over the nation (Figure 2.1).

European Integration, Neofunctionalism, and Transnational Identity Expansion

Aside from globalization processes, EU integration processes have considerably weakened, but at the same time rekindled to a certain extent nationalist tendencies. The early European political science literature, which builds on the seminal contributions made by Lindberg, Mitrany, Deutsch, and Haas, did not yet experience such developments. But the creators of integration theory already laid the foundations for current scholarship evolving from (neo)functionalism, transactionalism, intergovernmentalism, and, more generally, institutionalism (Rosamond, 2000; Niedermayer and Sinnott, 1995).

One of the main tenets of functionalist integration theory is that the governments of separate countries come together to create common institutions that over time shift powers to a new supranational center. However, functionalism alone was not able to supplant nationally oriented policy orientations and traditional diplomacy since "the EC states have increasingly wanted to define their relations with each other and with the outside in political as well as merely functional terms" (Duff, 1994: 161), a tendency that increased post-Maastricht. Neofunctionalist approaches extended the original functionalist theory by identifying essential prerequisites for political integration such as a change in public attitudes and the promotion of these processes through elites, in addition to spillover effects (from one level or area to a more integrated one). It is important here to note that neofunctionalism should not be compared to constructivist theories, even though they share some views on integration and spillover effects. "Even though there are connections between key aspects of neofunctionalist theorizing—e.g. processes of socialization, learning, transfers of loyalty, redefinitions of interest and, in general, the transformative perspective—and aspects of constructivism [. . .], such overlap should not lead to a conflation between one and the other" (Christiansen et al., 2001: 3). Constructivism is a social ontology and social theory dealing with ideas, identities, and interests in social relations, whereas (neo)functionalism as integration theory is concerned with policy formulation and, thus, tangible matters such as European monetary policy or foreign policy. Another distinction relates to the scope of analysis of both theories: constructivism seeks to understand the processes of identity formation and is therefore rather agnostic about the finality of the outcome. Neofunctionalism, however, is biased toward an ever more integrationist development inherent in its view (Checkel, in Christiansen et al., 2001).

Although neofunctionalist theories as one of the classic integration models are at the core of European integration processes, they focus primarily on "technical" measures of integration, explaining policy making by governments and elites. In doing so, they neglect the repercussions these processes have on the citizens. However, while neofunctionalists initially renounced the importance of public opinion and the role of the citizenry, they later extended an active role to the population. "Expectations, common identity or consciousness, and a 'sense of community' are acknowledged to be essential elements of political integration" (Niedermayer and Sinnott, 1995: 23). In a related matter, the "zero-sum game" theory proposes the linear transfer of power to the supranational center while slowly diminishing the national position. With regard to identities, this functional logic does not necessarily apply since human beings have a variety of roles available to them. While in some instances the impact of European integration can at least be perceived as a threat to or loss of national sovereignty, European cultural identity construction in the form of identity engineering through the Commission (e.g., by assigning a Europe Day or creating the European flag and anthem) is designed as an identity facet complementing and enriching national identities, yet with varying degrees of success, as the following quotation by Van Ham points out:

> The basic political (and psychological) idea behind the introduction of these European symbols is to gradually modify the consciousness of the peoples of Europe of the political entity to which they belong. But the strengthening of a European identity [. . .] is a process of both top-down voluntarist management and bottom-up attitudinal changes. Attempts to create a European identity through European symbols seem a dead-end. (Van Ham, 2001: 73)

Both models of identity expansion, the competitive and the complementary transnational one, constitute the traditional strands of theorizing about the mutual relationship between national and European identities. More recently the social sciences came to agreement that adding a new level of solidarity or allegiance as transnational identity growth does not take away from existing national ones. “The shifting of identity from a national to the European level [. . .] follows a dialectic of identity gain and loss which doesn’t necessarily turn out to be a zero-sum process” (Münch, 1997: 184).

The multitude of allegiances is currently theorized as a system of so-called nested identities, whereby nested identities are composed of lower- and higher-rank identities. The higher-ordered one encompasses the lower-ordered one, so that, for example, a citizen’s identity as resident of a city would be nested within his regional identity, which ideally is integrated into his national identity, etc. Similarly, each of these identities is functionally different: the superordinate identity secures inclusion into the collective, and the subgroup identity establishes distinctiveness within the larger social category (Medrano, 2001). While this theory in concept sounds promising for the future research of multiple identities, it raises questions about possible conflicts within this ranked categorization system (Risse, 2001). What if there is a tension between the regional and the national identity, as in the case of the Basque country or Scotland? Accordingly, theorists such as Risse provide us with other, more fitting models such as the crosscutting one assuming that some identifications are more problematic for a person’s characteristic than others, and the already mentioned interrelated or blended model, in which multiple identities interact and co-constitute each other.

The contemporary volatile political climates as well as contentious civil protests of the post-Mastricht period have shown that there is considerable popular opposition to the streamlining politics “made in Brussels.” Umberto Bossi, Jörg Haider, Geert Wilders, and Jean-Marie Le Pen enjoyed electoral successes founded on xenophobic and nationalistic rhetoric based upon the exclusion of most things non-European—or even foreign at all. In my case study, UK political parties committed to withdrawal from the EU gained in power in past elections. Opposition to European integration fits well in populist political ideology because of protectionist domestic considerations that demonize the harmonizing effects of European integrations. Then again, this kind of collective, even transnational, counteraction is not exclusively a case of citizens feeling threatened by EU policy making, as non-EU members such as Switzerland or Norway also exhibit some form of reactive nationalism, as evidenced in the recent debate about minaret building in Europe.

As a counterargument to the dichotomous discussion about (trans) national identity expansion, it has been argued that for once the increased attention, positive or negative, that is called to EU governance is in fact proof for the development of transnational social movements or even an evolving European public sphere (Risse, 2010; Imig and Tarrow, 2001)—even if they should contest European integration. Furthermore, the major societal change in most EU member states toward postmaterialism as proposed by Inglehart resulted in more popular demand for political participation and influence over European policy making. While Inglehart's concept of cognitive mobilization, i.e., the increased capability in acquisition of knowledge by citizens, as an influencing factor for support of European unification still holds true, postmaterialistic attitudes have been found to compete with individualistic, depoliticizing orientations in European populations (Inglehart and Reif, 1991). In view of the above, discontent with or insufficient knowledge of the EU cannot simply be equated with recourse to nationalism; a closer look at the causal underlying mechanisms and domestic political cultures that ultimately determine the values, norms, and expectations of each national community is necessary.

At times, EU governance is seen as technocratic imposition to national decision making, thereby underestimating popular demands. Paradoxically, the intended democratization of EU politics and the polity itself, as discussed in the past few years in European public spheres, are likely to increase this kind of popular protest and involvement. National identities could then more easily be politically mobilized, either in a justified fashion or at times abused for populist motives. The question of the EU's democratization and the connected evolution of transnational, politicized identities for citizens are theoretically related to the concept of citizenship. Especially so because the Treaty of Maastricht created a complementary "EU citizenship" reaffirming rights for citizens, such as the right to live and work in any of the EU states, to stand or vote in local or European elections, and to call upon an EU ombudsperson. So far, though, EU citizenship is still contingent on possessing the respective national ones and delivers few rights as an extension of the national citizenship. According to Eurobarometer surveys, it had no significant effect on the development of a stronger European identity (Delgado-Moreira, 2004), as those rights are granted to people possessing citizenship in one of the member states and therefore are not open to immigrants and third-country nationals already living in the member states (whose numbers are increasing). If citizenship is to be a determining factor in the development of a European identity, it would have to be redesigned as a title providing civic and social rights to all people that permanently live in and identify with the EU. Following this overview of the structural conditions in which identification processes evolve, a closer look at the complex characteristic of these is of the essence.

European Transnationalism and Identification with the EU

Regarding public support and mass attitudes toward European integration, few studies provide factual evidence and explanatory models for the impact of integrative EU measures on the European public. Within the classification of public support models into political-economical, solely political, and national identity approaches, the latter is considered in current research to be the strongest predictor (Marks and Hooghe, 2002; Niedermayer and Sinnott, 1995). This finding in turn validates the theoretical framework built above. With regard to the attitudinal content of support for EU integration, one of the main divisions to be drawn in this field falls between utilitarian (or instrumental) and affective support. The utilitarian mode expresses a concrete perceived interest, whereas the affective one resembles a more diffuse, emotional attachment for the ideals of European unity (Delgado-Moreira, 2004), although the latter is considered a "nonemotional" identity (Guibernau, 2007). Hence, a transnational identity should be conceptualized containing all three parts, the instrumental and civic support leading to increased identification with the EU in combination with the affective allegiance to the culturally based pan-European identity.

Very few scholars focus on the formation of a transnational pan-European identity in such a comprehensive manner. Only recently Bruter investigated attitudes toward the separate civic and cultural components of a sociopolitical identity, finding that possessing such an identity does not automatically translate into support for regional integration, but is linked to mainly civic ideas about the EU (Bruter, 2004). In general the literature on postnational citizenship and identity proposes that the transformation of identities in the EU is occurring as a result of various integration-related factors: differentiation and ascription from outside, below, and above (i.e., how Europeans see themselves as such and how they distinguish other "EU" Europeans); internal homogenization (e.g., the convergence of standard of living, of law, or of culture); and inclusion (e.g., of the societal peripheries to the center) (Münch, 2001). Most new research thus converges on the assumption of the existence of both civic and cultural or instrumental and affective components of an assumed European identity.

Jürgen Habermas, in a less tangible manner, proposes a transformation of Western European societies from national to transnational communities, moving from "ethnos to demos." This idea is linked with his ideal of a constitutional patriotism, according to which citizens should not identify with a cultural or ethnic identity but rather with constitutional principles that guarantee rights and duties in a postnational framework (Habermas, 2001). The step to create a common constitution for the EU revived Habermas' theory—and it fell with the treaty's rejection in 2005. Coincidentally, such constitutionalism clashes with some of the real existing problems, such as the exclusion of third-country nationals and minorities living in EU member states, e.g., the Roma population. The idea of liberal contractualism as a way to bind European citizens closer to the EU has also been explored by other political theorists who maintain that citizens accept institutions as legitimate if they can be justified by some kind of social contract (Rawls, 1993). So far, such legal norms have been mainly applied in the national arena, since there are few instances in which the EU established a social contract with its citizens as treaties are not recognized as such. Should the EU levy direct taxes and redistribute resources on an individual level, this would certainly constitute a valid example, although there has been little progress on matters of taxation.

The inclusive principle, then, is essential for idealists who maintain that a new European identity is emerging that encompasses national subidentities and at the same time allows for cultural and ethnic differences embedded in a broader societal context. This multicultural, inclusive conception clashes with the argument that the way the EU is promoting European identity is that of an official "Euronationalism," the promotion of an exclusionary political block. Theorists generally agree in doubting the suitability of the nation-state model for a just and plural system of transnational governance (Delgado-Moreira, 2004). Even though common characteristics are certainly helpful in fostering an identity, past examples have usually been particularistic and oppressive, and thus cannot provide a model for this new diverse transnational structure—yet they continue to figure strongly, as my research proves.

To complicate matters, most scholars agree that in current EU member states the Europeanization of domestic collective identities occurs according to nation-specific characteristics of their nation and Europe (Cowles, Caporaso, and Risse, 2001). That is why, for instance, France has pursued a more ambitious but also more civic construction of Europe and the EU than Germany or Britain. Whereas this has been true for the past fifty years of integration, in recent years this process started to work in a reverse mode. It is no longer the states' conception of their view of Europe that has a monopoly on domestic identity discourse; the EU as an active player informs collective identity formation in either a positive or negative way as well. Primarily so because the EU has developed a tight network of competencies and policies that tangibly influences domestic political spheres in an unprecedented way. Secondly, there now are too many member states now cooperating in the Union for that one particular notion of Europe or the EU to prevail. For instance, the Franco-German dominance in EU policy initiation is increasingly clashing with differing views of other member states seeking an equal voice. The enlargement waves of 2004 and 2007 made this process already apparent, in which Europeanization informed national identity to a large extent, e.g., with the debate about how much new member states should compromise national interests during their integration into the EU.

As a political integration project planned by European elites, a "European" identity lacks the natural, culturally based foci of identity as maintained by the essentialists. Most citizens of the EU aspire in some way or another to profit from the Union's policies, showing more instrumental support and less affective identification. Even so, it cannot be generalized that purely material interests determine public support for the EU. A transnational identity, which for the sake of a working definition should be regarded as the extension of the national toward a larger European collective identity, constitutes a seemingly complex and abstract phenomenon. In its current configuration in the EU, it is remarkable to find in this context a particularist call for more common identity factors such as history, politics, economics, and other sociocultural aspects on the one hand, and a pluralist-minimalist characterization of supposed European values that entail an inclusive, civic conception defining normative European standards on the other hand. The reality lies in an acknowledgement of both tendencies, as the last hypothesis states: so far, EU citizen posses a capacity to tolerate intra-European cultural diversity, but still want to maintain their own national way of life. At the same time, the necessity of more common policy actions conflicts with the ideal of European unity as well as with the reality of the native political culture under integration pressures. One important point of inquiry consists in the question in how far citizens perceive of their Europeanized identity as either particularist or pluralist, since this aspect hasn't received attention in previous works on this subject.

For the purpose of this study, the transnational object of research is at times also referred to as "European identity," particularly as ordinary citizens and interview respondents have a better understanding of this term and the media utilizes it as well. It entails the existence of two different yet closely related political identifications—the cultural one referring to the cultural common aspects of social groups, and the civic and instrumental components built upon political values and a system of rights and rules as increasingly realized by the EU (Bruter, 2005). Both concepts are often not distinguished for research and statistics (e.g., the synonymous usage in the Eurobarometer) as well as for the population, so that the synchronous usage cannot be totally eradicated here. If referred to in this work, it means the political transnational self-ascription of EU citizens, and it is differentiated according to its cultural or civic component. A useful characterization of the civic identity spelled out by Moxon-Browne captures the complexity of a common political identity shared by citizens in the EU: "Europeans share a common political identity inasmuch as they accept among themselves a redistribution of resources and an equitable pattern of rights and duties that can be upheld by common institutions responsible for the authoritative allocation of values" (Moxon-Browne, 2004: 196).

A distinction of the idea, identity, and reality of Europe, which distinguishes between those three approaches to Europe with regard to their ideological reading aids in the conceptualization of a transnational European identities. In his own words, Delanty attempts "to dispel the mystique of Europe in order to assess the extent to which the European idea can in fact be the basis of a collective identity unencumbered by the narrow normative horizons of national identity and the chauvinism of the 'Fortress Europe' project" (Delanty, 1995: 163). The question of whether a multicultural European society can evolve to a collective identity that is not based on ethnoculturalism is as important as matters pertaining to economic and political integration. Nonetheless, he is wary about the chances to create such a transnational identity in current societies of the Union. Delanty contends that the postwar European project was born as a model of economic, not explicitly political, integration resulting from the wish to overcome the disastrous European hegemonic history in the first half of the twentieth century, an argument that is still hotly debated in EU studies because it goes to the core of what European integration is about. That is why he calls for an "alternative" collective identity built on multiculturalism and linked to a postnational citizenship in the Union. Delanty's work is important here because it demarcates well the notions and ideologies behind the goal of a united Europe, but it also exposes the rift between normative visions and the volatile reality found in contemporary European societies. Delanty's as well as Bruter's works raise important questions about the relationship between transnational identity extension and the identification of the EU as a result of European integration. As will be evidenced in this book, the civic component is heavily influenced by the processes of European integration occurring today so that identification with the EU reflects the degree of transnational allegiance to the political system established across Europe. The cultural transnational consciousness, however, existed before the civic component emerged and was built alongside national characteristics, and therefore remains a competitor to the civic component that pursues nationally removed political goals. The following chapters explore these two different yet related components of transnational identity extension more closely and show that the civic component of the European identity, while slowly emerging, is being constrained by ethno-national cultural considerations and domestic reception in the member states.

Some researchers depict collective identity formation and integration as a rather divisive and excluding process, either within countries of the European Union or between them. With regard to the developments inside the affected states, the impact of the EU is theorized as a catalyst for disparities between socioeconomic different constituencies of the population, the winners of European integration being pro-EU and the losers opposing it (Fligstein, 2008). "European integration is going to open up a new gap between the mobile elite of people moving toward a European identity and the less mobile people sticking to national solidarity" (Münch, 2001: 1). While this view is generally true, it presupposes that mobility—which is not further specified here either vertically or horizontally—is the decisive factor. This dichotomy ought to be differentiated so as to include of other influential factors such as knowledge, political involvement, etc. Yet especially in view of European countries that are not (yet) part of the Union, the exclusionary idea is significant for researchers of collective identities. They raise questions about the future self-understandings of Europeans with regard to the impetus of widening (Strath, 2000; Neumann, 1998). While enlargements make changes in identifications necessary, in the existing member states as well as in the accessing ones, it will not be a main focus of this project since the emphasis here is on the dimensions of deepening, not widening, the Union. In many ways, the recent enlargement waves can be viewed as an EU internal test for cultural plurality, with Turkey still holding out.

Authors examining theories of identity constructions often concentrate on an elitist-institutionalist analysis of identity politics "made in Brussels" (Checkel, 2007; Burgess, 2002; Hix 2001). Early on, there existed a split between the majoritarian group of elite-driven neofunctionalists and the few mobilization theorists who argued that integration does require the support of the masses. However, over time this quiet, elite-driven style of EU politics came to an end and debates around the Maastricht Treaty signified the start of a wider debate in the European public. Even a "Charta of European Identity" was created in 1994 by the pro-EU civil association Europe-Union, including references to the cultural and political community of Europe. Although the Charta was one of the few bottom-up projects, it remained neglected and remote from the issues that the mass citizenry faced. To address the issue, the principle that the Union shall respect the national identities of its member states was added to successive treaties, symbolizing the recognition of the sovereign entities. Despite the fact that this insertion was important for policy analysts, it changed little in the perception of ordinary citizens who witnessed a continued increase in EU legislation and implementation with little popular legitimization. Accordingly, an emphasis of this work will be on the impact of recent integrative policies on European citizens, thus producing an analytical counterweight to the elite-focused analyses of many EU integration studies.

A concentration on the citizenry also provides us with a valid account of the transnational identities of European populations. In distinguishing between so-called elites (e.g., political and business leaders) and citizens, it is necessary to be aware of the implicit idiosyncrasies that processes of knowledge diffusion and cognitive mobilization among the population entail. Policy makers and other elites are said to lead the rest of society by their decisions and policy implementations on national level. Unfortunately, they often do not pay sufficient attention to the need to clarify and justify these decisions to the public, or even willingly manipulate their position in the multilevel governance structure. As a result, the lack of transparency results in mistrust and, in extreme cases, in protest. This situation differs slightly from country to country, but as a general observation of policy formulation in Europe, it holds true for all states. With regard to the effect this process has on public opinion, it can be expected that general attitudes are far more critical and static in their perceptions of European integration than the one of elites. Moreover, the continued trend toward postmaterialist attitudes will probably result in a more individualistic and rather instrumental attachment to the EU than in strong political loyalties like the ones evoked by the classic national states. The time frame chosen for the evaluation of the impact of European integration spans a little over a decade. Twelve years can hardly represent or mirror the half century of EC/EU activities and its repercussions on the European public sphere. But 1993–2005 are key years with regard to the acceleration of integrative measures and, thus, the related identity transformations in the member states. In the following chapters, a highly complex picture emerges in which nationally conceived notions of Europe determine the approval of supranational policies and the creation of transnational identities.

Conclusion

I am proposing that in the most recent integration period marked by the ratification of the Maastricht Treaty and its collapse with the Lisbon one, the subject populations of the EU have embraced the construction of a civic transnational identity within their specific national contexts to the extent that their national political culture allows it. As a way of reading those enfolding structural changes, self-identifications are split now between the ones that feel their identity is enriched by the addition of a transnational European one, the ones that claim "a different Europe is possible," and the ones that outright reject the dissolution of traditional modes.

A theoretical framework comprising the major factors influencing and transforming collective identities was established and the relationship of the various layers of identity toward each other were explored, taking into account the synergetic as well as contradictory effects of these interrelated phenomena. Lastly, several explanatory models for the change in transnational identities in Europe, based on European integration, were proposed. Recent research on this topic highlights the need for contextual and transnational explorations to establish middle-range theories that adequately address the complexity of the topic, moving away from strict disciplinary boundaries (Checkel and Katzenstein, 2009). In an attempt to do so, the following chapters will address these theoretical concerns through a variety of historical-institutionalist and other empirical methods.

Chapter 3

The Impact of European Integration on the UK, Ireland, and Germany—A Historical-Institutionalist Overview

The Europeanization of EU member states, i.e., their adaptation to EU laws and regulations, and to integration more generally, represents an integral process characterizing contemporary European civic and political life in Europe. As such, it has not only created new layers of supranational governance in the economic, political, and social spheres, but also embraced the European public with a network of elite and mass exchanges as well as discourses that go beyond the generally assumed statist focus on the (nation-)state. Some analysts even speak of an Europeanization of elite identities, with a corresponding impact on transnational identity formation (Risse, 2010). To better understand the contextual base of identitive positions of the populations in the three case studies, it is necessary to review the countries' histories and experiences within the framework of the Union, and to assess the transformation of their nationhood, that is, "the nationally varying ideologies of collective distinctiveness and purpose" (Katzenstein, 1996: 59). This chapter illustrates the claim made in the second hypothesis that national identity constructs as forged through historical experiences, and later, with the help of EU integration, have shaped each country's political culture and thus its potential for identity extension in a distinctive manner, thereby leading countries such as Germany and Ireland to develop a stronger transnational identity as compared to the UK. The politicization and institutionalization of European affairs in the domestic context ultimately determines the degree to which these countries' populations will identify with the Union. Hence, the following sections review the historical-institutionalist configurations of the respective collective identities in these states, distinguished by multiple levels of governance, from the broadest one being the EU itself to the national governmental and party level, ending with a look at some of the nongovernmental civic actors involved in the domestic arena.

The Republic of Ireland

Historical Introduction

The national identity of this small island republic on the westernmost edge of the European continental shelf was strongly articulated throughout its long history. Stemming from ancient Celtic roots, expressed by its EU-recognized Gaelic language and in the past 500 years tested by British colonialization and occupation, it survived the experience of being a partially independent yet divided nation. In its relative isolation, Ireland developed a sense of national unity steeped in Catholic tradition and belief. Similarly influential, but less appreciated, Great Britain also had a significant impact on the country in that it served as a dominating antipode to the nationalist aspirations of the Irish population from the sixteenth century onward. The differences in belief, language, and customs constituted a determining factor in the Irish fight for autonomy, ending in 1921 with the establishment of the Irish Republic. With regard to its international relations, the principle of neutrality has become one of the major identity features of contemporary Irish foreign policy today. Its nonalignment orientation is rooted in pre-independence national struggles for autonomy from Britain, and is still highly valued by the majority of Irish citizens, who are increasingly worried about its dissolution in the face of accelerated European security integration.

In postwar Europe, agriculture-based Ireland was little affected by the preceding conflicts and missed out on the reconstruction boom that occurred on the continent, with the result that living standards slowly deteriorated. In 1973, when Ireland became a part of the then European Community (EC), subsidies started to flow in and modernized the country's infrastructure and economic sectors. Joining the EC also brought about a widening of markets, thereby easing the dependency on the UK and, finally, attracting considerable foreign direct investment from the United States and other countries in search of favorable political, geographical, and economic conditions for production. Until the global recession of 2008 took hold, the "Celtic Tiger" excelled as a thoroughly globalized country (*Economist*, 2004) and became one of the most economically successful EU member states. Governmental overspending and a bursting mortgage bubble, however, led in 2010 to a bailout through an EU-financed emergency fund, with ambiguous repercussions for Irish EU-sentiments.

Experience with the EU

Accession to the EC has been the most important postindependence step for the Republic of Ireland, and with good reason: "Ireland saw EC membership as a way of furthering its industrial plans, reducing its reliance on agriculture, and loosening its ties with Britain" (McCormick, 2002: 70). Especially with respect to Irish dependency on Britain, the EC was not only perceived as a platform for economic expansion, but also politically as a step toward emancipation from a nation that historically negated and subdued Irish autarky, autonomy, and national identity. Historically the reliance on Britain as Ireland's only major market proved to be detrimental to domestic growth since the UK was trading agricultural products, which were simultaneously Ireland's main export with many other nations—thus keeping down prices for these goods and artificially impoverishing the island. Therefore, the island's economic potential was largely unrealized until EC accession. "The benefits accruing to Ireland from EC membership were immense—far greater in relation to the size of the country than was the case with any other member state. This was true in relation to the impact on agriculture and the net flow of Structural Funds, but most of all in relation to the expansion of exports" (Fitzgerald, 2003: 175). At the time of accession, the EU's Social and Structural Funds provided great help in catching up economically and sociopolitically with the older member states, and Irish politicians skillfully negotiated favorable terms for their nation's development: Ireland received at one time 13 percent of the European Social Fund, although its population at the time constituted only 1 percent of the EC's population. It also fared disproportionately well under the Regional and Structural Fund allocations (158–9). In this regard becoming a member state had positive economic, political, and sociopsychological implications for Ireland that led it to develop a strong instrumental gratitude toward the Union. Referring to its dominant neighbor, John Ardagh astutely observed with respect to its changed status that "it enabled the old unequal face-to-face relationship with Britain to change into a new, more relaxed partnership, within a wider club where both are equal members; and this has eased the old Irish complex about the English" (Ardagh, 1997: 328). But it also contributed to a rediscovery of Ireland in the eyes of a larger international audience, rather than being perceived as a satellite of the UK. This effect further contributed to the initial pro-Europeanness of its citizenry.

Impact on National Politics

On a state level Ireland's identity remains contested by the divide between the Republic of Ireland and Northern Ireland, a province formally incorporated into the UK after the war for independence ended in 1922. Even after EC accession, terrorist acts by the Catholic Irish minority in Northern Ireland occurred, in part brought about by human rights violations from Protestant authorities, which in turn resulted in street violence on a regular basis. Considerable economic, political, and social differences between Northern Ireland and the Republic of Ireland existed, exemplified by the separatist activities of Northern Ireland's Irish Republican Army (IRA). So as to hint at the underlying socioeconomic roots of the conflict, in contrast to the salient ethno-religious component, Laqueur points these out: "In some of the most acute cases of national strife in Europe, poverty and underdevelopment also played a significant role, with Northern Ireland as an obvious example" (Laqueur, 1992: 442). Thus, in the case of the island republic the integration into the EU has helped alleviate the above-mentioned problems because under the EU umbrella, member states are required to have peaceful relations with one another, and generous redistributional funding is provided for regions lagging behind the EU average. A well-funded EU program for peace and reconciliation, worth about 700 million euros, aided in transforming Northern Ireland's social and political disparities as well (EC Special Programs, 2005).

Under the previous British Labor government, the peace process led by Tony Blair resulted in a devolved Northern Irish region with its own assembly and regional prerogatives in 1998, though the autonomous status of Northern Ireland has since been suspended on several occasions. In addition, the earlier parallel accession of both Ireland and the UK into the EU had momentous effects on the relations between the Republic of Ireland and Northern Ireland. The subsequent abolition of border controls and establishment of free trade between them enabled both parts to return to a state of normality: "The ending of economic custom controls between Northern Ireland and the Republic also had the effect of removing one particular physical manifestation of the border. The removal of customs posts and custom officers from the 'approved' border crossings changed the way people, north and south, viewed and thought of the border" (Ingraham, 2005: 3). On a smaller scale than occurred in the borderless Schengen area, both parts of the island already experienced a limited form of unification.

The Republic's government stood firmly behind increased integration and embraced the Union's policies and funds not only politically but also ideationally. As apparent by the obvious modernization, industrialization, and generation of jobs and prosperity, the domestic administration justified EU integration to the citizens of this proud nation as an actual strengthening of national Irish-Irish identity through European integration (Jolly, 1998). Overall, "ten years of painstaking diplomacy, by both the British and the Irish governments and by politicians and paramilitary leaders on both sides of the sectarian divide in the north have largely put an end to the violence that for two decades disfigured Northern Ireland" (*Economist*, 2003: 10). But whereas on a political level peace has gained ground and a significant level of stability has returned to the Irish-British relationship, both Irish entities still possess a separate national consciousness, with Northern Ireland showing an antagonistically contested identity. Even though most Northern Irish people, no matter if Catholic or Protestant, consider themselves "Irish," a significant part chooses instead the label "Northern Irish" to distinguish themselves, and some Unionists even call themselves "British" (Trew and Benson, 1996). The current situation could best be described as volatile and proves the limitations of integration in the eradication of national consciousness.

While Irish politicians maintain the consensus on pro-European attitudes independent of their party affiliation, differences are apparent in the engagement of governing Fianna Fail politicians toward European integration: whereas former Prime Minister (PM) Ahern proved to be a skillful negotiator in the run-up to the EU constitutional draft negotiations and thus elevated Irish allegiance to the bloc, the political elite under PM Cowen has more recently been accused of negligence vis-à-vis the Union in its handling of the domestic post-constitutional repercussions following the rejection of the constitution in France and the Netherlands. After initially canceling the referendum on the constitutional treaty, the government under the then new PM Cowen promoted in 2008 the popular approval of the Lisbon Reform Treaty. Yet public opinion turned against it because of doubts about national infringements on everything from moral issues to fears about losing neutrality to disapproval of the government in power. In addition, the anti-Lisbon group Libertas agitated on the base of demanding a more democratic Union, in line with Irish political culture, which incidentally constitutes one of the most basic democratic ones of the EU. This put the EU in crisis mode again (Euractiv, 2008), and proved that instrumental attachments to the EU cannot outweigh issues of national importance. Finally, the approval of the Lisbon Treaty in a second referendum in summer 2009 relieved some of the fears that Ireland could turn Euro-skeptic. But it has led the Union to question the allegiance of the Irish population to the EU and to revisit premature assumptions about the compatibility of national identities and interests with European integration.

Impact on the Domestic Arena

Ireland's opening toward other nations in the context of European integration and market liberalization more generally transformed the traditional societal structure of the island. One nongovernmental institution was particularly affected by this change and therefore needs to be mentioned in this context. Where the Catholic Church and a strong national bond once dictated social values and mass behavior, unprecedented cultural pluralism and market orientation brought about by European integration, migration, and globalization now challenge and change Irish society. The experienced increase in prosperity as well as the exposure to secular attitudes and some political consequences of EU accession, such as immigration and mobility, have had profound significance for the reevaluation of Irish national identity throughout the various sectors of society. "Among elites these changes have led to a crisis of identity as the values of a materialist and increasingly pluralistic society become more common and stand at odds with the values inherited from previous generations. For the masses these new materialistic and consumerist values have not replaced nationalist values as much as they have managed to coexist with them" (White, 2002: 8). While the public in general seems to have no problem with the impact of modernization and integration, the elites are by virtue of the obvious economic advantages of EU integration committed to further deepening the bonds with Europe. The permissive consensus surrounding the pro-European public attitude is challenged, however, by two important factors: on a structural level, Irish society has internalized the Irish role as beneficiary of aid funds distributed by the Union and now finds itself confronted with the fact that these funds will be curtailed for the benefit of the new EU member states from Central and Eastern Europe. And politically, a small group of Euro-skeptics, interestingly coming from the left spectrum, has crystallized around anti-EU stances regarding issues of human rights, neutrality, ecology, and democratization of the Union (Fitzgerald, 2003: 160).

With regard to the former issue, the high amount of utilitarian support effected by material gains through EU structural funds won't be available in the future as enlargements have started to direct these funds eastward, and thus instrumental approval needs to be replaced with affective support. It is unclear if the reciprocal gratitude has been able to generate such feelings. EU opposition groups, in turn, can build on a strong sentiment of noninterference with regard to foreign policy and ecological protectionism, in addition to increased demands for a more transparent delineation of national and European affairs, which have been consistently important topics for the Irish and are unlikely to disappear anytime soon.

On the other hand, the economic sector in Ireland is in strong support of the EU (as it is in most EU member states). This is largely explained by the modernization and diversification of the domestic industry, which has received substantial subsidies through the EU as well. The internationalization and diversification of the export economy from the UK to the EU market and beyond made the Irish industry more competitive, and access to the single market was welcomed by a mobile inbound and outbound labor force, with substantial numbers of new EU member citizens from Central Europe flocking to the booming Irish economy in the post-2004 period, reversing long-held emigration trends on the island. Subsequently this process led to a strong increase in housing prices, which during the recent global recession led to a steep decline of economic output, so that the economic viability of Ireland is, for better or for worse, perceived as being closely connected to the politics on the continent.

Media outlets seem to recognize the contribution of the EU for the strengthening of Ireland's status and national identity, and reflect this in their broadcasts and publications (see Chapter 6). Simultaneously there exists a strong commitment to democratic and transparent policy making in Ireland, originating from its historical origin as an enlightened modern republic and its small size, thus enabling basic democratic political participation. Particularly in the past few years, however, there has been a certain amount of discontent, with EU decision making perceived as unaccountable and exemplified in the initial rejections of the Nice Treaty in 2001 and later, the Lisbon Treaty in 2008. Therefore, future public support will be in part dependent on measures decreasing the democratic deficit of the Union as well as assuring the equality of small member states, especially in a country with strong popular governance principles such as Ireland.

Overall, the republic's experience with the EU has been harmonious even though European integration changed the structure of Irish politics and society tremendously, with somewhat ambiguous repercussions for both the island and the Union. The attitudes that Ireland as a whole as well as its citizens show toward the EU result largely from the material gains acquired through market integration and the receipts of structural funds, but are in part also explained by a gratefulness for being politically recognized as an equal member state—the civic component. However, this kind of reciprocal relationship between the island and the bloc weakened in recent years in that the gratitude of the Irish is slowly being replaced by expectations to be a player on equal footing with others. The downturn of 2008–2009 certainly deteriorated instrumentalist approval, yet such a development should not be conflated with the civic and cultural attachments inherent in transnational identity expansion. These perceptions have a significantly distinct impact on Irish transnationalism, as I will show in the following chapters.

The United Kingdom

Historical Introduction

Britain has a long history as a colonial world power; it did not experience an existential threat to its existence comparable to the Irish or German cases. In contrast to the other two cases, it implemented selective patterns of colonially based immigration up to the mid twentieth century, thus retaining a clear understanding of its national identity based on notions of empire. Yet as with other ethnically based nations such as Germany, for example, Britain has sought to define its people by identifying those who don't belong as much as by establishing a community of those who may fit into the national category. Evidence of this thinking is apparent in the appearance of immigration laws and amendments that were enacted in the second half of the twentieth century after the arrival of many commonwealth citizens on the island. "It is difficult to interpret this [...] as the expression of a coherent civic nationalism, given the discrimination and systematic inequities which appear to have marked successive revisions of citizenship, or to have a great deal of confidence in the civic character of a nation that has felt impelled to define itself by keeping out so many others" (Spencer and Wollman, 2002: 109). This exclusionary route is partially reflected in the UK's hesitancy toward all things European, but it has not prevented British society from becoming more multicultural and open throughout EU membership, as will be explained in the following paragraphs.

Experience with the EU

Within the EU, the UK is considered to be mainly Atlanticist in its geostrategic orientation, reflected by its actual geographical position as well as by its close historical and political connection to the United States. This description was proven true again in spring 2003 when the British government decided, in spite of its population's wishes and the majority of EU member states' dispositions, to take part in the U.S.-led invasion of Iraq. This fact reinforced the idiosyncrasies of the geopolitical transatlantic position of Great Britain at the Western periphery of the EU together with Ireland and Portugal.

Alongside those spatial features, the UK had declined to join the EEC at its creation in 1957, and instead initiated the European Free Trade Association, then was refused EC accession twice in 1963 and 1967 by French president De Gaulle's veto, and was finally admitted in 1973. From the outset, the UK has been a somewhat reluctant member state, especially during the years of Conservative Prime Minister Thatcher's government (Dinan, 1999). What other historical or political constellations exist that could explain the general British hesitancy toward European integration? As Lunati maintains, "[T]he UK's Commonwealth links, a continuing legacy of the British Empire, its North Atlantic inclination, due to a perceived closer affinity and supposed wider shared interest and values with the U.S. than other European countries, and its island mentality have all meant an often detached and skeptical attitude toward the whole project of European economic and political integration" (Lunati, 2000: 229). Economically seen, the UK possesses a more strongly liberalized economic system as well as a less restrictive labor market, both systemic differences that associate the country with the United States rather than with continental Europe.

In addition, there are factors at work that have to do with the unequal distribution of EU membership contributions throughout all member states. Great Britain has been for the first ten years after accession, together with Germany, one of the main contributors to the EC budget even though its domestic economic output until the mid-1990s was only average in the EU and its agriculture-based sector comparatively small. In 1984, the British government under Margaret Thatcher obtained a special rebate to make up for its disproportionate contribution. More recently a debate commenced about a possible abolishment of this refund on grounds that it would be unfair for the new EU member states that need monetary aid for themselves, in contrast to an economically stable country such as the UK. This announcement has not fared well with the British public, and only a partial rebate cutback of 20 percent has been achieved in the 2005 EU budget negotiations. Now that the British public finances are under severe pressure, governed by a Conservative-Liberal coalition, any new EU-related expenditures are treated as similarly sensitive and contentious.

While some scholars perceive British public support for integration to be farther reaching than just possessing a utilitarian attitude in that they feel European, their economic and political interests are not necessarily served by EU policies, which is documented by an abundant and well-established literature on the phenomenon of British EU skepticism (Risse, 2010; Carey, 2002; Baker, 1998; Anderson and Weymouth, 1999). Those reservations materialized in issues such as food export limitations set up by the EU in the aftermath of the outbreak of "Mad Cow" disease, the decision to opt out of the Schengen agreement and not to join the Euro area, or the disagreement over a common foreign and security policy in relation to NATO and the United States, to name a few.

Overall, it appears that throughout its history of contact with continental Europe, the UK has constructed its national identity as being distinct from the rest of the continent. EU accession and integration has not changed this attitude much in this respect. As Thomas Risse points out rather pessimistically, "English identity is incompatible with federalist or supranationalist visions of European political order. It explains why British governments, whether Conservative or Labor, have consistently been reluctant to support a deepening of European integration" (Risse, 2001: 199).

Impact on the National Governmental Level

The consensus in various segments of the British public, especially among members of the Labor Party and the Conservatives, about the rather detached level of cooperation with the EU reinforced the existing resistance toward pooling sovereignty. In contrast to Margaret Thatcher, who opposed most noneconomic integration measures such as the Economic and Monetary Union, and her Tory successor, John Major, who was consumed by internal party and domestic divisions over Britain's relations to the EU, Tony Blair's premiership was marked by a conscious and explicit rapprochement toward Brussels with the motivation to make Britain a leader in the steering of European integration. During his government, however, proposed policy measures such as the introduction of the euro or the ratification of the constitution have fostered domestic opposition toward further deepening from the traditional conservative right wing as well as from the accountability-seeking left. "What is at stake in the European controversy in British politics is a major choice about Britain's role in the global political economy, which involves questions of interest, ideology and identity" (McLean and Trouille, 2001: 4). This leaves the UK today with few supportive mechanisms for the EU, such as, for example, the policy of enlargement, which in itself can be critically viewed as an alternative strategy to avoid further policy integration.

Two main factors for the strong attachment to its national unity and sovereignty lie, according to Risse, in the historical importance of the British Crown and the parliamentary democratic model of the UK government. The royal family symbolizes "external sovereignty" from the Catholic Church and the continent more generally, and the old parliamentary tradition constitutes "internal sovereignty" and power sharing for the UK. These aspects were fundamental in the construction of British history as a continuous national evolution (Risse, 2001: 204–5). There have been other monarchies with parliamentary democracies integrated into the EU with much fewer problems surrounding sovereignty, so the other factors at work—i.e., geography, political role in Europe and the world, etc.—make for a peculiarly strong case of national consciousness in the UK.

Such strong British identity and corresponding lack of EU attachment is enhanced by two domestic political factors: the relative failure of right-wing mobilization in the UK and the spatially contested concept of Britain's stateness. Extreme right-wing parties are of concern in this analysis insofar as they popularly impress on transnational identification, but neither in the UK nor in Germany or Ireland has there been sufficient ground for the development of a thriving extremist political scene as can be observed in other European states, such as France, Austria, or Belgium, for example, whose nationalist parties have seats in national legislatures. There are many reasons for the nonexistence of a viable British right-wing opposition; the most important ones being the absorption of these elements into the more moderate Conservative party and the limiting effect the single-member district electoral system has on small parties. "For all these reasons—the identification with foreign ideologies, the low profile of the party leaders and inner factionalism, the anti-racist counter-mobilization, the skillful containment operated by the Conservatives by raising and then suffocating the immigration issue, and the majoritarian electoral system, plus the cultural features of the British system—the extreme right never acquired a relevant status in Great Britain" (Ignazi, 2003: 186). However, the UK Independence Party and the British National Party, both known for their virulent anti-EU stance, have gained electoral access to the European Parliament in the elections of June 2009.

On the other hand, the spatially contested concept of what "Britain" geographically entails has been and still is a decisive issue in British identity. Since the Middle Ages, foreign influences and the power struggle for regions on the British isle like Scotland or Wales and neighboring Ireland have proven to the English powers in London that the establishment of a strong national identity comes only with control over these areas.

Contemporary efforts to devolve these regions and give room to their ever-present demands for autonomy—as evident in the Scottish National Party leadership, which wants to conduct a referendum on Scottish autonomy in the next few years—slowly dilute British monopolization of national identity. Based on their history and the potential to circumvent centralized governance through relations with the EU, the regions, England excluded, seem to profess more affinity for regional integration. In the former region, however, the UK Independence party, notoriously known for its demand to withdraw from the EU, formed in 1993 as a reaction to the Maastricht proceedings.

Up to this day British identity seems to be incompatible with a European imagination, a perception mediated by previous Labor administrations but not always well received domestically. It remains to be seen how European constitutionalization and enlargement will affect British transnational identification in the coming years, especially since Tony Blair raised the level of discussion about European matters such as defense policies, the EMS, and EU reform significantly, thereby advocating in principle a closer orientation toward the bloc, whereas Gordon Brown tended to be more cautious in his European politics and sideline EU affairs in view of domestic challenges. The elections of May 2010 further complicated the dynamic between the British government and the Union as the Conservative-Liberal coalition under PM David Cameron will position itself as even more distant, as his ambiguous treatment of the Lisbon Treaty in spite of the British parliament's ratification in June 2008 has shown. It is difficult to imagine that the Liberal Democrats as minority partner can sway the coalition's moratorium on the introduction of any new European integration measures for the remainder of their common term.

Impact on the Domestic Public Arena

Britain's public is not reflective of the domestic position of the political, economic, and social elites, which are split on EU matters between approval of closer economic integration, and apprehension of political integration yet overall displays a higher degree of pro-Europeanism (as in most member states). This does not translate to the general public, though: if one takes a closer look at more recent poll data, it becomes evident that although the annual execution of Eurobarometer and other surveys note a slight improvement in pro-EU attitudes, the UK still has the lowest proportion of respondents who view membership as a good thing, with only one-third of those polled agreeing, as compared to an EU-15 average of more than half (European Commission, 2004). The relatively high percentage of people not knowing or not having an opinion on this matter, around one-third of the respondents, can be considered an expression of the widely dispersed mistrust and disinterest in European affairs. As one Commission report from 2003 states, "The UK has historically tended to be the 'don't know' capital of the EU when looking at the level of public knowledge on matters European. What emerges from this report is a high level of distrust of the European institutions." (European Commission, 2003: 4). But there also prevails a chance for partial improvement in attitudes: the euro adoption, previously most strongly rejected in the UK, has become a topic of debate for the domestic government as well as for the public, which observes the surrounding single-currency scheme. The continuing debates about the euro, future enlargements, and, particularly, about a European defense policy worth its name, will in the long run stimulate more discussion among the British citizenry so that the monolithic resistance built upon national pride might at least be questioned—independent of the party in power.

The business community, while elitist, is overwhelmingly pro-European. Whereas British labor unions still debate the impact of European integration on their leverage, companies and businesses in the UK knew how to market themselves to international investors as an ideal entry point into the common market. As a result, the British economy fares well compared to other EU member states and has developed extensive communication and lobbying channels aimed at Brussels. That makes the British business community one of the strongest supporters of the EU in the UK. In contrast, other societal actors in Britain, such as the churches, agree with the general sentiment against increased EU interference in domestic affairs displayed by political parties and politicians, but are of lesser salience in British public life. The majority of domestic audiovisual and print media are certainly contributing to EU fatigue, as will be illustrated in the print media analysis chapter. Fairly commercialized, they appeal with their scandalous stories and customary "us against them" position with regard to many things European to a large uninformed strata of the population, and they keep the level of contention about membership high instead of discussing the contents and implications of EU policies.

In sum, the British stance toward the EU is one of widespread reluctance, opposition, and ignorance. In comparison to Ireland and Germany, the UK had more influence before the EU existed and therefore experiences integration as harmful for national sovereignty and identity because it is being constrained in its political decisions. Although recent governments appear more conciliatory vis-à-vis the EU, the majority of the public remains opposed to any further integration, and a continuation of such government Europeanism is doubtful in view of the incumbent center-right government. The aim in this case study, therefore, is to show how integration is affecting transnational identity formation under adverse circumstances.

The Federal Republic of Germany

Historical Introduction

In its equally long and eventful history, Germany, which constituted part of the (Holy Roman) Empire of the German Nation before its unification in 1871, based its national consciousness predominantly on language and on other ethno-cultural characteristics for hundreds of years. Its drive for establishing a European superpower, along with imperialistic ambitions, led to the First and subsequently, Second World War. The surrender in 1945 and total destruction as well as occupation of Germany, followed by the separation of the country into an eastern and western part, gave way to a new kind of national character in the Federal Republic. This postwar identity, however, was dampened by the immediacy of Germany's destructive past, and therefore a reorientation toward European multilateralism provided the only way for reestablishing its reputation on an international level. The reunification of East and West Germany in 1989 led to increased reflection on the newly unified national identity, and a discussion about resulting political expressions followed, which will be dealt with below.

Experience with the EU

Being one of the founding member states, its economic powerhouse, and currently the country with the highest population in the EU, Germany has been one of the driving forces of EU integration. This does not only relate to the historical circumstances of the creation of the European Coal and Steel Community (ECSC), but also to German usage of the EU for its postwar reintegration into the international political scene. Strong support for multilateral European policy making, mixed in the past with considerable economic performance and a weak national identity, has put the country at the core of the Union. Unfortunately the problematic economic situation since reunification has disillusioned many Germans about the focus on European rather than domestic affairs, and the country still needs to come to terms with its newly acquired powerful status in Europe.

After the annihilation of German nationalism following the Second World War, the country's successful reconstruction aided by the United States' Marshall Plan and the ECSC led to high approval for European integration from the beginning. As such, it ranked highest in pro-European support until the 1980s, when other European nations converged on the issue of pro-integration (Inglehart and Reif, 1991). It proved essential that the European reassurance of Germany was strongly connected to the guarantee of protection against the threat of communism at that time. As such, a large part of the German public saw the EU as a medium to realize not only European but also global economic and security objectives.

More recently it appears that this country has become rather preoccupied with itself, trying to manage the challenges posed by the reunification of East and West Germany in 1990, and the ensuing infrastructural, political, and economical problems: "A new international position and an internal situation in which two quite different political cultures had to be reconciled and a fifth of the population had to adjust to a completely new economic and political system inevitably led to a reassessment of the national consciousness and with obvious consequences for the German's European identity" (Splittler and Knischweski, 2003: 255). At the same time, both parts of the country clashed with their different identities, which evolved over the past forty-five years (Grix and Cooke, 2002), including a less trusting attitude of East Germans toward the EU—or any political institution for that matter. Even so, a Germanic European identity was closely interrelated with the reemergence of a national identity, perceiving the inclusion in the EU as prerequisite for an autonomous country in an embracing political regional structure. Some authors go as far as maintaining that the German postwar European identity actually informed the conception of German interests, with the economic and political reunification of Europe preceding the national one in 1990 (Banchoff, 2002). If this should be the case, Germany's post-unification identity is still being processed and formed, as the many domestic debates about its geopolitical role prove.

Contemporary attitudes toward European integration are still marked by strong EU attachment. A consistent majority of Germans look positively upon German EU membership, which compares to the current EU average. Interestingly for such a multilateral country, support for EU enlargement is relatively low among German citizens, who as direct neighbors are more affected than most other EU member states. "Due to the enlargement process positive expectations, such as a more important role for Europe in the world, and maintaining peace and security in Europe, are counterbalanced by concerns about rising unemployment, less financial aid from the EU for Germany, and higher costs for member states like Germany." (Banchoff, 2002: 266). As expected in the case of such a thoroughly Europeanized country, even nationally sensitive foreign policy issues have high approval ratings if perceived as EU tasks, with two-thirds of the population favoring a common European policy on defense and security or constitution (see Chapter 5). And although Germans agree with many citizens in the eurozone that the cost of living rose or that consumer prices have been artificially rounded up since the introduction of the euro, the positive attitude toward the monetary union as a means of European unification remained steady—until the German government agreed to disproportionately finance the EU 'bailout' funds of 2009-2010. Yet overall, a moderately permeating Europhilia is being complemented by the self-assessment of Germans as being well informed about current EU issues, making them, in contrast to the Irish or British, instrumentally critical of the Union but affectively in favor of it.

Its geopolitical location, historical idiosyncrasy, and economic development made Germany one of the strongest supporters of EU integration. First developed as a refuge of political reestablishment after World War Two, European identification has now been widely popularized among German citizens and is seen as indispensable, maybe even indistinguishable from a national one.

Impact on the Governmental Level

Because of Germany's political reinstatement via European integration, a consistent pro-integration consensus remained among the political elites and the citizenry throughout its postwar history. And while there have been at times public debates about contentious EU politics affecting the domestic realm, e.g., the loss of the deutsche mark in exchange for the euro or the implications of the last two enlargements waves, the "pro-integrationist elite consensus has had a symbiotic relationship with a permissive popular consensus" (Dyson and Goetz, 1999: 7). Even though the German public exhibited stable support for integration as such, I suggest that there exists now a qualitatively different and more critical public discussion about Germany's national identity and, therefore, its post-unification role within the EU policy-making framework.

Independent of party allegiance, German parties and governmental circles for most of the postwar period have strongly embraced and advanced European integration. Then, in the 1990s, during the painful adaptation of East Germany to the Western political and economic model, a considerable part of the governing elite of the former socialist German Democratic Republic was discredited, together with its "state security" system of control and repression. This process affected a larger part of the population besides the "perpetrators" and the "victims"—a whole national political culture vanished in the East. In the past two decades, the German government focused politically and economically on the internal reconciliation of the nation and on achieving unity rather than sovereignty, with the effect that Eastern German legislators adapted quickly to the Western model, while its public became increasingly alienated by it (Davidson-Schmich, 2007). This might explain why Germany was and still is much less concerned with the notion of sovereignty than with developing an "organic" nation-state—without considering the reality of Germany having become a "Zuwanderungsland" (immigration country) in need of sensible immigrant integration. In addition, the German state governments have increasingly used the protection of certain policy areas and autonomy of the Länder governments guaranteed in the basic law as an instrument to lobby for regional autonomy in Brussels—and indeed, at times for more control over Germany's EU involvement through the upper chamber, the Bundesrat.

Reunification of the country also had consequences for the reassessment of Germany's identity within the EU from a nonpower to a civil power and from the exclusive orientation toward Western Europe to Central and Eastern Europe. Its reunification was perceived as a major step toward normalization of the country, and with this process, a national reflection and debate began about changes for its future role in Europe and the world. Outside of Germany this debate was often perceived with the fear of a "Germanization" of Europe, in particular the exertion of influence gained by Germany through assisting Central and Eastern European countries in their modernization. While there has been elitist support for the accession of East-Central Europe, the outcome of enlargement has not led to a significantly stronger German clout, as certain countries, such as Poland, have their own bilateral issues. Germany actually lost the dominant Franco-German position in the enlarged Union, with more members aligning along policy issues rather than traditional diplomatic coalitions.

However, with regard to the post-unification debate about Germany's changed identity, the claim is made that instead of opening up to a real transnational state in the center of Europe, "it was nationalist ideology in its various forms which appears to have largely dictated and structured the terms of the debate, marginalizing democratic demands for equal rights within a multicultural post-national society, incorporating others into the nation on selective criteria (e.g. ethnic Germans from the East), whilst constructing a range of new barriers and gates" (Spencer and Wollman, 2002: 135). An institutionalized renegotiation of national identity is still taking place somewhere in between the facilitation of naturalization in 2000 and the newly introduced citizenship test for naturalizing residents.

Such transformation is also reflected by a more assertive stance of the German government toward the EU, no matter if previously under Social Democrat Schroeder or currently, Christian Democrat Merkel, emphasizing more often than before Germany's national interests in light of its economic and EU-budgetary clout. According to some scholars, Germany's "shift in tectonic plates" toward European integration has led to a stronger consideration of a cost-benefit analysis, something that is considered normal for other member states but has been a nonissue for most of Germany's postwar attitude toward the EU. The newly expressed self-confidence is more conditional opposite EU demands and is exemplified by, for example, the insistence on a German appointment as enlargement commissioner in 1999, repeated attempts to evade EU subsidy controls and fines for breaching the Stability Pact, and debates at treaty and constitutional negotiations about issues of national interest vis-à-vis other EU member states (Jeffery and Paterson, 2004). Still, Germany's general commitment to EU integration remains stable and its orientation fundamentally multilateral, reflecting in combination with Germany's new assertiveness what Anderson calls a pattern of continuity and change (Anderson, 1999). But, as Regina Karp contends, the EU and Germany seem to have arrived at a point in which "Germany has to stay integrated since the very meaning of integration is a function of how well the question of German identity and power has been resolved" (Karp, 2003: 537).

German national identity transformed slightly through critical junctures, such as the hosting of the 2006 World Soccer Cup, which justified the display of patriotism in a multicultural, peaceful framework. Yet twenty years after the fall of the Berlin Wall, there still exists a preoccupation with the creation of a "Gesamtdeutsche" national identity and its ramification for Europe and the world, which takes precedence over the various other identitive positions existing in the country, such as party-based or transnational ones. The previous Grand Coalition government and the reemergent Left, fashioned from the former East German socialist party, are expressions of an ambiguous national consciousness, and even the incumbent center-right government is under constant pressure to justify German power to its domestic society as well as its regional neighbors.

Impact on the Domestic Public Arena

One ought not to forget that national unification brought about a merger of two completely different popular bodies, each with its own set of priorities and ideological affinities. I have already touched upon the visible East-West divide regarding domestic popular support for European integration. The citizens of Eastern Germany seemed to feel general disappointment about national developments after reunification, which was only exacerbated by the cost-cutting measures initiated for the Eastern enlargement of the EU (Dyson and Götz, 1999). It also meant that the political and electoral stability of the new German system eroded, based on a lack of identification of the East German population with the country (Mushaben, 2010).

The unified civic German landscape has experienced a drop in general support for the Union, compared with levels in former West Germany. Lower percentages of people interested in European politics and people identifying with Europe are indicative of the delimiting effect of the integrationist policy of political leaders in the post-unification phase (Münch, 1996: 32). A distinction needs to be made, however, between the two levels at which German citizens perceive the EU: "those that are defined by the daily and increasing annoyance with policies emanating from Brussels, and those that are shaped by a long-lasting and ever-enduring 'love for Europe'—the latter assuming the notion of the political community as a solid basis for the EU polity. 'L'Europe profonde' can still be seen as a major part of German identity, even though empirical evidence for that statement appears less reliable and valid" (Wessels, 2003: 136). Even today, German romanticism and idealism sustains support for the vision of Europe as materialized, for better or for worse, in the EU.

The increasing contestation of domestic support for EU integration has not led to a sustained boost for right-wing extremists. While in the 1990s electoral gains of right-wing parties such as the Republikaner and xenophobic incidents occurred, these phenomena declined significantly with the consolidation of the Eastern German states. The extreme right has not been able to solidify popular support "because of a lack of legitimacy, linkage to the past, and inner structural weakness. [However], if the extreme right failed in the electoral arena it is still present (and aggressive) in street-level activity, especially in the East" (Ignazi, 2003: 82). This anomic right-wing extremism, however, reflects domestic adaptation problems to a "Gesamtdeutsche" identity rather than opposition to the EU. Interestingly, contestation of the liberalizing aspects of European integration has grown under an emerging Left party, which discredits increased competition and serves as a political refuge for the (mostly East German) losers of it.

A more complex though positive impact of EU regulation has been on the business associations and other industrial interest groups. Challenged by the market liberalization in preparation for the single market, these players understood to lobby directly EU institutions were more effective than their European competitors, and they also profited from investments in the new member states. They excelled through organizational strength and the advantage of being traditionally involved in major domestic policy making. Therefore, these interest groups contributed to a supportive elitist stance on European integration (Dyson and Götz, 1999).

Interest groups representing social, environmental, religious, and other political stances have not had much control over EU integration even though they are well represented on a civic level. One reason for this is that social and welfare policies are still a strictly domestic domain and, therefore, only very limited effects of EU legislation are visible. In contrast to Ireland, which is socially dominated by the Catholic Church, environmental interest groups are strong civil-society representatives in Germany, but they also structure debates and policy making through national parties, especially the Greens and the newly emerging Left party. They, in turn, relay national aspirations through their input onto the EU level. The strong influence of the German and European Greens on Brussels has shaped German consciousness as one of the environmental public advocates in the Union—while at the same time, German chemical and automotive industries lobby heavily for less environmental regulation.

In sum, with the exception of a shift toward a stronger national orientation after reunification, there have been limited effects of the unification on German (trans)nationalism. The main explanation for this phenomenon lies in the modeling of German postwar institutional foundations and collective identities toward European integration: "Processes of opinion formation, identity construction, and elite-mass interactions have not been notably affected, whether one looks at the party system, interest groups, or the media. The prime reasons are to be found in a strong pro-European elite consensus, which defines macro-political strategies at home as well as within the EU" (Padgett et al., 2003: 357).

Conclusion

After having reviewed the experiences of each case country with the EU, it is worth considering the meso-perspective of these countries with regard to their interaction within the EU, since their position toward each other in part influences their domestic political culture and their identification patterns. As mentioned above, the Republic of Ireland possesses a strong though ambiguous relationship with the UK, which stems from their fateful common history and the disagreement over Northern Ireland. It is therefore not surprising that Ireland appears continuously wary about any British attempts in Brussels to (re)nationalize European policy issues.

In fact, Ireland's Euro-optimism is in large part due to the fact that the EU is seen as providing a level playing field for both actors, thereby giving Ireland the chance to be present and visible on the European scene. Yet at the same time, Ireland demands this democratic balance not only from its neighbors but also from Brussels.

Related to the last argument is Ireland's position as a small member state, compared to the UK and Germany. As such it has unique interests among these three with regard to power sharing and institutional representation in the Union. In many EU policy debates there is a tendency for the big member states to overrule smaller ones, not only in terms of voting proportions, but also through their geopolitical diplomatic or economic and financial influence. In particular, the so-called "big three," Britain, France, and Germany, have used their clout to their collaborative advantage. As one of the successful smaller states, Ireland has made a point of insisting that the institutional reform initiated through the European constitution will not leave an unequal balance of power between smaller and larger states (Magnette and Nicolaidis, 2004). This is especially true after the 2004 enlargement, with most new members being considered small states. And it has realized such demands by dragging its referenda heels twice, thus threatening to slow down reform processes in the Union.

On the other hand, Ireland is in a position to bridge the transatlanticist and the so-called Europeanist positions that constantly confront each other on the EU level. While being an Anglophone country on the Western rim of Europe like the UK, Ireland is very much committed to deepening European integration, with the notable exception of the CFSP. The 2004 Irish presidency proved its skillfulness in coming to agreements needed for consent on the Constitutional Treaty. Simultaneously, Irish voters insist on their neutrality and recognition, and will make their voices heard even if it means stalling the EU's constitutional evolution, as occurred with the initial rejection of the Lisbon Treaty.

The British-German relationship is marked by the necessity of cooperation rather than conscious or willful collaboration. Even though under Blair's premiership, the UK was more willing to play a more significant role in EU construction compared to the reluctance shown during the Thatcher and Major years, disagreements over the EMS and foreign policy issues such as the Iraq invasion have highlighted the limits of British-German cooperation and intra-European consent more generally, and the current center-right coalition has come full circle in refocusing their priorities and demands toward the EU and its continental Franco-German backbone. The interaction between all three states is marked by negative collective memories and competitive attitudes toward each other with respect to assuming a key position in determining the EU's strategic direction. Hence, one cannot analyze the German-British relationship without extending it to a strategic diplomatic triangle between France, Germany, and the UK. The Franco-German cooperation, historically the main column of European integration, is regarded with suspicion by Britain. This reservation is in part due to the tendency of France and Germany to push ahead with integration proposals that leave out other member states, not only Great Britain. The British government finds it difficult to regain some of the influence and goodwill among its other two diplomatic counterparts who forged so strongly ahead with the creation of a unified Europe, so that the close collaboration between the two continental neighbors will remain a defining aspect of the EU in the years to come. Importantly, France and Britain share a historical role and continued ambitions as world powers and, equally important, a seat in the United Nations Security Council. The advantage point of their bilateral relationship is constantly renegotiated, and the German governments have opted in recent years to rely mainly on the support from its French neighbor, although these bonds appears more historically and politically forced than voluntarily sought, and are dependent in part on the personal relationship between both countries' leaders. But Germany, following the end of the Cold War, has somewhat reoriented its outlook from West to East in the post-2004 EU enlargement period as well. It becomes evident that none of the collective identities in these countries can be examined only in light of EU integration; they also are affected by and influence each others identitive positions. Leaving the individualized focus of the Union's impact on each of the case countries, the next three chapters empirically assess the degree and direction of transnationalism in these nations through interview, print, and aggregate data analyses.

Chapter 4

How Do Citizens Perceive European Integration?

Introduction

Presenting the first of three empirical chapters exploring the construction and constitution of (trans)national identities, this qualitatively oriented interview analysis provides an immediate and detailed view of identitive positions of citizens in the EU. Public opinion varies significantly among the population and statistics can only supply an aggregate overview, thus there are good reasons for including such an ethnographic method. For one, direct access to individuals makes for a good primary source. Moreover, it allows the reader not only to explore apparent, quantifiable statements, but also to aim at the underlying attitudes and cognitive preconceptions attached to European integration. The citations presented here are used to illustrate the arguments regarding the impact and meaning of integration policies, the perception of people's changing national identities, and the volatile evolution of European transnational identity formation. Additionally, interviews enable the researcher to direct the questions to obtain open-ended questions that cannot be collected by precoded surveys, such as the EU's Eurobarometer dataset. In designing a suitable questionnaire (see appendix), the aim was to enable people to share as much information as possible. This meant that the questions had to be for the most part open-ended and, on an intellectual level, comprehensible for citizens with different levels of education and cognition. Starting with a few simple demographic indicators, such as age, gender, educational degree, and political affiliation (question 1), four questions were inserted from the Eurobarometer surveys to obtain a certain degree of comparability. These dealt with a self-categorization in identity terms (question 2; see appendix) and a general judgment about EU membership (question 3), as well as two questions relating to the level of information about the EU and political news more generally (questions 4–5). The open-ended questions that followed ranged from spontaneous associations with terms such as Europe and the EU (question 6) to inquiries about personal experiences with the EU (question 7), judgments about EU membership in the past decade (question 8), and a probe into the EU's ability to constrain national sovereignty (question 9). The next set of four (10–13) covered each independent variable, asking respondents to voice their opinion about the common market, the euro, the Common Foreign and Security Policy, and the draft constitution. A second query posed a dilemma of choosing between national goals and common EU goals (question 14), and the last question asked about differences between EU and non-EU Europeans and delved into the ambiguous relationship between national and transnational European identity (question 15). Lastly, all participants had the chance to add or express thoughts that were not covered in the interview so far (question 16).

This section is intended to answer some of the hypotheses developed in the introductory chapter. Inquiries into the compatibility of national and transnational identities lend support to the first hypothesis, which states that for the majority of citizens EU integration is not perceived as a threat to national identity. The second hypothesis, exploring if and how post-Maastricht policies contributed to either transnational identification or protective nationalism, is strengthened through correlation of the statements relating to the various variables and is further operationalized in the question focusing on the respondent's opinion development on the EU over time. Questions 4 and 5 ask for information through media use and thus serve as indicators for the basis of opinion formation and attitude development. The last hypothesis, which states that more EU citizens are developing a particularistic conception of European identity versus a universalist or pluralist one, is reflected in the questions about preferences of national or supranational goals, as well as the relationship between EU citizens and non-EU third-country nationals. As the answers to both questions indicate limited support for a transnational orientation toward the EU, however, a universalistic and inclusive common identity cannot be concluded from the responses.

A sample size of sixteen respondents per country is theoretically sufficient to establish a matrix covering the major demographic distinctions among the population to receive a wide variety of responses in a four-by-four matrix: different age, gender, occupation/education, and location

(Gaskell, 2000: 89). Age and gender, for instance, are categories included in the initial demographic section, where I also obtained information about the respondents' occupation, their highest obtained degree, and their political affiliation on a left–right polarization scale. The distinction between urban and rural positions has been taken into account as far as the interviews were conducted in Ireland in the cities of Limerick and Galway, but also in the surrounding rural areas. In the UK, the samples are from London and the region north of the capital, and in the German sample, the respondents come from the city of Munich and the Bavarian countryside.

Demographic Characteristics

The first questions inquire about five demographic indicators and prepare the interviewees by asking for information that is readily available. Respondents are asked to provide their age, occupational status, religious affiliation, their highest degree earned in the educational system, and their political affiliation. This data is collected to obtain the most important constituent characteristics and to ensure that there is a wide range of opinions within the sample.

With regard to age, in Ireland, respondents' ages range from 21 to 68, with an average of 34 years and a standard deviation of thirteen years. In Germany, the age span starts at 28 and ends at 60, with an average of 37 and a standard deviation from that average of nine years. The British respondents are slightly older, with an average of 39 years and a standard deviation of twelve years. Ideally the gender distribution should be balanced because the literature has detected significant differences between men and women with regard to the "gendering" of support, with women showing slightly more Euro-skepticism (Liebert, 1997). In the German and British sample, there are eight and seven women, respectively, among the respondents, and the Irish sample consists of nine women and six men.

Similarly, religion is mentioned in the field as a significant indicator for the development of Europeanism or Euro-skepticism (Nelson and Fraser, 2001). While in theory religious people tend to be more supportive of the EU than atheists or agnostics, in practice a public debate occurred about the EU's secularizing tendencies that has preoccupied, for example, the Catholic majority in Ireland. Twenty-nine people, or about two-thirds of the respondents in the total sample, have been baptized as Christian, but are now either atheists or nonpracticing. The remaining one-third, consisting of sixteen respondents, identify themselves as practicing Christians, with Ireland having more practicing outliers.

The various levels of occupation and education range in all three countries from students to housewives to manual laborers to management executives and retirees. Similarly, the education level in the samples shows disparities: in the German case, for example, about one-third possesses a high school diploma and vocational training as their highest degree, and close to two-thirds hold a university degree of some sort. In the Irish and British samples, however, the percentage declaring a high school diploma or vocational training as the highest earned degree rises to around 50 percent, with the other half possessing some sort of university degree. The last of the demographic questions asks respondents to position themselves on a dichotomous political spectrum ranging from left to right, with left meaning socialist and social-democratic ideologies and right meaning conservative or nationalistic ones. This dichotomy is generally well established in most EU countries and is reflected as such in political science (Schmitt and Thomassen, 2005). However, one cannot link these ideological orientations directly to either Europeanism or Euro-skepticism. Support for or opposition to the EU is not directly related to either a social-democratic or conservative affiliation (Marks and Steenbergen, 2004).

In Germany, as in most other continental European states, a fairly clear-cut distinction exists between the left-leaning Social Democratic Party and the conservative Christian Democrats, even though the Social Democrats at least rhetorically appear to be more centrist than during previous decades. A similar phenomenon is visible in the UK for the Labor government under Blair and Brown, who repositioned their party as "the new left" with policies more closely located in the political center. Only in Ireland are the party families not distinguishable in an easy detectable manner: the biggest one, Fianna Fail, which regularly wins around half the seats in parliament, is a centrist party, leaving little room for other parties on both sides of the political spectrum except for the ones that are able to enter into a coalition with the dominant party (Gilland, 2002). Accordingly, two-thirds of the respondents identified themselves as neutral or centrist in the Irish sample. Only two respondents there considered themselves as either belonging to the left or to the right. In the UK, eight of the fifteen interviewees consider themselves as "left" or affiliate themselves with the Labor Party, while only four are conservative. The remaining three describe themselves as belonging to the center or didn't want to be categorized at all. Germany is the exception to the rule: of the fifteen respondents there, no one wanted to be identified as conservative or even belonging to the right. Five people associated themselves with the Social Democrats, and nine occupied the middle ground using terms such as neutral, centrist, or liberal to describe their position. One person identified herself as conservative, albeit with some social-democratic values.

Such atypical self-ascriptions point to a certain hesitancy among Germans to consider a rightist self-classification as a political option, most probably stemming from the country's fascist past.

Questions Taken from the Eurobarometer Dataset

While the previous questions supply us with the demographic information necessary to interpret the results and to control for balance and outliers, the following four were taken from Eurobarometer to achieve comparability with its outcomes. They also include some of the most important questions in this interview, such as the one asking respondents to identify themselves in terms of national and/or European identity. In the Eurobarometer codebook, the question probing how people see themselves supplies only four categories as possible answers and ranges from a purely "national" identification, to professing a "first national and then European" identity, to a "first European, then national" category, and, finally, an "only European" self-assessment. Since I wanted to encourage more open-ended questions, I also allowed for other categorization at a global or local/regional level and inquired *why* people chose a certain category. In Germany, eleven people answered that they would feel German first and then European. This is congruent with the results of the Eurobarometer surveys, in which this category is continually chosen by the majority of Germans. One person felt that she was first European, then German, while another one identified himself as only European. Interestingly, one person used a triple classification, speaking of himself as first (regional) Bavarian, then European, and only then German. And one respondent in particular had an interesting way of answering this question, citing the broader context:

> "German, from my cultural roots, but Europe is the sociopolitical context in which I live and which I support. In that case, I think of Europe as the more important goal. The one is where I come from, the other where things should be going." (D-2)[1]

Asked why they chose a specific categorization, most people in Germany referred to the fact that they were born or grew up there and that they are in possession of the language and the customs of their country. With regard to the second identity preference, "European," chosen by almost all respondents, the argument was often made that because of the country being in the EU, one automatically is European. It seems that the merging of the two distinctly different notions of Europe and EU, used by the latter as strategy for a common identity construction, is readily accepted in Germany. Two people argued that traveling and knowing residents from other European countries made them feel more European. On the other end, an externally differentiating proposition was made by one person who argued that he felt European to distinguish himself from the United States.

In Ireland the number of predominantly national identifiers is much higher. One responded as being exclusively Irish, while a majority—thirteen people—fell into the "Irish first, then European" category, with one exception who felt her allegiance first to Ireland and then to all English-speaking countries. Only one person felt primarily European and then Irish. Lastly, one interviewee didn't want to be classified in the given categories, but rather preferred to be noted as a world citizen. Again, some mentioned that their national identity would come "naturally" first because they grew up in that particular country's culture. With regard to their European attachment, most of the interviewees argued that the EU has opened up Ireland economically and socially, and that Ireland has profited from being part of the EU, which in turn made people feel more European. Such reasoning is problematic for the exploration of an affective EU commonality in that it corresponds with an instrumental outlook on EU membership.

In contrast, the British sample reveals an even higher degree of national consciousness. Four people in this sample identified themselves as being exclusively British, compared to one exclusive identifier in the Irish and none in the German sample. Eight felt primarily British and then European, while only one mentioned first European and then British allegiance. Another person didn't like national categorizations at all and didn't want to be classified as such, while a single person preferred the term world citizen. A typical example for the exclusive nationalist, transatlanticist response appears below:

> "British only, really. Because we are an island, quite separate from them. So I can't really relate to being European, I am sorry. Although I will be honest. If I am going to Europe, I sometimes feel European because I realize we have more in common with them than with America. When I come to America, even though we speak the same language, it does feel like an alien culture, whereas any country in Europe, it doesn't." (UK-11)

The people expressing a transnational identity extension, making up half of the sample, argued either more enthusiastically that they liked being part of Europe or stated rationally that they were part of the EU and, as such, considered European. One person also mentioned that she had relatives that were from other European countries, and one talked about the impact her work had on her identification, since she frequently comes in contact with EU regulations through her profession.

The next question consists of a utilitarian judgment on the EU, asking respondents if they feel that membership of their country is a good or bad thing. Again, the question "why" was added to elicit a content-based response. In Germany almost two-thirds felt that EU membership is a good thing, while the remaining third expressed that it had both a positive and negative impact. Six of the supporters argued primarily with the economic advantages that being in the EU brings, with a special emphasis on the importance for the country's export-led economic growth. Overall, five people stated that Germany's place in the EU is necessary in view of its nationalistic past and that such integration enabled peace:

> "Germany is too small to be important in the world, and it is an export nation. It is also the nation with the most traveling people in Europe. Germany's historical heritage is to occupy a leading role in peaceful transnational coexistence." (D-14)[2]

The people who were split on the issue of EU membership felt that while it is generally a good thing, there are some problems with some of the Union's tendencies. Fears about increased immigration, loss of national identity, the power imbalance of the member states after the 2004 enlargement, and, lastly, increased pressures for employees indicate the problems that Germans have with EU membership.

In the Irish sample, however, membership is evaluated in a more positive light. Eleven citizens said that Ireland's membership in the EU was purely a good thing, compared to four who saw both positive and negative implications of membership and none negating it. A typical but well-phrased example, below, connects utilitarian and affective elements in line with theories about transnational identity formation:

> "I think it has been good for the people in Ireland just from an economic point of view. There is no way we have the standard of living we have now unless we have been part of such a big trading bloc. I do identify myself with some of the European ideals, which try to transcend national sovereignty and to increase cooperation. It's better to trade and talk than have barriers and wars." (IRE-8)

What follows is a longer piece of my conversation with a man who had a critical yet differentiated picture of the rewards as well as the disadvantages membership brings:

> "It has its positives and negatives. On the positive side, we don't want to be regarded as being on the periphery and have nothing to do with Europe. But on the negative side it has meant to lose some of our identity."

> *You made an interesting point. Do you want to elaborate?*
> "The EU is a federal Europe, right? Although many people don't want to say that, it is exactly what it is. You have to be a country like Germany, or France, if it comes to the important issues. If those countries and the UK differ, then Europe comes to a standstill. Whereas all of the other little countries mean nothing." (IRE-11)

In the interview excerpt above, there is a theme apparent that seems to be of major importance for the critical attitude toward the EU in parts of the Irish public opinion. In the question dealing with national identity, people have consistently referred to the problem of Ireland being a small state and therefore too dependent on or powerless in the Union. Issues of representation, however, are overarching structural problems that cannot be eradicated easily and therefore will remain salient in the Irish public opinion.

EU membership is regarded differently in the UK, however. In contrast to Ireland and Germany, where no exclusively negative judgments were obtained, two British respondents felt that being a member state of the Union was actually something negative. Only six participants found "being part of the EU a good thing" compared to nine in Germany and eleven in Ireland. The others produced both positive and negative arguments for membership. The positive voices were of a liberal kind, stating that involvement in the EU brought economic advantages, peace, and openness to the island. Interestingly, the negative views expressed came from very different angles: while one felt that the EU was too exclusive of an organization, stating, "If you dig deeper, you'll find that the one-Europe approach is very unjust to the undeveloped world. There's a notion of 'fortress Europe' " (UK-7), its nationalist counterpart found that "if we get swallowed into that, all this prosperity and wealth which we have now gotten in this country will just be eaten up by Brussels." (UK-10). One person who precisely pitted the contradicting views of EU membership against each other professed:

> "I think it's a mixed blessing. I am worried by the British tendency to try and go it alone. We think we are superior to everybody else on the planet, and there is obviously a huge importance to being part of Europe. I can see that intellectually, the fact that we haven't had major wars for fifty years. But on gut level, I am an isolationist." (UK-12)

Many British share this contradictory feeling toward the EU, realizing the necessity of being in it yet having problems to emotionally accept or even effectively support it, hence negating diffuse support necessary for civic identity development.

The following two questions about EU knowledge and media usage appear in the Eurobarometer surveys as well, giving an indication of the level of knowledge and cognitive mobilization of the citizens. The question asking specifically about the level of knowledge about the EU, including its institutions and policies, is scaled from one to ten, with one being the lowest and ten the highest point. In Germany, the average self-professed level of knowledge was 5.5, whereas in Ireland the average knowledge was measured at 4.9, an indication that many respondents in the overall sample opted for the safe middle value. The UK had the lowest self-acknowledged average at 4.2.

To understand how the level of media usage alone and in combination with the level of EU knowledge affects the views of the interview participants, I asked about the frequency of use of television, newspapers, radio, and other sources, such as the Internet, to obtain political news coverage. It is assumed that knowledge of political news and, therefore, the obtaining of this information through mainstream audiovisual and print media generally has a positive effect on attitudes toward European integration, according to Inglehart's concept of cognitive mobilization (Inglehart, 1970). Here, I found that while there was little difference in the frequency of use of these media, a recognizable distinction in the preferred choice of medium became evident. In Germany and Ireland, twelve and ten people, respectively, access at least two of the three mainstream media on a daily basis to obtain political news, while in Great Britain only half do so. There, seven respondents state that they use only one medium daily, mostly TV, compared to two people in Ireland and none in Germany. These patterns of media consumption broadly confirm the above theory linking political awareness and positive attitudes toward European integration, since in my overall sample, the subgroup provided with the least information about the EU, the UK, shows the lowest levels of support and transnational identification. However, the negative press that the EU receives in the UK contributes to the negative EU attitude of citizens as well, resulting in an equal number of people who are insufficiently informed and citizens who are influenced by an EU-skeptic media.

Open-Ended Questions

The sixth item in the questionnaire asks for associations with the notions of "Europe" and the "EU," and aims at distinguishing images and perceptions about Europe in general and the EU specifically. It has become customary for the Brussels institutions to use the term "Europe" for the

Union's reach and self-understanding, be it in the usage on its website or in the way the questions in the Eurobarometer are posed. The EU, however, does not include all countries of the European continent, and while it may assume that the public might not be able to make a distinction between the EU and Europe or to identify with a political organization as opposed to a spatial-historical concept, my findings below show that most people in fact perceive a distinct difference in both terms. The synonymous use of the words Europe and EU is evidence of the bloc's political instrumentalization to apparently monopolize the right to speak for the continent.

Yet the public seems to realize the different notions behind these two terms, viewing Europe in predominantly cultural terms and attaching political notions to the EU. With regard to the answers supplied for "Europe," four distinctive terms seem to be mostly associated with it in all three member states: cultural plurality, European history and civilization, the geographical notion of the continent of Europe, and the images of different countries that are located there. While cultural plurality assumes the top spot in Germany and Ireland, in the UK the idea of Europe as the continent is often used to distinguish Britain from the mainland. Other items, such as a European way of life, vacations, etc., also aspire to the same notions of Europe as mainly a cultural and geographic phenomenon. Not among the most frequent, but nevertheless an often occurring idea is the concept of Europe as a distinct civic model, with history, common values, democracy, welfare states, wars, and peace, which is of particular importance in that the rather culturally determined notion of Europe can indeed be linked to civic ideas. One German participant in particular phrased the meaning of Europe in these terms and, at the same time, delimited it to the EU: "Europe as potentiality, whereas the EU is the actual realization of it" (D-8).[3]

Many of the respondents in all countries argued along a similar line, distinguishing both strands according to the geographical/cultural and political divide:

> "Europe, I think as the continent and the countries that form that. When I think of the EU, then I think of the Commission and the countries that come together, and I think of Britain as part of that. When I think of Europe as a continent, I don't think of Britain." (UK-8)

When talking about the EU, however, the answers differ dramatically in scope and judgment. The associations are purely political, and while negative images were hardly conjured up for Europe, the responses given for the Union are significantly more critical in all three countries. Among the most often mentioned responses in Germany and Ireland is the negative connotation of bureaucracy, which tops the German list and appears third in the Irish listing. The ideas of economic cooperation as well as of the EU's subsidies are also evoked with high frequency in Germany. In Ireland, people tend to think instrumentally when thinking of the EU: politics or policies are on the top there, followed by the notions of money and prosperity, a sign of the beneficial impact the Union has had on the island. A quite different picture emerges for the UK, in which the theme of different political cultures within the EU appears most often, followed by the euro and then by the notion of rules and laws. This prioritization provides an indication for the way British citizens construct their image of the Union by putting issues of political heterogeneity and intergovernmentalism as an overarching theme before more technical issues such as the euro adoption or bureaucracy. A comparison of negative connotations across the samples aids in understanding the extent to which attitudes toward the EU are negative. While in the German case, 25 percent of the total was categorized as negative under the headings of bureaucracy, chaos, corruption, and Euro-skepticism, in the Irish sample, 21 percent were negatively listed under bureaucracy and fear of losing national identity. In the UK, however, 35 percent of all responses were of a purely negative kind and referred to hard-to-reconcile political cultures, an expansive bureaucracy, a political organization being too big and too expensive, and, lastly, an accusation of the EU treating its members differently. The analysis can be summarized with the discovery that, in contrast to the EU's frequent use of the term Europe, most citizens make a conscious distinction between Europe and the EU, referring to two different yet connected entities altogether, a fact that corresponds with other research in the field (Ruiz-Jimenez, 2004).

The next set of questions relates the experience of being a part of the Union on a personal level to the time frame of ten years. The seventh question asks precisely if and how an individual has been personally affected by living in the EU and in what way. Intended to obtain a more personalized account of the lives of EU citizens than the initial inquiries, this query was met by some participants with hesitancy because it demanded making a connection between the organization and their personal lives. As a result, many people began answering initially with "not really," but were then adding aspects of belonging to the Union. Here is a typical example: "No, except if I travel I find the borderless travel and having the same currency very good" (D-2).[4] In Germany six participants expressed their relationship with the EU in this format, and two totally negated any personal connection with the EU. Overall, twelve Germans saw the removal of borders and the resulting ease of travel as a connecting element, while eight mentioned that the euro has directly affected their life in a positive way by eliminating currency exchanges and facilitating price comparisons. Only one regretted the introduction of the euro because of her nostalgia for the experience of being in a "foreign" country, something that was deemed lost through the use of the common currency. Two people each referred to the student and labor mobility in the EU, as well as to an emerging yet vague sense of commonality between European peoples. And one person reported that he had directly benefited from EU funding.

In contrast, citizens in the Irish sample have a more internalized picture of the Union, with less than half of the respondents denying having a personal experience with the EU. Again, the mention of borderless travel is the most frequent sign of the Union's presence here, with eight responses, followed by the euro. Three people stated that the labor mobility option made them realize the benefits of the EU. One respondent in the rural area said the Common Agricultural Policy had a huge impact on her personal life, and another actually had a family member working in Brussels.

Citizens in the UK seemed to have the most remote relationship with the EU: nine of the sixteen interviewees saw no direct experience of the EU in their lives, which, considering the huge impact the euro had on the other countries, is in part attributable to nonmembership in the EMU. One person, however, was in favor of the euro because, as she stated, it would make traveling easier. Four respondents argued that the open borders helped them realize the existence of the Union, while one was in contact with EU institutions and regulations in her workplace. Another participant remarked that the EU has eased her life as a lesbian with her nonnative partner through EU-initiated harmonization of same-sex partnership and mobility laws. Interestingly, one respondent answered that in her personal life, the EU was only visible through fears about the EU's interference with Britain's sovereignty, e.g., through policy harmonization:

> "Only to the extent of sometimes being ruffled about the decisions made, points of law that have gone to Europe and the British Lords being overruled. But it has not affected me personally except that I get angry about it. And I also feel anxious about the euro. On the other hand, the ease of travel is very pleasant." (UK-12)

Nonparticipation in the EMU has obviously decreased the Union's influence in the daily lives of the British, albeit considering that the most often named example overall was the experience of borderless travel, which applies to the UK as well, there is a higher than expected lack of the EU's salience there. Nine of the British respondents expressed having no connection with the EU on a personal level, compared to a minimal two in Germany and three in Ireland. To summarize, the country-specific foci of experience are strongly related to travel and the euro in Germany and Ireland, whereas the occurrences in the UK were limited to travel opportunities alone, together with fears about too much EU interference. It appears that policies that make people experience the EU in their lives create a base for the development of transnationalism.

Having established a link to the personal connections with the EU, I then asked if and how the opinion about the Union has changed over the past decade. The reason behind specifying this time frame is that it lends itself to a purposeful reflection. Again, the picture looks very different for each of the examined countries. The most positively inclined sample consists of the Irish, with ten people stating that their opinion about the EU has become more positive in the past decade. In the UK, six people responded in the same positive manner, leaving Germans at the bottom with five positive responses. The main arguments in the Irish case referred to the fact that the island has prospered, modernized, and opened up internationally—and in the case below, that EU membership has led to a more sustainable environmental orientation:

> "People cannot dump their waste in the countryside anymore. Ireland was a very, very dirty country and it cleaned up a great deal rurally, compared to what it was. And I would say that is a direct result of EU policies." (IRE-6)

Of the sixteen Irish citizens, two voiced that their image of the EU has worsened over the past years, citing fears about the enlargement to Eastern Europe and an anticipated decrease of benefits and national importance of the island. In the other anglophone nation, the most often mentioned response was that the opinion stayed the same over the past years. When asked why, ignorance about the Union or simply indifference toward it was acknowledged. For three people, the EU's image has actually suffered from fears about overregulation and issues over immigration policies. Still, some participants stated that their opinion about the EU has changed for the better for a variety of reasons not always indicative of the larger Euroskeptic sentiment found there:

> "Well, I fell in love with a Swedish woman, and because Sweden came into the EU, then it was very easy for us to move together because we were in the EU. So I have to say, definitely so." (UK-2)

> "Before I started working as a transport planner here I had only rudimentary knowledge of the EU. Now that I am working here it is much more part of my everyday life. So, I think, I went from having little knowledge to a much greater sense of what it is about and as a result, developed a more positive view." (UK-6)

With regard to Germany, a more balanced picture emerges here, with four respondents each stating that the EU's image has changed for the better—or for the worse. In addition, two people mentioned that their opinion has remained as positive as ever, while six feel that it made little difference over the past ten years. While a majority of positive judgments for the activities of the past years prevail, there are also more expressed negative views apparent than in the other samples. The positive answers refer to the way the EU has managed to successfully integrate a substantial number of less developed countries and express some differentiation toward the outside world:

> "I was always pro-European, but my support has increased. Especially with regards to the global political developments—i.e., the U.S. as global hegemon—it is important to build a strengthened Europe that acts with reason and power." (D-2)[5]

In contrast, the negative judgments referred to the overregulation in many areas and the conflict of interests in a widening community, but also to policy making by using the lowest common denominator, not to forget issues dealing with cultural identity:

> "I believe it has gotten worse because it became too intrusive. I prefer a more loose community instead of forcing too many commonalities. I do not think that I am very nationalistic, just like most Germans, but I am proud of my region and identify with where I live." (D-7)[6]

The next question was specifically designed to probe idealistic opinions and assumptions by asking people what they think with regard to their country's autonomy or sovereignty in view of the integration process. Of all three countries, Ireland is in an exceptional position, being a very small member state. This is reflected in the responses to this question, which are split, seeing either the EU as major supporter of national economic and political power, or, on the other end, feeling that they have to guard against the encroaching limitation of sovereignty by Brussels:

> "I think we have been given, considering we take such a small place in the EU, sufficient areas to voice our opinion. Ireland has done very well. I don't think we have been kind of booted out as in 'you are the small guys.'" (IRE-4)

In the UK, a majority of ten people would like to keep as much of their national sovereignty as possible and regret having given up autonomy in the course of EU integration. The importance of the British empires' sovereignty still reigns in many minds, and questions of accountability and representation are raised as well: "I think we are afraid of the EU because we have been so used to being in charge. It's not like we have a lot to lose, but it's just such a pompous country" (UK-2). Another view questions the democratic credentials of transnational market integration:

> "That does worry me. Where is the democratic accountability for all kind of policies? It seems an awful lot of decisions that will affect our nation are made in places other than our parliament, and not even in the European Parliament. They will be made by finances." (UK-12)

German public opinion, as represented in this sample, is colored by its dramatic past. Even though about half of respondents find that the country has been too streamlined along the demands of other EU member states, they indicate the strong role historical guilt plays in continual German support for the Union:

> "Because of integration, Germany is not sovereign anymore. But I see this as positive because it prevents crazy leaders from going it alone. Instead, they have to be accountable to a community [. . .] But Germany's position on the Iraq crisis shows that one can still retain one's own viewpoint." (D-10)[7]

The next set of questions covers the central argument of this work by focusing on the identity-extending aspects of the main integrative measures. Initially, I asked if people know and are aware of the single/Common market, the Common Foreign and Security Policy, and the plans for a common constitution—obviously it was not necessary to ask about the euro's salience since the new currency is well known even where it is not applied, such as in the UK. Once I established the extent of knowledge on the respective subject matter, I inquired about what each individual measure meant to people and how they feel about it.

The completion of the common market as one of the cornerstones of European integration was not only hailed in the 1980s and 1990s as a significant achievement with respect to the regulation and enhancement of intra-EU trade, but was also promoted as establishing a wider variety of consumer choices and increasing job creation for EU citizens. It is unlikely that people know about all four components that can be freely moved within the Union's single market—goods, services, people, and capital—but for this issue to be indicative of the market's impact on the building of a transnational consciousness, a majority of respondents should be able to make a valid reference to at least one aspect. When asked about the knowledge of the single market and its major components, a third of the Irish sample did not know or had not heard of the term. And of the ten people who responded positively, three stated that they would not know enough about it, describing only vaguely about communally made decisions in the Union. Only one person recited all four main components. The ones who were able to describe its meaning referred to the free trade of commodities between member states, with greater competition and consumer choices as second-most-mentioned items:

> "Free imports and exports. That makes it a lot easier. It kind of opened up huge markets in Europe for us. We were very dependent on Britain. Now we have access to the rest of Europe." (IRE-4)

While people in Ireland seem to have only a limited sense of the impact of EU-wide economic deregulation, the results in the UK are not any better: seven of the fifteen people asked had no idea what the common market entails. Of the remaining nine who heard about it, six were able to specify one aspect of the single market. Interestingly, here again, as in the previous question regarding the personal impact of the EU, we see the UK-specific phenomenon that two respondents actually voiced negative views about this EU measure, albeit from very different angles reflecting developmental and ecological concerns:

> "There can't be an EU single market because any trade in anything—money, or goods—is quite inseparable from the market outside Europe. Any developed market in the world today will only be doing this on the back of markets outside of Europe." (UK-7)
>
> "I think it's bad for the environment. All this moving, France sending a lot of stuff we don't need, us sending an equal amount of stuff there [...] Just because of minor cost differences." (UK-11)

The German sample, in contrast, seems to be sufficiently informed about the implications of the common market, which should come as no surprise considering the fact that Germany is the biggest export nation in the EU and therefore trade issues are highly visible there. Being on average also better educated than the Irish or the British sample, all of the participants said they heard or knew about the single market. Of these, three described the *Binnenmarkt* in general terms as an economic arrangement. The other twelve were able to mention one or more of the major functions of the market. Some of them made a differentiated judgment on its positive and negative aspects:

> "On the one hand, because of easy access to other national markets, the single market produced more economic growth. On the other hand, because

of European competition law, each state has less control ability, which can be problematic." (D-1)[8]

"The single market enables free commodity trade within the EU. The euro was introduced, and Europe-wide comparison of prices is possible, which together with the Internet gives the consumer lots of advantages." (D-9)[9]

Major differences in each country's perception with regard to the single market become evident. The German sample possesses the most knowledge in quantitative and qualitative terms. The tested Irish population seems less knowledgeable, with a third not recognizing it; however, they are most enthusiastic about the opening up of their economy. The UK population seems largely uninformed, with almost half of the sample unaware of the term and the remaining few having purely negative views about the single market. Congruent with my findings here, in a Special Eurobarometer 2002, a majority of Germans—53 percent—felt well informed, followed by the Irish populace with 49 percent. As expected, the British are located below EU average, with 44 percent expressing knowledge about the market (European Commission, Flash Eurobarometer 131, 2004).

Of all integration measures, the most visible is without doubt the common currency, the euro. Materially introduced in 2002 to the wider European public, its official adoption occurred in 1999, preceded by years of financial and regulatory planning. In Ireland, a country with high national pride in the Irish pound, the euro had been anxiously expected. This is reflected in the opinions collected: six interviewees expressed a purely positive judgment of the common currency, followed by five negative assessments of the changeover period. The remaining third finds both positive and negative aspects. The overwhelming advantage mentioned was the ease of price comparisons between countries and the fact that currency exchange is no longer necessary when visiting most EU countries, a sign of the outward orientation of the Irish:

"Oh, it's definitely good. You don't have to change money and deal with the banks. Now you can go abroad and check prices elsewhere and see how bad prices are here." (IRE-10)

The comment below reflects a common worry about inflationary price increases for consumers that, as all of the negative responses cited, coincided with the euro introduction. But some of them were also quite differentiated in their judgment:

"I am quite happy with it. I had reservations in the beginning. I don't blame Ireland's inflation problem on the euro. Problems with it began prior to that. Before the euro was introduced, there was a huge increase in going to the supermarket." (IRE-6)

In Germany the initial resentment to the new currency was even more pronounced than elsewhere in Europe since the deutsche mark was seen as a symbol of economic power and stability, and in that sense closely connected to German identity. In my interviews this connotation was of minor importance. Interestingly, a plurality of seven opinions made mixed statements about the (dis)advantages of the euro's takeover, while four responded either positively or negatively to the common currency. Of those mixed judgments, most refer to the cost increases but also to the facilitated price comparisons and travels, supplying an overall instrumental picture of euro support:

> "A loss of German identity really. On the other hand, now there's a better price comparison in other countries available and it is a connecting topic to talk with other nationals about." (D-12)[10]

The people responding predominantly negative were mostly concerned about the price increases, but they also lamented the removal of a characteristic symbol of German economic and political stability and expressed nostalgia for the old currency:

> "Euro is a 'teuro,' definitely. Politicians may argue differently, but for the normal family it is. Negatively, because with the deutsche mark I got more than with the euro." (D-5)[11]
>
> "I have a problem with it because the currency is something typical for a country, a point of identification. Now this characteristic is gone. Of course, when I go to Austria, I don't have to change money anymore and for the economy it's important. But I feel differently." (D-7)[12]

On a positive note, four respondents appreciated the ease of travel and the euro's increasing currency stability, the latter being a prime focus of attention because of the previous deutsche mark's value: "Overall a good thing. It is relatively stable as well. I can imagine the euro becoming an alternative to the dollar" (D-2).[13]

The citizens in the two samples above deal with the euro in their daily lives, whereas the citizens in the UK only gained firsthand experience of it if they traveled to other EMU-participating states. Astonishingly, opinions about the euro abound in the interviews, attesting to a lively debate in the British public. One would expect the views on it to be fairly negative; the people I interviewed, however, expressed varying feelings on the topic.

Three would not comment on the euro and six people were against the euro and its adoption. But two respondents actually support the introduction of the common currency on the isle and five saw the good as well as bad sides of it. Most of the negative statements referred to losing of the British national identity bound closely to the pound, and to the fear of no longer having control mechanisms for currency stability:

> "It is a loss of national sovereignty, and it does mean that your government has no control over economic policy and you are handing it in to a central bank. I do quite like that fact that we haven't decided. But I wouldn't be totally upset if we would join." (UK-11)

The people who were judging the positive and negative sides of a possible euro introduction in the UK felt that it was more of a necessity than a wholeheartedly taken step toward more integration, as another instrumental but fatalist opinion shows:

> "I think we should have it. It's a good idea just because it will make things easier. I don't understand finance economics a bit and I think that lots of people seem to be objecting to it on grounds more of a kind of a 'nostalgia.' I think a lot of people, if you ask, 'Why do you object,' they want to retain their 'British identity.'" (UK-4)

The above respondent as well as the speaker in the next excerpt differ in their knowledge about the economic consequences of the euro, but they still come to the same conclusion:

> "It's clearly useful to have one currency in use. I am not particularly attached to the pound per se; as an economist I judge the downside to be tied into the EU monetary policy and not having any freedom of setting interest rates. That's a cyclical thing." (UK-6)

In a synopsis of the countries' experiences with the euro, the most supportive one appears to be Ireland. There a small majority of respondents stand behind the euro as a symbol of further integration and connection to Europe, while a third feel that the cost of living has increased. In Germany, the highest percentage of opinions was of a mixed nature, balancing the advantages of exchange-free travel and commerce as well as stability against perceived price increases. And even in countries that do not use the euro, such as the UK, there is much discussion about it, resulting in comparatively well-informed opinions compared to many other integration measures that are already in place in Britain. A look at the Flash Eurobarometer survey from summer 2002 confirms these findings: while 60 percent felt that the euro's advantages outweighed the disadvantages, a whopping 83 percent felt that prices have been rounded up. With regard to the most mentioned advantages, 93 percent of all EU citizens feel that the euro made traveling more convenient and 90 percent said it facilitated cross-border commerce. Most important, however, 60 percent of eurozone citizens stated that the introduction of the common currency made them feel more united as Europeans (European Commission, Flash Eurobarometer 139, 2002).

The common currency is probably the most tangible symbol of the EU's continued integration policies. In contrast, the notion of a common foreign policy, as expressed in the Common Foreign and Security Policy (CSFP), is far more removed. Yet like the euro, it is a vital component of a national identity. Whereas the Union has managed to establish and further peace within its territories, there have been conflicts in proximity of its external borders in which the EU was not constructively involved. Historically and practically, NATO forces and/or European national contingents have played a more important role in conflict resolution and peacekeeping there. And disagreements over the handling of the Iraq crisis have shown how difficult it can be to reach a common position in the Union, as will be testified in some of the opinions below. Currently, the CFSP is the main instrument of a common EU foreign and defense policy, therefore I will use these terms interchangeably in the following section.

When asked about plans for a common foreign policy in the EU and what they thought about it, the German participants overwhelmingly supported it. Nine of the sixteen participants believe that a common EU foreign policy is important, whereas three found that the track record has been mixed and two actually lost trust in such a common-oriented policy. Among the respondents, the issue of how to reconcile diverging foreign policy approaches dominated the interviews, being mentioned few times:

> "Yes, that's the only viable concept. Take the Iraq war, for example: here, national interests were put above European ones, which led to a loss of influence. But individual nations need to be able to conduct their own foreign policy as well." (D-9)[14]

The importance of becoming a united global player was explicitly mentioned twice; in addition, the plans for a European foreign affairs minister were hailed two times. Four citizens seemed particularly concerned with individual nations' ability to voice their opinion under the pressure for unity. On the other end, two opponents were not ideologically opposed to a common foreign policy; rather, they were disappointed about the efforts so far:

> "The European Foreign Policy has been disappointing in the last years. The Europeans were not able to convince the U.S. and not able to form a

streamlined foreign policy within. What's missing aside from consensus is the ability. It will remain an idea." (D-12)[15]

In the UK, a strong difference in public opinion is recognizable: here, half of the respondents are supporters in principle but have doubts about the ability to make an impact, while the other half outright oppose a common foreign policy, citing a stronger U.S./NATO allegiance. Two interviewees were not aware of such a policy.

"I find it very hard. It might be a bad thing because, again, there are so many conflicting interests that we may end up being paralyzed and not being able to do anything. For reasons that have nothing to do with the immediately presenting situation, this particular nation is going to veto unless they get what they want." (UK-14)

While many of these respondents have a rather pessimistic outlook, they do criticize their leadership's decision to go to war with Iraq, which contrasts with the German sample, who mostly validated their government's step to oppose military action there. This critique is closely connected to the British policy orientation toward the United States, which interestingly is mentioned as de facto political handicap manipulated by the press:

"This war in Iraq, for instance. I wished we would have gone along with Germany and France instead with America. But then again, we will never speak with one voice. [...] The debate that takes place in the tabloid newspapers about if we are more transatlanticist or European comes from the right wing." (UK-11)

The Irish are well known for their adherence to the principle of neutrality, and in the interviews this affinity becomes apparent: a third of all respondents mentioned neutrality as an important but potentially impeding factor with respect to the development of a common foreign policy. Of the whole sample, only three people embraced an external representation of the EU, while four were against it because of reasons having to do with their neutrality or fear of domination by bigger states. The remaining few did not know enough to comment or did not want to contribute. Among the proponents, some felt that involvement in foreign affairs was needed to develop a stance and to become recognized as such:

"I think the idea of a rapid-reaction force or whatever. If you see the pluses and minuses of the EU, this would definitely be a minus. [...] the fact that it hasn't an active enough role means that... there is a lot Europe could do in Africa that it doesn't get done, let alone on our own doorstep." (IRE-8)

Each of the three countries possesses a very different outlook on the idea of a CFSP, thus reflecting their idiosyncratic political culture. While the Irish sample is worried about their tradition of neutrality, people in the UK are strong Atlanticists still adhering to their former Empire status, and the Germans remain Europeanists. There seems to be an indication among the Union's citizens that the EU should preferably take action in European defense matters: according to a Special Eurobarometer survey from 2001, 43 percent of all citizens felt that the EU should have decision-making rights in defense matters (European Commission, Special Eurobarometer 2001). It appears that people are more supportive of a common defense policy if it does not interfere with national prerogatives, as the astonishingly high support for the purely auxiliary rapid reaction force shows: 73 percent of all EU citizens give their support and 70 percent of Germans, 60 percent of the British, and 55 percent of the Irish agree. And while 71 percent of the respondents argued that the main objective of a European army would be to defend the EU territory and 63 percent say it is to guarantee peace in the EU, the goal of symbolizing a European identity is advocated by 19 percent of the population. So while the chosen case countries represent more skeptical samples, a European common defense is without doubt a measure that is regarded as desirable and necessary by most Europeans.

The European constitution was the latest of the four examined political initiatives and, incidentally, the least tangible one, a fact that may have contributed to the rejection of the draft treaty in 2005. A European CFSP is more removed from people's experiences but still remains highly important for the desecuritization of national identities. On the other hand, the EU constitutional project, even though it represents more than a reform of previous treaties in that it would give the Union a distinct political and legal identity, presents an abstract yet ideal case for the advancement of a civic transnational identity. At the time of the interviews during the summer of 2004, at the conclusion of the constitutional convention, knowledge about the then constitutional draft was rather limited in all three countries. Later, the Constitutional Treaty experienced a terminal blow with its rejection in France and the Netherlands in 2005, but main parts have been rescued with the Lisbon Treaty.

In Ireland, half of the sixteen people had not heard or did not know about the constitutional draft, while seven reportedly had at least some knowledge of it. Of these, two were of the opinion that the new constitution did not really matter, considering that each country possesses already a national one. The remaining five respondents felt that such a treaty would be positive for Ireland and the EU, provided that it stands for human rights (mentioned twice) and that it would not interfere with national laws and traditions (three times)—again an indicator for the prerogatives of the national political culture. The latter has simultaneously been perceived to be also an impeding factor for the utility of a constitution based on the smallest common denominator:

> "I think it would be very good. Except that there are so many countries in the EU, and a common constitution would be kind of neutral. Though it's good to have more linkages." (IRE-3)
>
> "It can be good, but it so happens that there are certain things in our constitution that we don't want to give up. We have provisions for our identity, like speaking Irish to work in the guard. It would have to make provisions for the different national identities." (IRE-11)

In Great Britain, a country without a written constitution, the situation is not much different, although people there seem even less knowledgeable and supportive than in Ireland. Nine participants had not heard of the Constitutional Treaty before, and of the remaining seven who knew about it, two were rejecting the constitutional draft outright. The negative responses occurred on grounds that there was no need for it and that it would be only another step to a more bureaucratic Union, while the skeptical ones provided a more differentiated comment, arguing that, on the one hand, popular input was needed, and on the other hand, divergent national interests would make this enterprise difficult:

> "A federal Europe? If it can be done without making us all the same I actually think it can bridge the vast cultural differences. A constitution is a good thing in itself, and common standards are good, but it worries me that it becomes a melting pot." (UK-12)

One of the two supporters put it simply yet argued in line with one of the convention's main objectives to frame the EU's legal and political identity accordingly:

> "Like a Magna Charta. It's an important part, isn't it? It would basically complete the Union. But I hope there will still be room for individuality for each country. It completes the project." (UK-9)

Citizens in the German sample are the most enthusiastic, with nine responding in a positive manner. The remaining seven are split into two negative opinions, two skeptical ones, and three ambiguous responses. The respondents rejecting the constitutional draft referred to the vast differences in interests and the need to respect of the individuality of each country. The skeptics expressed that a common constitution is theoretically positive for human and citizen's rights, and they fear risks with regard to diverging interests that became obvious during the preceding convention:

> "A sensible constitution containing not only human but also civil rights, as kind of a minimal social charter, would raise the EU's profile. The difficult negotiations are rather pitiful, however." (D-12)[16]

Most of the supporters of the constitutional project did so with reference to the streamlining of national policies on a European level and the prospects for a more harmonized Europe, on the condition that Germany's basic laws and values are not curtailed, a recurring doubt indicative of the general ignorance of the document:

> "If we don't lower our standards, then it's a good thing. And when Europe in the future becomes more united, with one official language its own law, then a constitution makes sense. It could be used as 'rulebook' for candidate countries." (D-2)[17]

The widespread unawareness of the content of the constitution is not only evident in these interviews, but also confirmed by recent Eurobarometer data. In Special Eurobarometer no. 214, from January 2005, a third of the EU population had not heard about the constitution. And while Germans are in line with the EU average of 33 percent who had no knowledge of it, Ireland and the UK fared much worse with 45 and 50 percent, respectively. When tested on their familiarity with the draft constitution, the latter two countries were in the bottom (European Commission, 2005).

The previous questions focused on the four functional measures that are hypothesized to have an impact on the transnational identification of the citizens. After having clarified the extent to which people identify with the policy measures of the Union, in the last question I concentrated on the possible existence of a transnational European identity. Beforehand I asked one more question probing the respondents' willingness not only to agree idealistically to the goals of European integration, but also to actively support these objectives even when a win-win situation for their nation and the EU is not available. Specifically, I inquired what the reaction would be to an EU decision that might be good for the whole of the Union, but that may be unfavorable to the respondents' own country, such as enlargement of the Union with loss of funds for their own country. The last part of this question was intended to simulate a real problem, one that in the financial framework of 2007–2013 will start to appear when structural funds in Ireland, the UK, and (East) Germany will be shifted toward newer member states.

In Ireland the reaction to this scenario has been overall very positive as a result of the Irish experience as beneficiary of these funds. Ten of the sixteen asked said they favored a measure that would contribute to the greater good even if it brought disadvantages for Ireland, while only one person declined this request. Four people responded in neutral terms, stating that it depended on the issue. The positive remarks referred mostly to the fact that Ireland has profited from the EU's structural and development funds, and now that wealth has been created, reciprocity is the appropriate response, not least in order to assume a different, more important role in the Union:

> "I think Ireland cannot keep getting the grants it has been getting to the detriment of East European countries such as Poland, etc. It is time for Ireland to stand on their own two feet [. . .] It has to take an identity as a mature country that has benefited a great deal but cannot continue to benefit as in the past." (IRE-6)

The last answer in particular refers to the need for reciprocity, which was mentioned five times overall. It appears that the Irish sample understands in light of the country's development the need for redistributive politics of the EU. Influencing variables are also the existing Catholic belief systems and/or the politicians' and media's communication to the Irish citizens in that matter.

The answers in Great Britain were decidedly different. When reciprocity was mentioned, it was in a negative way, stressing that the UK is one of the main contributors to EU funds and therefore should receive more. Accordingly, six respondents said that Britain should not make sacrifices for other EU member states, while four stated they would be willing to. The remaining third responded neutrally or were not able to answer appropriately. The declining respondents argued on a variety of grounds, such as general discontent with the enlargement of the EU to Central and Eastern Europe. Some respondents who agreed with the request for solidarity argued with economic and moral reasons, supplying simultaneously ideational and instrumental justifications for it, in an illustration of the interconnectedness of both reasonings:

> "The Christian part of me says: If they need it, that's justice. I might not like it much, but it's fair. And those countries are important because they change the power balance in the EU." (UK-16)

While we find in Ireland a positive reception of solidarity appeals on the basis of reciprocity and in the UK a rather hostile environment, there is a permissive yet supportive momentum recognizable in Germany. Seven participants in this sample agreed with a theoretical common interest overriding national ones, even if this would mean the removal of funds or additional taxes. Four people declined this request and four expressed their opinion in neutral-permissive terms, referring to the downplaying of German needs:

> "I think the ability of Germans to suffer is pretty high. And I have to accept it because the common good is above my interest. It's okay if it is a reasonable decision. I wonder if Europe is strong enough to proceed with a viable enlargement." (D-4)[18]

A few negative answers to this scenario were mainly based on domestic problems that Germany currently faces and that connect enlargement (funding) to a possible loss of jobs, interestingly with a diametrically opposite view of reciprocity than in the Irish cases:

> "I think, fourteen years after the reunification, Germany has more problems within its own borders and has to voice its interest more strongly. It's time that Europe does something for Germany, not only vice versa." (D-12)[19]

The seven approving responses to the scenario were not enthusiastic in essence, but rather led by a routinized permissive agreement as well as strategic calculations: "It balances out. Once it is us, then the British, and then the French. Everybody has to take turns. One cannot always win and needs to compromise" (D-6).[20]

For some people, the EU remains synonymous with Europe, and vice versa. Even though the EU has encompassed in the last year much of Central and Eastern Europe, there are still states remaining outside the Union. I therefore asked participants to tell me if, in their opinion, the EU made a difference in how they perceive non-EU countries compared to other EU member states, aiming at the internal cohesiveness of transnational identities within the EU as compared to external European ones.

In Ireland the opinions regarding this matter were almost evenly distributed. While seven interviewees stated that the EU would not make a difference in how they perceive other Europeans, six respondents argued that EU membership is in fact a distinguishing feature. Three people would not comment on this issue. The ones negating that they have more in common with other EU citizens than third-country nationals stated that they would differentiate based on cultural similarity. Some argued, however, that the cultural diversity within the EU makes such a unitary distinction between EU states and non-EU states impossible, yet two others mentioned the linguistic and cultural closeness to the United States as a more profoundly connecting link:

> "No, I think we have more in common with Americans. Yes, the French, the Spanish, the Germans, I think we have totally different identities within Europe. Maybe we are more like England. It could be the language, it could be the culture or something." (IRE-9)
>
> "We have the English language in common with America, Australia, and the UK. We identify with them. That is stronger than the euro." (IRE-11)

On the other hand, respondents who made a distinction between EU states and other non-EU European countries argued that increased linkages on national, regional, and local as well as professional and private levels, encouraged by integration, have brought them closer to fellow EU citizens.

> "Yes, definitely, I have more in common with the EU member states. The currency helps, and the fact that we all have, to a certain level, the same government and elected MEPs and things like the Maastricht Treaty, because the non-EU countries are kind of 'outsiders' now." (IRE-4)

In the UK, nine of the respondents denied having more in common with EU than non-EU countries, while only four said they felt closer to other EU citizens, so the percentage of people denying a qualitative difference was double that of people acknowledging one. Three participants did not really know and often referred wrongly to the distinction between Europeans and non-Europeans more generally, even after my clarification. As in Ireland, British citizens referred to the cultural identity of Europe existing prior to the EU:

> "I am not sure it's the EU that makes a difference, but the fact is, yes, we do. It's a combination of culture, values, and all those things. And we in Britain are and always have been closer to Europe than to any other parts of the world." (UK-6)

In fact, one person criticized the Union's attempt to construct a common identity in view of the exclusive potential of such identification:

> "I think the EU by its political behavior tries to encourage European nationalists to feel as one, to regard themselves as similar. There has to be a strong aspect of racism. The EU regards its citizens as being the same and it encourages in a quite doctrinaire, subtle fashion Europeans to regard

themselves as different, possibly even superior, to members of third-world countries." (UK-7)

The few proponents of a distinction between EU member states and non-EU states in Europe referred to the same argument, stating that the EU countries are held together not only by a common cultural identity, but also by the harmonizing effects of integration:

> "It's now very easy for somebody from London to go to Brussels, Amsterdam, wherever. Even further, Germany...and there doesn't seem to be that stigma that was there years ago, that the English didn't like the French and the French didn't like the English, that type of thing. That's gotten much better in Europe." (UK-10)

In Germany a more balanced relationship between the two sides is visible: Like in Ireland, of the sixteen interviewees, a small plurality said the EU would make no difference in their feeling of closeness to other European nations, with six people saying it would. Two people would not answer. People declined to make a distinction with regard to cultural affinities to countries that are not part of the EU such as Switzerland, but are supposedly more closely aligned with a Germanic character, pointing to a limited tolerance even within the Union:

> "I would not say so, no. You can see it now, with the Germans and Italians, which have a totally different mentality. Germans would find more in common with the Swiss, for example. You cannot determine such things with political boundaries." (D-4)[21]

One interesting voice counterargued such a cultural distinction on other grounds, pointing at the acculturation effects of living in the EU for non-EU immigrants:

> "Not really. I believe that if you look at the Turks in Germany, they are just as European or even more European than some of our neighboring countries. I believe the EU doesn't make a difference; there are enlightened people outside the EU as well." (D-2)[22]

In all three countries the aspect of possessing a common cultural heritage as a link between Europeans was taken for granted by a majority of people, irrespective of the question asking whether the EU made a difference between member states and European nonmember states. The people mentioning differing mentalities and languages within the EU as an obstacle were clearly a minority. The predominant statement that Europeans are similar in many socioeconomic and cultural aspects is already proof of a common linkage between Europeans, with half of the people in the samples giving the EU an identity-building function.

The last item on the questionnaire specifically poses the question of whether a transnational identity exists or whether people are oriented instead toward their national identity. As I laid out in the theoretical chapter, the literature in the field recognizes the simultaneous existence of both in a complementary and also competitive fashion. Here, I aimed to see how people judge the existence of a "European" identity, even if they might not apply it to themselves. In the Irish sample, seven respondents stated that there exists such an identity, while three denied its existence, and the remaining ones argued that it depended on the exposure to the EU's activities and the person's background. Of the seven who proposed such a common reference, the primary identification through the nation still existed. A recurring theme, mentioned three times, was that it will take more time for such a European identity to develop:

> "It is a bit of both, really. There is a kind of 'Europeanish' identity. People always think, 'I am Irish,' outside of Ireland and, 'I am European,' outside of Europe. There is a certain European common cultural identity. People are happy to be part of that." (IRE-10)
>
> "It depends on how much contact you had with Europe. If you talk to somebody who hasn't had much experience with Europe, he would say, 'I am Irish,' but myself, I feel more European. And my children will probably feel more European than I am." (IRE-12)

The three respondents denying the existence of a common identity emphasized spatial and cultural aspects that leave the Irish outside of a common European experience mediated by the EU:

> "I think you can't be an EU citizen only. You are German, British, or Irish and that's it. It also has to do with culture and knowledge and where you come from, traditions and such. And the EU hasn't invented any of those. It's an organization and that's it." (IRE-4)
>
> "In Ireland, we will never see ourselves as being European. You have people here in the Aran Islands. If you asked them, they will say, 'I come from the Aran Islands; secondly I come from Ireland. First and foremost, I am Irish. Then, I am European.'" (IRE-11)

Interestingly, this question triggers more positive answers in the UK than in Ireland: nine of the sixteen participants agreed with the existence of a common European identity, while seven denied it. Many supporters of a European identity acknowledged that it's still weak in the UK, but that it exists and is expected to grow over time:

> "I don't think that the European identity is particularly strong here. I think the primary for most people is their country. But it may be weak, but there is one. And I think it will get stronger with time. That's something that will probably take fifty to one hundred years." (UK-6)
>
> "We all have a European identity. And the EU has brought that out. People are moving around, there are more intermarriages between countries or communities. For your parents, if you married somebody from the next village, that was terrible at that time. And now, you can marry somebody from a different country." (UK-9)

The negative responses are based on the fact that, from a British perspective, Europe seems rather removed. Aside from this classic reasoning, some people actually find identity-related classification ideological in itself:

> "National identity, Englishness, and patriotism are very similar, indeed, to a more popular nationalist mentality. To me—and a lot of people wouldn't agree with me—you cannot really define Englishness [...] If you go back 150 years, you had Prince Albert, who was Germanic, and so the First World War created a lot of trouble. And German became part of the English bloodline." (UK-7)

Germany, in contrast, appears thoroughly "Europeanized." Thirteen people subscribed to the existence of a common identity versus three who had their special justifications of their negative response. One participant saw only an external ascription of commonality among Europeans, while the other argued that a pan-European identity was not really significant in relation to other classifications in a globalized world:

> "No, I don't feel European, but German. I cannot identify with Europe. In Spain, I am foreigner because I cannot speak the language. In France it is different because I do speak the language. But I believe a Spaniard would always consider me as foreigner. One always identifies with one's country." (D-7)[23]
>
> "The identities we have are not necessarily German or European, but they end at the borders of the media or the global consumer industry. Levi's, Coca Cola, Microsoft, and Madonna are a big part of our identities in Germany, in Europe, and the world." (D-10)[24]

While the notion of a necessary protection of national identities seems prevalent among the German sample, many recognize the existence of a common link strengthened and subsequently furthered by EU integration:

> "I think our next generation, our children, will grow up with a stronger European identity. They don't know the deutsche mark anymore and the borders, then it's much easier. But I think it's okay that each one keeps his national and local identity as well." (D-3)[25]

Conclusion: Three Different Identity Frames on the Same Process

One can conclude from the interview analyses that most citizens in the German sample indeed adopted a transnational identity, whereas respondents in the UK and Ireland saw less commonality among Europeans. A transnational civic identity in contrast to a broader cultural and geographical European one was recognized by only half of all respondents, providing some evidence of transnational identity development as a result of EU integration, but certainly not enough to posit an identity spillover of sorts.

Recurring themes in the exploration of collective identity transformations point to more transient as well as persisting issues. For example, the notion that Europe's cultural and linguistic diversity and the various national interests are permanent factors preventing the development of a transnational identity was prevalent in many responses that dealt with future developments of certain policies or the Union as a whole. On the other hand, people recognized in many instances that the EU is a relatively young organization compared to the long history of many nation-states, and that with time and further integration the EU may establish a more pronounced civic identity as an institution. The following figures provide a graphic overview of the most frequently appearing notions connected to European transnationalism in each of the three case countries providing a succinct summary of the respondents' identitive positions.

These diagrams were established using the qualitative analysis program Atlas.ti by highlighting linkages among and frequencies of important terms appearing in the interviews. As can be seen in the figure below, German transnational identity is, in quantitative and qualitative terms, closely connected to the EU, and backed by cultural and democratic notions, but firmly positioned in contrast to globalization. In the interviews, the euro features heavily, as do foreign policy and enlargement/border considerations. This contrasts with the extroverted view of British respondents, who see themselves not only linked to Europe and, to a lesser extent, to the

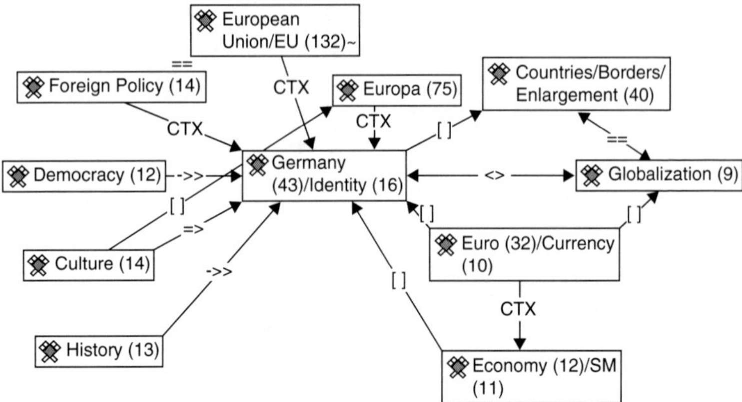

Figure 4.1 Germany: Frequency and Linkages of Keywords (in parentheses)
(CTX = Context; < > =in opposition; [ ] = is part of; -> = contributes to; == = associated with)

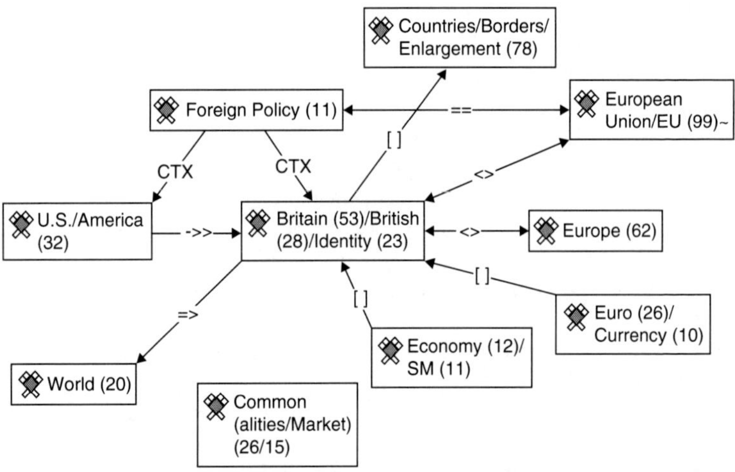

Figure 4.2 United Kingdom: Frequency and Linkage of Keywords

EU, but also to the United States and other countries across the world. In fact, notions of the EU and Europe stand in contrast to British identity and appear less often than in the other two countries (Figure 4.2).

Aside from the ubiquitous external references to the world, other countries, and the United States, in the British interviews, the common market plays an important recurring role, as does the euro. Overall, fewer intrinsically European aspects appear, whereas the majority of expressions point to more generalized outward-looking orientation emphasizing global diplomatic and economic relations. In contrast, the overview for Ireland displays a majority of people responding positively to the dramatic developments and changes brought about by the Union in the past thirty years, as evident in the frequency of the terms change and difference, but they also view EU integration as an opening toward other countries and people as well as a distancing from the previously dominating UK (Figure 4.3).

Besides the two notions of change and opposition toward the UK, Irish respondents highlight the participation of their country in the EU as "being part of Europe," as well as the mobility aspect of citizens, be it for leisure or work.

Returning to some of the initially posed research questions, the length of membership does not play a significant role in this analysis, as in the two cases with the same admission year, Ireland and the UK, both countries display very dissimilar orientations. These results are of particular interest taking into account that both the Irish and British governments displayed pro-European attitudes over the past decade, and indicate that the variation in identitive support might be founded upon other factors, such as media portrayals of the EU—a hypothesis examined in Chapter 6. Germany as a longstanding founding member state shows a highly internalized and supportive stance, but also exhibits critical attitudes to an extent that best describes Germany's inclination as limited permissive Europeanization.

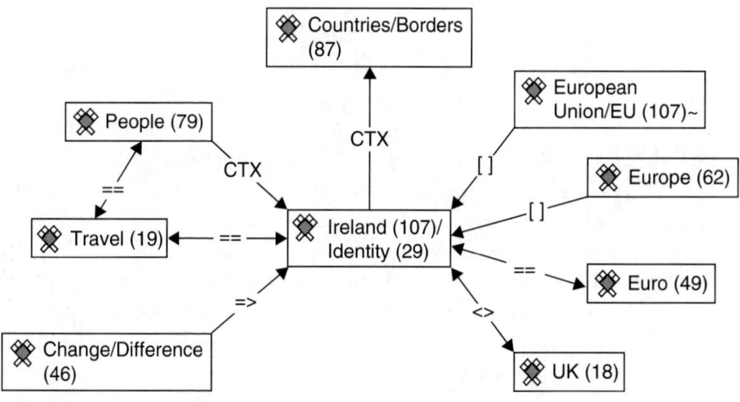

Figure 4.3 Ireland: Frequency and Linkages of Keywords

Aside from temporal issues, some respondents also emphasized the fact that people's exposure to the Union determines their probable attitude toward it. Interestingly, this argument is validated in the overall assessment of the interviewees in regard to the Union's salience and its impact on these: the people who had the most contact with the Union's policies and institutions, be it through their consumer behavior, workplace, or mobile lifestyle, had the most positive and differentiated opinions. The less a person experienced the EU directly as an institution or indirectly through implemented policies, the less he or she was inclined to make a qualified judgment about the organization, which lends support to the proponents of a more visible Union and measures that showcase the civic aspect of European integration. In a related matter, an augmented visibility of the EU in the daily lives of its citizens needs to be accompanied by increased transparency of the Union's initiatives, laws, and regulations, otherwise people will view integration as outside interference in the domestic sphere, as has been argued by some respondents.

The above-mentioned issue is closely connected to the question of democratic accountability of the Union. While this important topic is not the focus of this work, it is noteworthy that although some participants in Germany and Ireland commented on the EU's dominating influence on their state's policies, almost no one called explicitly for more democratic input into the Union, except one person each in the UK and Germany, who wished for a better representation through the European Parliament. The limited knowledge of EU affairs, together with the low turnout for European Parliament elections and the ambiguities about and difficulties of passing referenda on European issues, hints at a need for more visibility and transparency of the EU in the national public spheres. This does not necessarily entail increased democratic input from the citizens, which is much harder to judge in its effect on future European integration.

With regard to the confirmation of the hypotheses, the interviews have shown that most of the assumptions were at least partially verified. The answers to the interview questions dealing with the reaction to the four independent variables, as well as the ones asking about respondents' development of opinion about the EU over time, provided sufficient knowledge to confirm that post-Maastricht measures resulted only in a limited expansion of collective identities toward a transnational civic one. In particular, the euro, despite initial public hesitancy and accompanying price-adjustment problems, is now accepted by two-thirds of Germans and Irish in the sample and is hotly debated in the non-EMS participant UK. The strong support for the euro that exists in Ireland and Germany as a transmitter for the everyday experience of the Union's benefits is a sign of the EU's salience in these countries. The single market as the oldest of the four measures receives broad approval from the Irish and German citizens, with reference to improved travel and work opportunities and expanded consumer choices, but is generally underrepresented in people's knowledge about the EU's action, especially in the UK, where half of the respondents were not familiar with it.

The Common Foreign and Security Policy, while being more closely connected to the political consciousness of the EU in the sense that national defense is an important feature of national identity, receives a mixed reception in the countries observed: in the German sample, two-thirds supported further strengthening of the Union's defense capabilities, which is seen in Ireland as a threat to its longstanding neutrality and in the UK as a strongly disputed issue reflecting the UK's ambiguous position in the midst of transatlantic relations. The constitution, however, aside from being an elite document, was the youngest product of integration among the member states. It is therefore not surprising that in Ireland and the UK, half and two-thirds of the sample, respectively, were not aware of such a document. Of the remaining people who had knowledge of it, most were conditionally supportive. In contrast, most of the Germans had heard of the constitution and two-thirds approved of it. All three countries display an idiosyncratic national outlook that continues to delimit the extent of transnational European identities among EU citizens, as suggested in the hypotheses.

The responses to the development of these indicators confirm the above hypothesis. Ireland appears to be the country with the most extensive spread of transnational identity. There, almost two-thirds of the respondents stated that their opinion of the EU has improved over the past decade, citing increased knowledge about the positive effects of EU membership. UK public opinion is marked by indifference, with a slim majority stating that their opinion and/or disinterest in the EU has remained the same, but there are also some encouraging voices who positively comment on the Union's activity. In Germany, the opinion about the bloc is split equally among people whose support increased, decreased, or remained stable during the observation period. Overall, the public in these countries realizes that the Union delivers more benefits than in the past, but also interferes more often in previously domestic spheres, which at times produces antagonistic attitudes toward it.

With regard to the first hypothesis, the fear of losing national identity was not among the most-mentioned responses when asked about mental associations with the term EU. It did not appear in the German or British list at all, while only two of the statements in Ireland referred to it. Furthermore, the last item on the questionnaire asked if a European identity existed or only national ones, aiming to see whether respondents viewed the relationship between both identity forms as competitive, threatening the national one, or as complementary, signaling an unproblematic acquisition of both. In the responses to this question, none of the three samples contained any explicit reference to a fear of losing their identity. Even if a minority stated that there was no transnational identification or that it was still weakly developed, most allowed for one and proposed its further strengthening in the future.

The only instance where a loss of national identity was expressed occurred in the judgment of the euro. A few respondents found that the replacement of their national currency with the euro led to a loss of their collective identity. In an experiment to see how negative integration—meaning the removal of previously nationalized policies—affected support for the EU, I asked a few participants what their reaction would be if the national citizenship were replaced with a common European one. The answer was almost unanimously negative. Taken together with the identity-eroding criticism of the euro, this leads me to conclude that the second hypothesis is valid under the condition that any future integration measure, in order to receive support from the citizens, should not curtail or replace existing national institutions or symbols, but rather should be an additive, complementary element.

With regard to the last posed hypothesis, the findings here allow for a confirmation of the proposition that a particularistic and possibly exclusive European identity is developing. From the overall responses, in particular the ones from questions 9 and 14, it appears that while there is a propensity for a transnational solidarity and commonality within the Union, and even culturally with non-EU Europeans such as the Swiss or the Norwegians, differences are made with respect to non-Europeans. The evolution of transnational European identities, with somewhat common cultural roots and fortified civic elements supplied by the EU, appears to be of a rather particularistic nature when it comes to cultures and peoples outside of Europe and even of non-European minorities within the boundaries of the Union. While the latter produces its own set of difficulties, this finding supports my overall argument in that it shows that the identity changes toward transnationalism in the EU have not been effected primarily by globalization, which could theoretically also lead to a universalistic cosmopolitan attitude, as shown only in two of the forty-eight cases, but rather by EU integration measures emphasizing common historical and cultural ties in a potentially exclusionary manner.

In sum, these open-ended interviews not only permitted a partial validation for the hypotheses, but also provided valuable immediate information about the underlying motives, attitudes, and (trans)national identities of the citizens in these three countries. However, the UK sample deviates from the German and Irish ones in the extent of transnationalism; there, attachment to the EU is much lower than in the other two samples, and is in fact lower than in every other EU member state. Overall, this cross-national survey supplies an approximation of the status quo of a transnational identification with the EU and Europe as a whole and delivers key indicators for support, but also presents factors that impede and constrain these developments. To examine the data's generalizability, the next chapter details the aggregate impact of the EU and its policies on identitive positions of Europeans as expressed in public opinion surveys conducted by Eurobarometer.

Chapter 5

Large-Scale Survey Analyses through Eurobarometer

To ascertain the validity of the previous individualized interview section, some longitudinal, quantitatively, and qualitatively analyzed data from the EU's Eurobarometer survey provides an aggregate look at the current state of transnational identity development among EU citizens. As an accompanying statistical instrument to the previous analysis, this section supports the generalization of identity-related macroprocesses in the EU. Data taken from the Eurobarometer archives has been widely used in the literature to test theories and hypotheses of public opinion formation in the EU, but few have examined country data comparatively. As an evolving tool, these investigations have been modified over the years to respond to the needs of researchers and the Commission itself. For example, the identity-related question in this survey has changed from the one originally posed in 1979 asking respondents to hierarchically order their loyalty to town, region, country, and the EC; the question utilized in this section inquires if people consider themselves as only national, or partially or fully European.[1]

This chapter attempts to validate the primary hypothesis that, following the Maastricht Treaty, the majority of citizens did not linearly develop a stronger sense of transnationalism by way of supporting the common four policies of the single market, euro, CFSP, and constitutional draft. Rather, the results yield a constructivist assertion of identity transformation as a contested, malleable and nonlinear process, even in a harmonizing context such as is provided in the Union. A second objective is to confirm the hypothesis that European integration is, on the contrary, not being perceived as threatening to national identity. A longitudinal examination pertaining to this statement is provided in the last section of this chapter. The chapter contains a graphical inquiry of the neofunctional impact of the four integrative measures on national public opinion in the three case countries, as well as in the EU-15/25. A shortcoming of some Eurobarometer analyses consists in their statism, thereby neglecting the dynamic aspects of collective identity development and reducing them to an observation at one point in time. The time-series graphs presented here, however, explore and display trends for the observed time frames. After searching for a relationship between the variables' impact on an EU-wide scale, a more detailed view of the three case countries enables us to see specific commonalities as well as differences that reflect the constraining impact of domestic reception based on national political culture and interests.

To verify the research assumption that there is no threat to existing national identities observable through public opinion, I assume the percentages of people expressing fear of losing their national identity will remain relatively constant and at a low level throughout the observation period. The last section details respective Eurobarometer surveys highlighting the course of threat perception throughout the observation period. They also add a qualitative perspective on the "meaning of the EU" as collected in these surveys.

Time-Series Graphs

This section visually presents the main indicators as they have been perceived by the public over time. Beginning with the dependent variable, the indicator "European identity" below, juxtaposed with the dummy variable "support for EU membership," provides a visual display of the development of transnational identity extension. Starting from a fairly advanced position of around 60 percent, the percentage of people expressing that they feel "European to some extent" remained fairly constant, except for the dip in 1996, a result of the enlargement to Austria, Finland, and Sweden. These countries have initially had very low identity ratings for Europe, but converged over time with the EU average. Despite a lack of data, the more recent assessment of transnational attitudes continues at a balanced level of 57 percent. There is no significant increase in European identity over time, yet it is remarkable that the ten new mostly Central and Eastern European states contain similar levels of "European identity" or have quickly converged, as there is no substantial deviation recognizable in the post-2004 period.

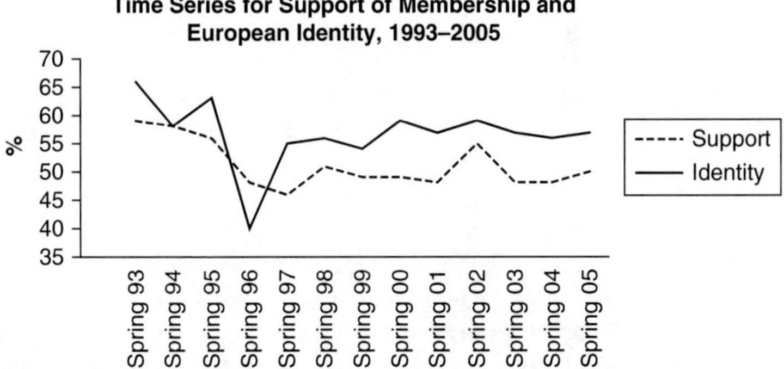

Figure 5.1 Time Series Sequence for European Identity Versus Support for EU Membership

A comparison of the time series for transnational identity and the instrumental indicator "support for EU membership" makes for an illuminating comparison distinguishing purely instrumental and ideational attachment: while, as can be expected, both time series experience a synchronized development, the values for EU identification are generally a few percentage points above the graph for the more utilitarian question of membership support, which actually started above the identity value, at 60 percent. Even more striking is the observation for the past three years, in which support for membership actually stagnates, increases, and again decreases (as is to be expected for a utilitarian component that depends for the most part on structural stimuli such as political gains or economic cycles), the transnational identity variable crystallizes around 60 percent and remains above the volatile utilitarian benchmark, signifying an evolving independent affective category (Figure 5.1).

Time-Series Comparison between the Three Case Countries

To better understand the progression of the four indicators over time in the three case countries, I extrapolated the values for these cases and contrasted them with the EU average. This procedure allows for testing the assumption postulating that with time, a convergence of national reception of those policy measures occurs according to nation-specific constraints provided by political culture and discourses (the second hypothesis). A note of caution: the following data spans vary according to the availability of the country-level data.

With regard to the single market as perceived in the UK, Ireland, and Germany compared to the EU average, one can easily depict the obvious positive outlier Ireland, with an average support for the single market of over 70 percent, which is congruent with the interview and print expressions about the diversification and opening up of the island through EU membership. This contrasts sharply with the EU average and with the approval by Germany and the UK, whose values both hover below the EU average in the 40 and 50 percentage points at all times.The majoritarian support for the single market and the contradictory lack of knowledge in certain countries corresponds to a Eurobarometer special survey held in 2002, which attests to an overwhelming support in the EU-15 for the individual functions of the single market with a minimum baseline of two-thirds approval and a wish for more information on the subject (European Commission, Flash-Eurobarometer 131, 2004) (Figure 5.2).

The euro, when observed in the individual cases, shows a more interesting pattern. While, as expected in conjunction with the repercussions of the common market, Irish support is again the highest among the three countries and higher than the EU average, the contrast between the UK as a nonparticipant in the EMS and the remaining cases is noticeable in its deviant stagnation. All participating countries have slowly increased their support, Ireland more softly, whereas Germany experienced a fast growth in approval after the mid-1990s, reflecting the confidence in the convergence criteria for membership in the EMS. All countries show a slight slump

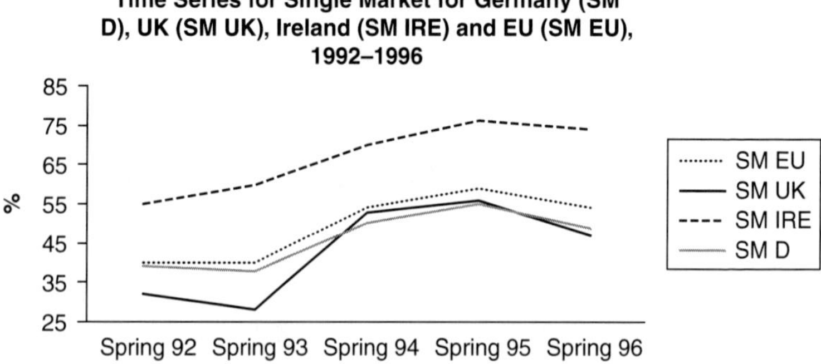

Figure 5.2 Time Series Sequence for Single-Market Support in the Case Countries

around the year 2000, when the euro became politicized and the loss of the national currency became more imminent. The upward trend to over 60 percent for the EU average at the end of the observation period seems to show confidence in the new currency. A look at the Flash Eurobarometer survey from summer 2002 confirms this trend: 67 percent of all EU citizens were quite happy with the euro and 60, percent felt that the euro's advantages outweighed the disadvantages. Sixty-eight percent thought that the euro would become an internationally recognized currency; this percentage should have increased in the meantime with the steady rise of the euro's value. In addition, 64 percent hoped that the euro would be a guarantee for economic growth in the eurozone. Interestingly, even during the difficult Eurocrisis of 2009–10, favorable opinion of the Euro outweighed, with two-thirds supporting the single currency yet a similarly high number of respondents stating that it did not automatically increase their 'European identity' (European Commission, Flash Eurobarometer 306, 2010), therefore delimiting the identity-crafting power of this integration policy among the general population (Figure 5.3).

However, the graph for the development of support for the CFSP reveals a different pattern: It is here that German public opinion overwhelmingly supports the establishment of a common foreign and defense policy, with 75 to 80 percent throughout the period—a seemingly idiosyncratic Teutonic preoccupation with war issues—while the Irish population seems to be the most skeptical group, with support below 60 percent throughout. German foreign policy is deeply rooted in multilateralism based largely on historical determinants. Ireland, in contrast, has for the longest time been a neutral country and feels that a common policy in this area is not

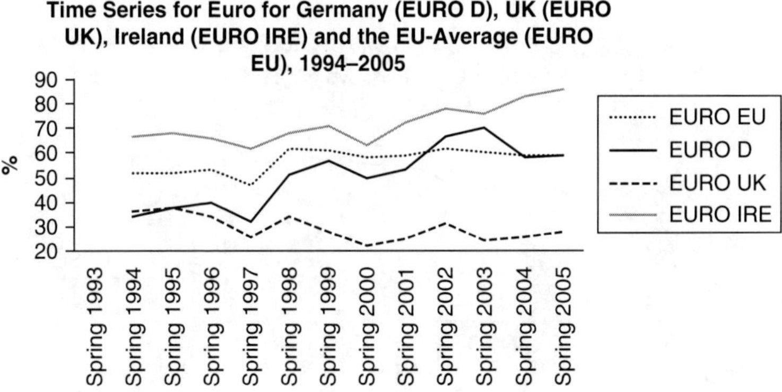

Figure 5.3 Time Series Sequence for Euro Support in the Case Countries

only a "foreign" concept, but also infringes on the much-appreciated Irish neutrality. The British, while initially showing high support above the 60 percent mark, quickly grew disillusioned with the weakness of the CFSP in the Balkan conflicts, thus support dropped to 40 percent, which likely has to do with the divergent opinions over the involvement in the Yugoslav crisis—just as the short peak following September 11, 2001, expressed hopes for unified action thereafter (Figure 5.4).

There seems to be at least unity among the Union's citizens that the EU should preferably take action in European defense matters: according to a Special Eurobarometer survey from 2001, 43 percent of all citizens felt that the EU should have decision-making rights in defense matters, with only 24 percent relying primarily on their nation and 17 percent entrusting it to NATO (European Commission, Special Eurobarometer, 2001). However, the numbers for the case countries are lower, with only 39 percent of Germans and even fewer British and Irish citizens choosing the EU (22 and 29 percent, respectively). These observations clash with the high support that an EU common foreign policy enjoys in regular Eurobarometer surveys, which indicates that there is a considerable gap between the idealistic wish for countries to unite their defense capabilities and the actual operationalization of a CFSP.

The time series for approval of the EU constitution, measured over the period of five years, discloses yet another constellation among the four data sets. Here, the EU average, together with the German indicator, reaches the highest levels, in the 60 to 70 percentage bracket. About 10 percentage points lower, one finds Irish support, and, almost parallel, British support another 10 percentage points below, reflecting general antipathy to legal integration and possibly unfamiliarity with constitutional governance

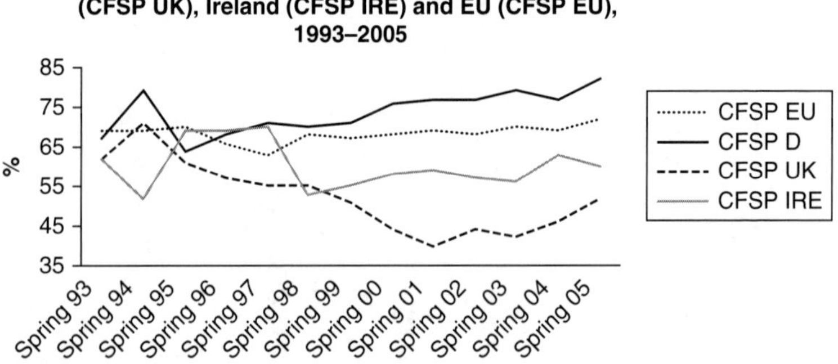

Figure 5.4 Time Series Sequence for CFSP Support in the Case Countries

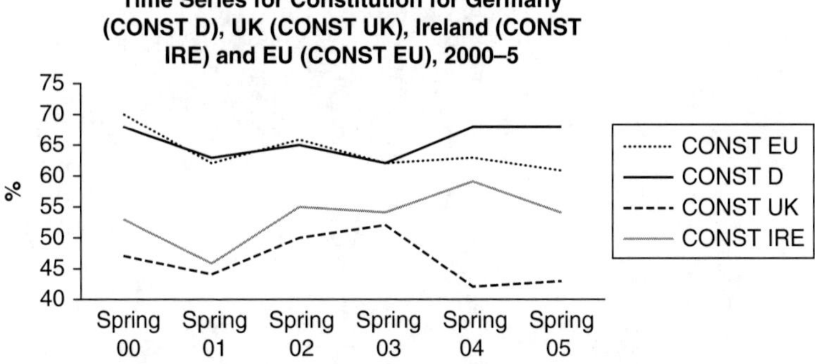

Figure 5.5 Time Series Sequence for Constitution Support in the Case Countries

models more generally. In all observations, after an initially increasing support during the convention in 2002–2003, a slight downturn occurred in the following approval period, marked by disagreement and negotiation among the individual member-state governments. The public contention about the constitutional draft has obviously had a negative impact, though not significant, among EU citizens. Despite some hesitations regarding their country's autonomy, the German data reveals a surprising yet foreign-policy consistent trend supporting a deeply engrained pro-EU orientation (Figure 5.5).

Lastly, a comparison of the development of European transnationalism in terms of "feeling European" in the case countries produces some noteworthy comparisons and results. The evolution of EU-average attachment to the Union has already been previously explored, but the country results diverge in a quite obvious manner that supports the overall thesis of this work. The UK population displays the lowest identification values throughout, which should come as no surprise after the interview and press analyses, but they particularly drop in the run-up to the single currency and later in the preconstitutional period of 2000 and beyond. Interestingly, the emotive attachment of the Irish and Germans seems to develop fairly congruently, in that the drops and rises occur almost in parallel, except for the past three years, when the German poll improves steadily whereas the Irish seems to rise and fall with the referenda issues brought up with the Nice and Constitutional Treaties (Figure 5.6).

In sum, it has become graphically evident over the course of this analysis that statistically, few of the assumed independent policy variables showed a significantly linear progression on transnational identity development by way of convergence of citizen's position over time. Rather, each country pursues interests and develops identification with policy measures

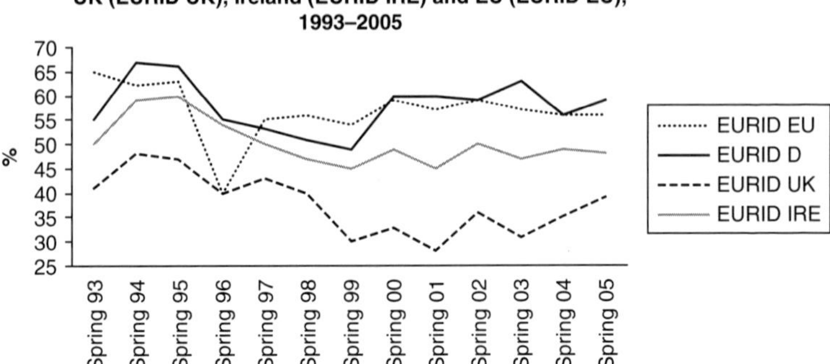

Figure 5.6 Time Series Sequence for European Identity in the Case Countries

and the EU in accordance with its national political culture, taking into account nationally determined historical and political criteria. After visually examining quantitative indicators, the following section provides a more qualitatively oriented Eurobarometer measurement, which supports the basic hypothesis relating to the assumption that European integration is not perceived as a threat.

Qualitative Eurobarometer Survey: The Meaning of the EU

This dataset statistically validates how the EU is perceived in the countries observed, and how those meanings change over time and are replaced by others. Respondents were asked to qualify the "meaning of the EU" by choosing from a particular list of notions about the EU. In particular, the first hypothesis stating that European integration in general is not perceived as threatening to national identities is here confirmed for all cases except the UK. The section is particularly useful as background information and control for my interviews, in which similar claims are qualitatively supported. Data for the closed-ended question asking about the personal meaning of the EU for Europeans is available for the years 1997 (EB 47.2), 2001 (EB 55.1), 2002 (EB 57), and then again, reformulated and reintroduced, with EB 61 in spring 2004. All of these reflect the views of the citizens in the fifteen member states at the time.

A comparison over time reveals the change of meanings during the first wave of this question, starting with the three most-mentioned responses by each country in 1997. In addition to listing the associations mentioned for the EU, I included in the bottom row of the table the data for the response "(risk of) losing cultural diversity/identity," because it reflects the object of research on the other end of the identification spectrum.

As can be seen in Table 5.1, one of the three most significant features of the EU consisted in the "freedom of movement," which remains part of all three top categories in varying order. This aspect of the EU has a rather

Table 5.1 Most-Mentioned Responses to "Meaning of the EU" in Case Countries, 1997–2004

	%	Ireland	%	UK	%	Germany	%
1997 (EB 47)							
Freedom of movement	35	Better future for young	49	Better future for young	27	Freedom of movement	49
Means to improve economy	34	Way to create jobs	40	A European government	25	Means to improve economy	34
Better future for young	34	Freedom of movement	40	Way to create jobs	25	Better future for young	33
Risk losing cultural diversity	12		7		14		12
2002 (EB 57)							
Freedom of movement	50	Freedom of movement	43	Freedom of movement	35	Euro	54
Euro	49	Economic prosperity	41	Euro	24	Freedom of movement	47
Peace	32	Euro	40	Waste of money	23	Peace	46
Risk losing cultural identity	13		8		22		8
2004 (EB 61)							
Freedom of movement	51	Euro	50	Freedom of movement	45	Euro	58
Euro	50	Freedom of movement	45	Waste of money	31	Freedom of movement	51
Peace	31	Economic prosperity	32	Bureaucracy	29	Peace	44
Risk losing cultural identity	14		12		29		13

obviously practical yet positive meaning for EU citizens. In the same vein, the responses "means to improving economy" and "way to create jobs" are similarly instrumentally situated in the consciousness of Europeans. However, the aspect of "creating a better future for the youth" can be interpreted as a more idealistic notion of enabling the next generation a life in peace and prosperity. One exception represents the second-most chosen notion of "a European government" in the UK, which indicates the existing realization and, I would add, fear of being governed by Brussels. The EU is a kind of factual European governance institution and therefore could have theoretically been mentioned by all three countries' respondents—or none. That it only appears in the UK's top listing indicates a special preoccupation with it. Of particular interest for this analysis is the response to the notion of losing cultural diversity or national identity in Europe: while the UK, as expected, shows a higher than average value, Ireland in particular does not seem to have any issues with European governance in this respect.

Five years later, in spring 2002, the same question was reintroduced by Eurobarometer, this time with a more balanced row of optional answers expressing both positive and negative views, thus giving us more information about the identification of respondents, but not changing the original question about the meaning of the Union. Importantly, the euro has been integrated as a possible response after its introduction on January 1, 2002. The introduction of the euro is shown here as having significant impact on the transnational connotations connected to the EU. In all three countries, as well as in the EU-15 average, the euro is among the top three responses. Even in the UK, a nonparticipant in the European Monetary System, the euro is the second-most chosen answer, a sign that discussion about the euro is prevalent in the UK, as evidenced by the interviews and print coverage as well, though it also reflects a further differentiation of the island from the continent using the single currency. In Germany, the euro as a symbol of European integration tops the agenda, with more than half of the respondents choosing it as the major reference. Also, the notion of "peace" has received more attention among the German population and the EU-15. This category was available in the first wave as well, so its increased significance seems related to the events in the international area, in particular to the post-September 11, 2001, changes in the international system. The positive notion of "economic prosperity" in Ireland is a reflection of the success of Ireland's economy over the past few years. For the first time, a strictly negative response to the EU, "a waste of money," is elevated to third place in the UK and constitutes, together with the relatively high percentage of residents feeling culturally threatened by European integration, a strong indication of British citizens becoming rather preoccupied over the period observed, signifying a trend toward a protective nationalism. However, such augmented threat perception is missing in all other cases.

The last published ranking during the observation period dates from spring 2004 (EB 61) and confirms the post-2000 changes in meanings related to the EU. It becomes evident that the impact of the euro as a unifying symbol of European integration has further increased and now occupies the first place in two of the three countries, Ireland and Germany, while it vanished from the UK priority list. The former two countries remain consistent in their value listings, but the Euro-skepticism noted earlier in the UK seems to have expanded over the past two years. In addition to relating to the EU as a "waste of money," the notion of the EU being a bureaucratic institution has been added to the top of the list. Being mentioned by one of every three British respondents, there is a significant increase in negative feelings toward the EU. Both indicators, however, seem to express a more general discontent with the institution than with specific policies. In addition, there seems to be an alerting—or, in the case of the UK, alarming—expectation of identity loss prevalent among EU citizens (up 9 percent up from 2002, representing more than double all other cases). In all observed cases, the responses for the identity-related notion increased only slightly.

The years 1997–2004 saw a significant change in meaning of the EU for its citizens. In the EU-15 average as well as that of Ireland and Germany, the most stable indicator has proven to be the freedom-of-movement notion associated with the establishment of the single market. After the change from previously nationalized currencies to the euro in January 2002, the euro as a symbol for the EU has become an essential reference for the citizens. The notion of peace also gained in importance after the 2001 survey, which can be traced back to the international crises after September 11, 2001. This section provided aggregate evidence for the hypothesis that European integration is not experienced as a threat to national identity, at least not for the majority of EU member states. In Germany and Ireland, the percentage of people fearing a threat to their cultural national identity has remained low throughout the observation period. On the negative side, however, the most worrisome development occurred in the UK. Over the time frame observed, the UK has doubled the responses for losing cultural diversity and national identity, and has replaced neutral or positive associations for the EU with predominantly negative ones, which is congruent with the quantitatively collected data above. Nevertheless, the values for the EU average expressing fear for national identity remain consistently low, in the 12 to 14 percent bracket, over the observation period, which in turn shows that for these countries, the threat to national identity has not increased over the observation period, as spelled out in the first hypothesis.

Conclusion

With regard to the utility of the time-series analyses offered in this chapter, small but largely insignificant trends in the temporal development of EU public opinion are detected for the attitudinal and identity-related changes initiated by EU integration policies. As an auxiliary instrument for the triangulation of interview and print media data, the main hypothesis of nationally constrained transnationalism according to each country's political culture is observable, ruling out any significant independent effects of integration variables. While support for individual measures and the development of European identification received only little augmentation over the observation period, a partial convergence in the development of support has occurred among most EU member states, except for the British case. On the other hand, a possible prediction for future incremental changes in most of the analyses is not possible. Rather, mere trends can be identified that open up the opportunity for further research into the direction of the relationship between the assumed independent and dependent variables and expansion of the observed time period.

Despite generous support levels for the CFSP, as noted in the graphical survey, attachment to a unification of foreign policies appears only in the notions of "peace" and "building a better future for the young" in the qualitative listings. The euro seems to be more important to the respondents of the qualitative surveys, as it has moved into the most-mentioned notions for three of the four observations. Both indicators, however, embody the main achievements of the EU, peace and monetary union, which are indicative of the Union's purported symbolism and which are simultaneously recognized by citizens as major unifying policies (the single market and the constitution are more limited in their explanatory power). German and Irish public opinion on the chosen indicators and the dependent transnational variable in both Eurobarometer analyses show signs of convergence over time, whereas the UK displays outlying values for all of the indicators, as well as for the values associated with the EU more generally. The slight increase in transnational attitudes recognizable in Ireland and Germany has morphed into a form of protectionist rejection of the EU as a governance institution in Britain and lacks any form of common transnational denominator indicative of most other member states.

The main outcomes of this chapter consist in the validation of the first and the second hypotheses, in that it has been shown that, for one, support for the integration policies has not resulted in a converging emergence of transnational identities as observable by the differing country graphs. Rather, these outcomes evidence country-dependent identitive support for the EU and its policies, and thus preclude generalizations of a common pan-European identity attributable to all member states. Secondly, European integration is not (yet) perceived as a threat to existing national identities for the majority of EU citizens, as evidenced in the last section. After providing individual views and illustrating the potential and limits of transnational identity expansion on a larger scale, the question remains of how discursive processes contribute to the framing of collective identities. In the following chapter, discourse analysis drawn from the countries' major newspapers is analyzed to test the background conditions existing in European public spheres.

Chapter 6

Newspaper Discourse and Public Spheres

Introduction

This final empirical chapter explores the construction and reiteration of journalistic messages with respect to their domestic focus and their institutional EU and broader European content. The content analysis conducted here concentrates not only on the prevalence of EU-related print content, but also, more importantly, , redraws the dynamic treatment of the integration-based independent variables over the twelve-year period. Derived from selected print media in each of the case countries, representative quotes reveal not only the extent of coverage of EU and European issues as part of the public (identity) discourse claim laid out in the third hypothesis, but also how the salience of these measures has changed over time in quantitative and qualitative terms, thereby reflecting the supply side of public perception as part of the domestic reception of European integration. Approaches pointing to the media's potential as transmitter of transnationalism are fairly novel and have received more attention only in the past few years (Wessler, 2008; Hurrelmann et al., 2009). Taken together, the span of observation, the breadth of sources, and the linkages between those, as well as the quantitative and qualitatively examined variables, support this methodology as a way to discern the print discourse in European public spheres.

Europeans witnessed the technological revolution of the past decades, which augmented the importance of communication of political content as a means of democratization and political control. In the process, traditional and new web- and satellite-based media have gained in significance as well. With regard to EU politics, the "permissive consensus" by which the masses would follow the lead of political and economic elites has been weakened by media-supported public spheres, where, in particular in the previous decade, citizens have demanded an alleviation of the Union's democratic deficit and more transparency and say in EU matters. These public spheres, originally defined as a discursive societal space allowing for interactive exchanges on social matters (Habermas, 1989) have in turn provided additional power to the media outlets based on their control function, although it also resulted in a reevaluation of their linkage role in the process of public communication.

The Extent of Transnational Coverage in Europe

A transnational European public sphere with open, standardized, and synchronized communication channels does not exist in contemporary Europe. While Europeans possess a compartmentalized system of audiovisual and print media, differences persist in the "Europeanization," i.e., the depth and timing of transnational articulation of coverage and interactive resonance, in these outlets (Trenz 2010). The European television landscape is by virtue of its technology more transnational than the print media in that television broadcasts easily reach above and beyond national borders into neighboring regions with the same language regime, with 3SAT, Arte, and TV 5 being prime examples for the German-speaking and French-speaking European markets, respectively. Print media, however, is produced mainly for national, regional, and local markets, except for a few products such as *The Economist*, the *Financial Times*, and *The International Herald Tribune*, which are published for a relatively small group of internationally minded elite.

The role of the media in the political process has become more important over the previous decades with the technological transformations and the emergence of the so-called information society, in which the continuous acquisition of knowledge is seen as essential. Over 50 percent of EU citizens rely on their national print media for getting information on the Union and other European affairs; only television is more often utilized. According to Eurobarometer data, the preferred sources of information about the EU and general politics are television (70 percent), followed by daily newspapers (49 percent). Online news consumers, while increasing in numbers, are still a minority (17 percent) (European Commission, Eurobarometer 61, 2005). Thus, the use of major newspapers makes sense particularly as online consumers often consult the online presence of the print outlets anyway. But news media outlets are primarily formatted for national and regional markets, and supply their audiences with messages that they think have priority and that are attractive for them. After all, in an increasingly commercialized media market, the pressure for a large market share of the viewership and readership is high. More important, the diversity of European languages and thus the multiple language formats of European national newspapers prevent the development of a tightly integrated transnational public sphere. Notwithstanding, the media fulfill valuable functions for a democratic public life: "The role of the media in a democratic system is also considered with reference to the provision of information relevant to political decision-making and participation, the provision of platforms for debate on European political and cultural issues, and the media's role as watchdog on the democratic process" (Kevin, 2003:7). Whereas the news media are essential for the framing of domestic issues and collective identities, as most famously stated in Benedict Anderson's "imagined community," their impact on agenda setting of transnational and EU-related topics is limited for a variety of market and political reasons.

If indeed at least half of the population in the EU consumes print coverage, the essential logic of the conveyor function of the press for the development of any kind of transnational identity remains, and thus a print discourse analysis can tell us about the context in which attitudes and identities are being shaped through the framing of specific issues. It suggests that "what consistently modifies specific perceptions and appraisal of policies and institutions may, in turn, affect the deeper beliefs and, ultimately, the very identity of an individual" (Bruter, 2003: 1149). In addition, the national perspective of print media outlets does not negate a Europeanized media landscape: recent research has moved from the strict conceptualization of an integrated European media sphere to a more differentiated model of the Europeanization of each individual national public sphere (Risse, 2010; Trenz 2010; Wessler, 2008). Behind the idea of several Europeanized national media landscapes is the argument that "since politicians aim for reelection by their domestic electorate, it can be assumed that decisions made on the European level are packaged as being in the national rather than the European interest. In this way Europe does enter a broader public sphere, although more often than not through the looking glass of the national perspective" (Voltmer and Eilders, 2003: 178–9). It is this persistent national perspective, together with national political cultures and domestic print markets, that constrains the development of a strongly Europeanized public sphere.

In most European countries print coverage can be distinguished along the political spectrum. Therefore, in each of the three countries, two widely circulated daily newspapers representing each end of the left–right continuum were selected. In the case of Ireland, the ideological contrast between the chosen papers is not as stark, because there is no corresponding strong ideological disparity among the political parties. But even in other countries, the increasing shift of political views toward the center has led to a less pronounced difference between more conservative-liberal and social-democratic parties (Kevin, 2003: 50), with a resulting moderation in political ideologies expressed in media outlets. Even if readers choose to select certain outlets according to their ideological stance, the consumption of "Europeanized" coverage still contributes to the formation of their (trans)national position.

The selected papers for this analysis are among the most widely distributed national dailies and stand for different political views for each country; e.g., in Germany, the *Frankfurter Allgemeine Zeitung* (*FAZ*) represents the more neoliberal-conservative view and the *Süddeutsche Zeitung* (*SZ*) the more leftist-progressive one. Similarly, in the UK, the rather Euroskeptic tabloid *Daily Mail* and the progressive daily the *Guardian* are chosen to represent diverging views, and in Ireland the *Irish Times* and the *Irish Independent* are comparatively examined. While some of these outlets can be described as being more traditionally conservative, particularly the *FAZ*, the *Times*, and *Le Figaro*, others can be seen as leaning toward the left, such as *Le Monde*, the *Guardian*, and the *SZ* (Kevin, 2003). Included in this study are factual reports and editorial opinion pieces, reflecting the whole spectrum of coverage of each topic. Similarly, I opted to include all transnational references; while some researchers may differ and would count only opinions of "external" actor representations, I perceive transnationalization as a two-way process. Such analysis required the categorization of these pieces into positive, neutral/balanced, or negative coverage. Those with semantic signs of positive coverage were classified in the positive category, the opposite ones in the negative category, and value-neutral reports or pieces containing both positive and negative statements into the balanced category.

Quantitative Overview of Keyword Distributions

Among the few more progressive broadsheets in the UK, the *Guardian* as an elitist broadsheet represents the more liberal, leftist spectrum of political coverage. In contrast, the *Daily Mail* is a tabloid that has—not least because it is the second most widely read paper in the UK, with a distribution of over two million—a substantial effect on mass opinion formation. While the *Daily Mail* contains predominantly populist coverage, analysts attribute to the *Guardian* a pro-European stance because of its perceived support of European integration in its journalism. My examination, in contrast, produced results that would classify the paper as less pro-European.

For this study I reviewed a total of 9,010 articles that appeared between January 1, 1993, and December 31, 2005, and contained keywords related to the EU and, in particular, the keywords "identity" in combination with the four variable keywords "single (common) market," "euro (currency)," "'Common Foreign (and Security) Policy," and "constitution."[1] The articles, taken from the LexisNexis database, were distributed as shown in Table 6.1.

As can be seen in the table below, the distribution of articles and their value judgment with regard to European integration varies significantly in these outlets. In both UK papers, the euro received the most attention, with 478 articles in the *Guardian* and 535 in the *Daily Mail*. In the case of the *Guardian*, however, the second-highest priority receives questions of an EU-wide identity, with 419 pieces dealing with that subject. The *Daily Mail* presses the issue of an EU constitution, with 314 articles appearing under that heading. And while the next highest prevalence in the *Guardian* falls to the constitution, the *Daily Mail* picks up questions of identity in third place. In comparison, topics such as the CFSP and the single market seem to be of less importance. Regarding the value judgment of the EU-related contents, an editorial could also be classified as neutral if it supplied a balanced opinion on a certain matter. For the two chosen papers in the UK, a significant difference exists between both newspapers: the *Guardian*, with an overall centrist average of 48 percent in all keyword areas, shows a tendency for balanced coverage that considers equally advantages and disadvantages of each subject or objectively reports facts without much or any polemic judgment. Most of the keywords analyzed also received some positive coverage, ranging from 11 to 25 percent for the individual topics. The one exception was the EU constitution, with only 11 percent of approving titles and a third of negative coverage. A look at the *Daily Mail's* journalistic stance reveals a much higher degree of anti-Europeanism, as can be expected from a center-right tabloid outlet. Here, the biggest category is not the neutral one, but the one containing negative articles, with 59 percent. There is less balanced coverage available than in the comparator, and the small percentage of positive reporting overall, 4 percent, differs substantially from the *Guardian*'s pro-European coverage of 18 percent. Despite their differences in the overall perception of EU integration policies, the constitution receives the least support in the *Daily Mail's* coverage, with zero

Table 6.1 Distribution of Keyword Articles According to Coverage in the Six Newspapers

	Articles	Positive	%	Negative	%	Neutral/ Both	%	Total %
Guardian: Keywords								
EU + Identity	419		25.3		30.3		44.4	100
EU + Single Market	158		25.3		34.2		40.5	100
EU + Euro	478		17.8		38		44.2	100
EU + CFSP	187		13.2		33		53.8	100
EU + Constitution	327		11		33.7		57.3	100
Numeric Totals	1569							
Average % Coverage			**18.1**		**33.8**		**48.1**	**100**
Daily Mail Keywords								
EU + Identity	213		2.7		49.2		48.1	100
EU + Single Market	169		10.8		43.7		45.5	100
EU + Euro	535		3.9		56.3		39.8	100
EU + CFSP	103		2.2		58.9		38.9	100
EU + Constitution	314				85		15	100
Numeric Totals	1334							
Average % Coverage			**3.8**		**58.6**		**37.6**	**100**
FAZ Keywords								
EU + Identity	446		17.9		31.8		50.3	100
EU + Single Market	313		21.3		31.9		46.8	100
EU + Euro	531		16.8		32		51.2	100
EU + CFSP	296		14.2		27.7		58.1	100
EU + Constitution	387		19.8		27.5		52.7	100
Numeric Totals	1973							
Average % Coverage			**18**		**30.2**		**51.8**	**100**
SZ Keywords								
EU + Identity	245		22.1		24.4		53.5	100
EU + Single Market	352		21.3		32.1		46.6	100
EU + Euro	464		18.3		35.1		46.6	100

Continued

Table 6.1 Continued

	Articles	Positive	%	Negative	%	Neutral/ Both	%	Total %
***SZ* Keywords**								
EU + CFSP	276		20.6		24.2		55.2	100
EU + Constitution	245		22.6		26.3		51.1	100
Numeric Totals	1582							
Average % Coverage			**21**		**28.4**		**50.6**	**100**
***Irish Times* Keywords**								
EU + Identity	332		23.3		24.4		52.3	100
EU + Single Market	311		28.1		24.2		47.7	100
EU + Euro	369		15.4		25.9		58.7	100
EU + CFSP	175		18.6		33.5		47.9	100
EU + Constitution	227		16.1		32.8		51.1	100
Numeric Totals	1414							
Average % Coverage			**20.4**		**28.2**		**51.3**	**100**
***Independent* Keywords**								
EU + Identity	202		24.3		21.9		53.8	100
EU + Single Market	223		27.6		23.5		48.8	100
EU + Euro	311		18		27.1		54.9	100
EU + CFSP	168		19.6		37.2		43.2	100
EU + Constitution	234		18.4		34.4		47.2	100
Numeric Totals	1138							
Average % Coverage			**21.6**		**28.8**		**49.6**	**100**

positive reporting about it, making it apparent that the constitution in both outlets is reviewed in a critical light—but significantly more so in the *Daily Mail* than in the *Guardian*.

In the two German papers, the variation in topics occurs in a more similar manner. In the two outlets, the highest number of articles deals with the euro as common currency, with 531 in the *FAZ* and 464 articles in *SZ*. The second most prevalent topics are identity-related in the case of the *FAZ*, but in the case of the *SZ* economic issues of the single market seem to take precedence over identitive issues. The least preoccupying topics in the *FAZ* relate to CFSP and in the *SZ* deal with the EU constitution. Not surprisingly, since it is the paper of choice for lawyers, the number of constitution-related articles in the *FAZ* is higher. With regard to the judgment of the individual topics in these two newspapers, the tables provide valuable information as well, confirming the more pro-European stance of the *SZ*. There, a little over 20 percent of the coverage is of positive nature, whereas it totals only 18 percent in the *FAZ*. The extent of negative reception of EU issues is only slightly lower in the *SZ* than in the *FAZ*, with 28 versus 30 percent, constituting a third of all coverage. With more than half of all articles being in the neutral category, both papers appear rather nonideological in their stance toward the EU, though positive reporting is slightly higher in the *SZ*. A look at the quantitative distribution of the issue-related articles indicates when a specific topic was popularized. In Table 6.2, one detects only minor chronological differences in the coverage of the examined themes.

In the overview of both Irish papers, one can see the above-mentioned difference in the frequency of reporting specific topics. The *Irish Times* shows a higher absolute number of articles dealing with EU-related issues than the *Irish Independent*. Both media outlets emphasize the euro, allocating it the highest number of articles, with 363 and 306 reports, respectively. In both, the single market and identity-related articles are of high priority as well, occupying the second-highest priorities in terms of quantity. Overall, the value judgments of both papers appear to be similar, with the *Irish Times* showing a higher degree of balanced reporting and lower figures for the positive or negative categories.

A chronologically oriented inquiry into the distribution of articles per topic per year yields an indication as to when the various issues were most intensely debated in these papers (see Table 6.2). For the four integration measures, one must also take into account the time of their proposal and implementation. The distribution of articles on each variable tells us about the progress or salience of these; for instance, the EU constitution has been treated predominantly after the year 2000. A distributive table looks like as shown in Table 6.2.

Concerning the UK's coverage of issues of European identity as well as British identity, the annual overview reveals that following the Maastricht Treaty, identity issues were published infrequently, with less than 10 percent of the total observation period falling in each year. Interestingly, the number of identity-related articles increased in the period 1999–2001. As detailed below in the textual analysis, this rise has to do predominantly

Table 6.2 Annual Distribution of Keyword-Related Articles from the Total (<10% Treatment Shaded)

	1993	**1994**	**1995**	**1996**	**1997**	**1998**	**1999**	**2000**	**2001**	**2002**	**2003**	**2004**	**2005**	**Total (%)**
***Guardian* Keywords**														
EU + Identity	4.4	6.1	1.2	3.6	3.2	2.9	8.8	8	7.9	6.6	**12.4**	**16.2**	**18.7**	100
EU + Single Market	6.2	2	1.4	4.1	4.2	**8.3**	4.9	5.6	5.6	10.3	**16.1**	18	13.3	100
EU + Euro	2.5	1.4	2.6	4.3	7.3	**10.1**	4.5	8.8	7.9	8.4	**16.4**	**14.6**	**12**	100
EU + CFSP	6.9	5.7	6.4	8.7	4.6	**11**	8.1	4.1	4.6	8.7	6.4	**21.5**	3.3	100
EU + Constitution						0.3		0.6	0.6	7.7	**16.8**	**30.8**	**43.2**	100
***Daily Mail* Keywords**														
EU + Identity	1.2	4.8	5.3	6.5	1.2	8.5	7.7	**13.8**	**10.9**	7.3	**11.7**	**10.1**	**11**	100
EU + Single Market	2.9	7.5	4	4.6	3.5	6.4	**20.3**	**11.6**	9.3	**11**	6.7	6.4	5.8	100
EU + Euro		0.7	2.7	3.2	0.4	9.5	**13.1**	9	6.7	6	**23.6**	**13.2**	**11.9**	100
EU + CFSP		2.5	2.5		1.7	8.5	**10.3**	**12.8**	**16.2**	**10.3**	9.4	**21.3**	4.5	100
EU + Constitution		0.3				0.3		0.3	1.4	7.7	**27.3**	**27**	**35.7**	100
***FAZ* Keywords**														
EU + Identity	3.6	2.5	1.7	3	3.5	3.3	5.1	4.8	6.3	**13.1**	**13.7**	**19.1**	**20.3**	100
EU + Single Market	2.8	2.5	2.7	2.2	2.5	3.7	4.9	8.5	8.5	8	**17.4**	**21.5**	**14.8**	100
EU + Euro	3	3.7	2.8	5.3	8.1	**10.4**	8.7	7	8.1	9.4	**12.3**	**12.1**	**9.1**	100
EU + CFSP	0.8	3.3	6.7	4.6	5.7	5.9	**10.5**	5.1	7.9	7.8	**16.3**	**15.1**	**10.3**	100
EU + Constitution		0.6	0.4	0.6	0.8	0.4	2.6	2.6	4.5	5.5	19.6	18.4	44	100

Continued

Table 6.2 Continued

	1993	1994	1995	1996	1997	1998	1999	2000	2001	2002	2003	2004	2005	Total (%)
***SZ* Keywords**														
EU + Identity	2.1	1.7	1.7	4.4	5	3.7	3.9	5.2	5	9.7	**14.9**	**19.7**	**23**	100
EU + Single Market	5.2	3.1	3.9	5.6	7.8	8.2	**10.2**	9.3	8.1	**10.2**	8.7	**12.3**	7.4	100
EU +Euro	4	2.7	3	5.6	7.9	**10.8**	5	7.2	6.9	8.5	**14.7**	**12.7**	**11**	100
EU + CFSP	1.5	4.5	7.8	5.4	6.3	8.1	**10.1**	7.5	8.4	9.1	**10.3**	**11.3**	9.7	100
EU + Constitution	0.9	0.7	0.7	0	0.9	0.5	2.3	4.6	3.2	4.2	**15.3**	**25.5**	**41.2**	100
***Irish Times* Keywords**														
EU + Identity	0.9	1.1	3.3	4.1	2.4	6.3	8.5	8.3	**11.3**	7.4	**15.8**	**16.7**	**13.9**	100
EU + Single Market	1.4	0.8	3.8	4.3	8.2	**10.3**	7.5	7.7	**11.3**	**10.5**	**11.1**	**12.2**	**10.9**	100
EU + Euro	0.3	0.9	3	6.1	6.1	**10.8**	3.8	7	5.6	7.1	**19.4**	**17**	**12.9**	100
EU + CFSP	2	6.2	5	7.9	6.8	**14.3**	3.7	6.8	5.5	12.5	7.8	**11.5**	**10.1**	100
EU + Constitution		1.1						1.5	2.6	4.2	**25.9**	**21.7**	**43**	100
***Irish Independent* Keywords**														
EU + Identity	0.9	4.3	5.2	5.4	6	**10.3**	9.7	9.1	9.4	8.3	9.5	**11.7**	**10.5**	100
EU + Single Market	0.4	3.6	3.1	3.2	4.2	4.6	**10.8**	**14.3**	11.3	9.6	**11.3**	**13.8**	**10**	100
EU + Euro		0.8	3.1	4.3	5.1	9.4	9.7	9.8	**10.6**	**10.8**	**10.1**	**12.5**	**11.6**	100
EU + CFSP	0.4	0.8	1.6	1.8	2.9	8.7	9.5	**12.8**	**14.6**	**13.9**	**12.3**	**11.1**	9.6	100
EU + Constitution					1	0.8		0.6	1.3	5	**25.2**	**35.4**	**31.1**	100

with either the preparations for euro introduction or reflections on the UK and its relationship with the EU on the eve of the new millennium. Noticeably, the steadily growing frequency of such pieces in the year 2000 and beyond gives an indication of the growing importance of these issues for both print outlets. Within this topical classification, I further categorized all articles according to the subtheme covered in each article to find out not only *how* they report (positive, negative, neutral), but also *what* they report about (national identity, European commonalities, cultural policies, etc). A look at this topical listing reveals that of all analyzed *Guardian* articles dealing with identity, 19 percent deal with the EU's impact on Europe in general, followed by 18 percent looking specifically at the Union's impact on the UK and 17 percent reviewing solely the question of national British identity.

With regard to the German coverage, a similar trend toward increased media salience of all the variables toward the end of the observed period is recognizable. The constitutional draft as a late-developed measure received more attention only after 2002, when politicians started to debate the constitution in the convention. Surprisingly, the single market has been covered significantly only after 2002 in its extension to services and linkage to EU enlargement, despite expectations that its coverage would be more pronounced in the years following its implementation in 1992. The only topic that was emphasized particularly in the midst of the examination period was the euro, as the year 1998 shows a coverage increase to double-digit percentages as a result of the prevalent discussion about membership criteria for the currency union and the stability pact more generally. The figures for both newspapers are similarly distributed, thereby demonstrating the domestic consensus regarding the agenda-setting function of the German media.

The temporal distribution of the Irish papers recognizes no stark differences in the annual treatment of the keywords. In both cases, the number of reports increases dramatically in the second half of the observation period, again attesting to the augmented salience of these integration measures over time. The *Irish Times* seems to put more emphasis on the coverage of the euro introduction during 1998, when the topic of eurozone membership was hotly debated. Both papers, however, show peaks for the years of the Amsterdam Treaty referendum in 1998 and the Nice Treaty referenda in 2001 and 2002, both of which are particularly relevant in the context of the required popular assent to EU integration there. Following this quantitative overview, the remainder of the chapter provides a qualitative, descriptive illustration of the changing notions attached to the examined variables in each country.

Treatment of Variables in the National Presses

UK

Looking at the *Guardian*'s identity-related content from a qualitative perspective, it appears that a discussion surrounding the Maastricht Treaty ratification provided ample opportunity to argue about Britain's increasing involvement in the Union and the resulting impact on the island's identity. In an early Euro-skeptic commentary by Martin Wollacott, for example, it is asserted

> that the discussion of the European future is being inhibited and distorted by the Maastricht Treaty, with its unreal aims, to which opponents have added their unreal objections. Maastricht was a Franco-German compact to which the rest of us acquiesced. ("A Redundant Routine of Prayer," *Guardian* Martin Wollacott, July 24, 1993)

Years later, in 1997, the question of a European identity in relation to the national ones is still a focus of reflection and confusion, as belonging culturally to Europe now includes simultaneously being part of the EU, thereby marking a transcending of nations.

> What does it mean to be European? There are the near-infinite Europes of memory, and there is the not so new 'Europe', which is neither public in the old sense, raising armies or confidently dispensing laws, nor wholly certain of what it is there to do. Somewhere between them lie the old nation-states of Europe, which are starting to look distinctively tatty. These Europes coexist but they have no real connection to each other. ("What State Are We In?," *Guardian* Nicholas Fraser, September 13, 1997)

In 1999 and 2000 the high frequency of pieces relating to identity issues are expressively reflective commentaries about the EU's direction and acceptance in the UK at the start of a new millennium. In 1999, Peter Shore asks in a feature article questions about the final shape of the Union, and Britain's place in it:

> What is the purpose, direction and destination of the European Union? It really does matter whether it is a Europe of nation states or a European state. The failure to put, let alone realistically face, this question is what distorts and demeans the whole British debate about its place in Europe. ("Britons Deceived," *Guardian* Peter Shore, January 6, 1999)

Aside from politicians calling for a change in newspaper coverage about the EU ("Cook Calls for More Positive Reporting of Europe," *Guardian* David Grow, November 4, 2000), Labor politicians under Blair's leadership make the case (to the opposition) that Britain should utilize the chance to make its own significant contribution to a speedily integrating Europe instead of viewing it as a danger for British national identity—something Prime Minister Blair consistently argued during his term:

> To regard each pooling of sovereignty as a diminution of a national identity, is to retreat from modern reality. And for a nation with such a proud history as that of Britain, it is to show a lack of self-confidence wholly at odds with our true potential for leadership. ("Blair Sets Out Vision for New Patriotism," *Guardian* Anne Perkins, May 26, 2001)

This optimism fades after the constitutional rejection, and a new soberness sets in both in the UK and within the Labor Party struggling to justify its own pro-Europeanness, particularly during the country's EU presidency in 2005, which is mirrored by low public opinion on the EU:

> On the one side is the familiar centre-left case that the EU exists to protect its citizens against the pain of globalisation. On the other is the claim that the old vision of an integrated social Europe is now bust, and the challenge is to embrace open markets, not raise walls. ("Blair and Brown Agree on This: Europe Isn't Working," *Guardian* Jackie Ashley, October 24, 2005)

With regard to the second, qualitatively oriented analysis, the classification of the *Daily Mail*'s coverage of identity-related articles shows that issues of national and regional identity in relation to the EU are treated 35 percent of the time, while smaller, miscellaneous issues such as the impact of immigration or the question of the British rebate on EU contributions make up 32 percent of all related articles. Finally, 11 percent of these articles debate the (non)existence of a common transnational identity. Overall, despite putting identitive content as the highest priority quantitatively when reporting about the EU, the *Daily Mail* possesses a rather critical stance when looked at qualitatively. At the beginning of the post-Maastricht observation period, the treaty is described as a threat to national identities throughout Europe, and the European Parliament elections of 1994 are being taken as example for its popular rejection:

> Calculating the size of Britain's anti-Maastricht vote in the Euro-elections is tricky, if not impossible [...] The French vote is telling. Throughout the Community's history, the apparent readiness of France to submerge its powerful identity in a European superstate has been a puzzling anomaly. Sanity is returning. ("Back to the Old Order: Sanity Returns in the Face of a Threat to National Identity," *Daily Mail* Andrew Alexander, June 17, 1994)

Aside from particular problems that the UK faces with regard to its regions, the *Daily Mail* responded harshly to accusations that the British press is in part responsible for the Euro-skepticism there and depicts the EU as fighting the validity of national identities—reminiscent of the "superstate" idea prevalent among UK interviewees as well:

> The EU's accusation of 'bias' in this newspaper, soundly rebutted yesterday, suggests they can't even use the English language honestly. 'Bias' means unfairness. I wish to be fair about the EU. It is run by unelected and largely unaccountable failed politicians, and it has a recent history of gross corruption. It hates the idea of national identity and wishes to create a federal superstate. ("Why Tony Is Running Scared," *Daily Mail* Simon Heffer, April 15, 2000)

The idea of the EU trying to create a kind of superstate is a recurring theme in the British media, and in particular Tony Blair's assertion that further integration of the UK in Europe would be patriotic receives lots of critical press ("A Dubious Kind of Patriotism," *Daily Mail* Simon Heffer, May 24, 2001). A good example of populist rhetoric is represented in a 2001 article dealing with supposedly drastic changes, listed from A to Z, that were initiated throughout the EU and their corresponding impact on British life ("R.I.P. Farewell to a Uniquely British Way of Life," *Daily Mail* Edward H. Amory, May 24, 2001). In 2002, another essay posits that an identity crisis takes hold in the UK, for which the EU is made responsible. Note the way the EU's interference in domestic politics is linked to the areas over which the EU actually has no jurisdiction, such as regional dialects or customs:

> The European superstate will finally finish off our traditional sense of belonging. When pounds and ounces are forgotten, and a single standard for vehicles, buildings, beaches, taxes—even water—rules us all, who will remember the glorious days of regional accents, local customs, village rivalries and national pride? ("History, Pride, and Crisis of Identity," *Daily Mail* Max Hastings, May 4, 2002)

Concerning the coverage of the single market in the *Guardian*, articles dealing with the topic do not, as initially suspected, appear more often in the years immediately following the official completion of the common market, except in 1993. Rather, their frequency notably increases in the latter half of the observation period, with an annual distributional share of upwards of 10 percent, further corroborating the claim of the media-supported politicization of the EU. With regard to their content, the articles dealing with implications of the integrated free trade area appear throughout the whole period in a relatively critical light. The single market is often reprimanded on grounds of loosening control over UK trade, with warnings spelled out even before the bovine spongiform encephalopathy (BSE) cattle crisis occurred in 1995, but is on the other hand seen as a probable mechanism to avoid further damage to the domestic beef market, for instance by referring to single-market rules allowing for nonlabeling of product origins ("Label Ruling Could End Beef War," *Guardian* Andrew Sullivan, November 20, 1999). After the euro introduction on the continent, the increased costs of doing business there poses an additional question mark ("EU Costs May Force Out Anglo-Saxons," *Guardian* Patrick Minford, June 13, 2005). And while the market becomes an increasingly important topic in aspects of tax harmonization and service deregulation, the domestic implementation of existing EU directives is deemed unsatisfactory and portrayed as external guilt ascription:

> Britain has the worst record in implementing EU directives. Brussels accused the UK of 'backsliding' and said its lack of progress was 'particularly worrying'. Britain's performance in adopting EU legislation aimed at bringing about the fabled Single Market in which consumers from London to Luxembourg pay the same price for goods and services has deteriorated. ("Brussels Says Britain Is Worst Backslider over EU-Law," *Guardian* Andrew Osborn, May 29, 2001)

In the *Daily Mail*, the coverage of the single market is quantitatively similarly distributed as in the *Guardian*, with a slight increase in the years following the establishment of the market, then there is a drop in interest and a renewed increase in reporting at the end of the observation period. Overall, the contents here emphasize the impact of the common market on the UK, with a share of 32.9 percent of all articles reporting about it, followed by articles dealing with the market's competencies and contents, at 25.3 percent. Even though these quantitative distributions do not significantly vary from the ones in the *Guardian*, the tone and style in writing about this particular integration measure do. While the single market as a liberal economic policy instrument is positively received by the *Daily Mail*'s journalists, the actual implementation receives lots of criticism early on:

> British firms are often unable to benefit from the much-vaunted Single Market because of Euro-bureaucrats, a survey showed yesterday. A year after the EU supposedly became barrier-free, firms say trade is still hampered by red tape. Last night, the Government pledged to take on Brussels

> and campaign to whittle down the daunting mass of regulations. ("Single Market Is a Singular Failure," *Daily Mail* David Norris, January 4, 1994)

Facts and figures are repeatedly reported, asserting that even with the single market the UK's extra-European trade is higher and more profitable than trade with other EU member states. One particular issue seems of special concern: the single market is considered as a prerunner to the single currency, which the majority of British oppose. In a telling example, an editorial in 2000 previews the common market creation and links it to all other potentially unfavorable repercussions:

> The *Mail* has always argued vigorously that membership in the single market offers huge opportunities. The tragedy is that those opportunities are consistently being undermined by the bureaucratic meddling of Brussels, the economic sclerosis endemic in the EU, the lack of democracy in European institutions and the obsession with the single currency and political union. ("Increasingly Dictatorial and Out of Touch: Why Mr. Blair Is So Wrong on Europe," *Daily Mail* February 24, 2000)

Coverage surrounding the single currency is not an important issue for the *Guardian* in the first half of the decade. The appearance of articles around the issues of convergence and stability criteria for participation in the EMU peaks only in 1998. As expected, the frequency distribution is skewed toward the years 2000–2005, testifying to the importance the single currency has even for the nonparticipating UK—something I found confirmed in the interviews. From the outset of the EMU's inception in the Maastricht Treaty, the editorials were filled with headlines resisting any attempts to unify monetary politics ("EC Is on Monetary Suicide Mission," *Guardian,* May 3, 1993). A few years later, in 1996, the political conservative leadership under John Major actually set a pro-euro course for his and the succeeding Labor governments, but the Euro-skeptics in both parties continued to fight over Britain's commitment to the EU and eventually saw an electoral change as its direct result. In the paper, this process is vividly illustrated:

> Tory Euro-sceptics last night vowed to fight on in their campaign against the single European currency after John Major decisively aligned himself with the Cabinet's Europhile heavyweights [...] The Chancellor even denied slaying Euro-dragons in Brussels this week. ("Major Backs Clarke on EMU," *Guardian* Michael White, December 4, 1996)

Two years later, when the future members of the eurozone were determined after passing the convergence criteria tests, the *Guardian* reported several times about the rising support for the single currency among the

UK public ("UK Warms to the Euro," Alan Travis, *Guardian*, February 11, 1999). The actual currency introduction on January 1, 2002, in the eurozone member states is perceived positively by the *Guardian*, with constant reference to the UK's exceptional status: "It is hard to avoid the question of whether Britons will follow where 300 m other Europeans have boldly gone" ("Arrival of the Euro-Reaction," Ian Black, *Guardian*, January 2, 2002). And although the British public initially seems to be warming up to the idea of a euro next to the pound, an argumentation against euro participation is portrayed as broad societal consensus justified mainly by possible cuts in public services for the stability pact and the current strength of the British pound, altogether economic-instrumental rather than identity-based reasons ("The Pound's 10 Billion Price Tag," *Guardian* Alan Howarth, April 10, 2002). In 2003, both papers closely follow the adoption discussion in the UK, particularly its five-criteria test, and the referendum on euro introduction in Sweden, which ultimately fails.

In contrast, the *Daily Mail* provides less coverage of eurozone members' experiences with the single currency, and while in both papers the discussion about a possible euro introduction is the most pressing issue, with 46.1 (*Daily Mail*) and 36.1 (*Guardian*) percent of the total coverage pertaining to this debate, the *Daily Mail* also highlights the problems of giving up the national currency, with a third of the articles devoted to the maintenance of national identity. Early on, the topic of monetary union was criticized and seen as a project favored by Germany and France. In 1995, an editorial articulated the worries of many Britons in an ever more integrating Europe with a particular emphasis on the threatened national autonomy in fiscal matters, with reference to a German preeminence:

> The mantra has been recited mindlessly by those who yearn for a federal Europe. A single currency, they declare, will not seriously diminish our national sovereignty [...] Any economist worth his salt knows that the control of exchange rates, interest rates and therefore inflation is central. Yet that is the control which advocates of a single currency propose to give away to a German-dominated Euro Bank. ("Sovereignty and the Single Currency," *Daily, Mail* June 19, 1995)

In particular, the years 1997 and 1998 are key with respect to the debate surrounding a possible participation in the single currency scheme. In the news, a particular strategy of the British as well as other EU governments is noted that sees the fact of the euro as a nonnegotiable issue removed from popular decision making:

> The euro will be commonplace in Britain in just over 13 months—years before Britons are given the chance to vote on monetary union. ("A Thumbs

Up by Brown for Euro through the Backdoor," *Daily Mail* David Hughes, November, 11, 1997)

After the euro's initial launch in 1999, it was heavily scrutinized because of its fall in exchange value on the global financial markets; this is noted by the *Daily Mail* with a certain amount of glee ("The Euro Is Flopping in Europe, EC Admits," Paul Eastham, *Daily Mail*, January 4, 2000; "A Snub for Euroland," *Daily Mail*, October 4, 2000). With time, the UK as well as the rest of the European public developed a more critical stance toward the slipping single currency, and public appeals by the Blair government to join the eurozone were repeatedly rejected. The debate intensified in the period leading up to the material introduction of coins and notes, which started in 2002, so that the Labor government, itself split about euro participation, set forth a five-item economic test that the euro had to pass to be considered a viable option for the UK. Whereas this test gave some leeway for the protection of British sovereignty, the coverage about monetary integration is perceived by the *Daily Mail* as another element in the creation of an EU superstate:

> The euro can only survive if countries using the new currency hand over control of their economies to Brussels, it was claimed yesterday. Taxes and welfare systems must also come under central control, or the euro will collapse. The warning, by French finance minister Laurent Fabius, could not have come at a worse time for Tony Blair as he steps up his drive to persuade a sceptical British public to embrace the euro. ("Now They Say the Euro Means They Must Have Total Control," Paul Eastham, *Daily Mail*, January 16, 2002)

In contrast, the frequency distribution for coverage of the CFSP in the *Guardian* shows no accumulative effect paralleling the continuous development of the Union over the past decade. The annual coverage seems to be much more dependent on world events and the national stakes in these. That explains the small increases in coverage in the years following the crises in ex-Yugoslavia and Kosovo. A qualitative exploration of the material recognizes an incremental push toward greater leadership role of the UK within the CFSP as a result of the foreign policy crises that the Union did not respond to adequately, but at the same time expresses a strong disappointment over these and the persisting disunity over common actions taken in this field. Initially after the Maastricht ratification, angst existed over a diminished sovereignty through the CFSP provisions spelled out in the treaty, as one article in 1993 shows:

> The Foreign Secretary, Douglas Hurd, struggled against a barrage of interventions from Eurosceptics on both sides to reassure MPs that Britain could

> not be told what to do by other EC members over common foreign and security policy. ("Maastricht Debate Runs into Night," *Guardian* Nikki Knewstub, March 31, 1993)

The realization of impotence during the civil war in the Balkans led to a further alienation of the public and press from what was perceived to be an elusive policy, mirrored by Eurobarometer data as well as a 5 percent drop in approval. One piece in particular questions not only the current CFSP configuration, but also the idea behind it:

> The Bosnian disaster, until the Americans wearily took the lead again with serious military force, is usually exhibit A. The latest venture in the Gulf, in which most Europeans are politely holding the Anglo-American coats while waiting for the return of business as usual, could turn out to be another. Curiously, the argument never seems to focus on whether or not a European foreign policy would be a good idea. ("In Defence of Europe's Civilized Impotence," *Guardian* Martin Walker, February 7, 1998)

One the other hand, the appointment in 1999 of Chris Patten as EU commissioner for external relations gave the British a sense that they have a decisive say in the construction of the EU's foreign policy. This is reflected in the number of articles dealing with his appointment, and later, his juxtaposition to CFSP high representative Solana:

> Britain can show its muscle as the EU plans to push ahead with a CFSP. George Robertson is NATO secretary general; Chris Patten is commissioner responsible for external relations. Javier Solana, Robertson's Spanish predecessor, is the EU's new 'Mr. Security' and anglophile. Last month, Robertson called for a debate about Britain's role and standing and how it could gain by being 'leader in the field'. ("On the Defensive," *Guardian* Richard Norton-Taylor, December 11, 1999)

This resounding appeal to the UK to direct the development of the future common defense was hampered by domestic debates about the reconciliation of CFSP plans with existing British responsibilities toward NATO, further stirred by the United States, and more recently, a frustration over the disunity regarding the reactions to September 11, 2001, and the mounting foreign policy crisis regarding Iraq. This situation is problematized in the reports debating the complexity of EU external actions as a global power:

> In a year that has seen much agonizing about Europe's role in the world, few things are more frustrating than the complex division of powers in the realm

> of what the wonks call CFSP. Very few Europeans outside Brussels have any idea how it works. Americans and others are simply baffled. It looks like staying that way. ("Inside Europe," *Guardian* Ian Black, July 15, 2002)

The *Daily Mail*, on the other hand, is more defensive in that it views the CFSP as a project that is hardly feasible, and in essence not wished for by the UK public. From the beginning of the formulation of common EU defense in the early 1990s, the Tory and later the Labor governments are portrayed as denouncing a common EU defense policy as a betrayal of the traditional transatlantic ally. Any attempts to cooperate more closely on defense issues with European partners, in particular with the continental rival France, from the St. Malo declaration onward is seen as an unworthy project of the Europeans and is presented as infringement on British military power.

> The fact is, the French are profoundly hostile to the Anglo-American alliance [...] True, there is not the slightest sign that Europe has any idea how to operate swiftly, effectively or with any unity of purpose. Look at the feebleness of Europe over the break-up of Yugoslavia and later the war in Kosovo. ("How Can We Ever Trust the French?," *Daily Mail*, November 26, 1999)

Over time Tony Blair developed a more pro-European approach to EU defense capabilities, seeing this as an opportunity to make Britain stronger in the EU rather than to marginalize it. This initiative, however, does not fare well in the coverage of the *Daily Mail*, which almost automatically assumes the primacy of NATO for European defense:

> The PM wants to persuade us and the new administration that Britain can play a full part in the development of a European army and still retain our special relationship with the United States, defending NATO from those who wish to marginalize it [...] For the truth is that the 'defense dimension of the EU' will involve an exact copy of NATO's military and political structures. ("Blair, NATO, and the Euro Army," *Daily Mail*, February 26, 2001)

The coverage surrounding the constitution begins in the *Guardian* only in the late 1990s and increases steadily after its official project launch with the Laeken Declaration in 2001. At the start of the convention in 2002, the project receives inquisitive attention:

> Nothing like it has been attempted before. If the Union's problem has been that vital decisions have been made behind closed doors, with insufficient

> democratic scrutiny, the idea now is for a great and open debate [...] It poses thorny questions about institutional arrangements, democratic legitimacy and the division of competencies between national capitals, regions and Brussels. Some sensitive decision-making matters were tackled in horse-trading at the Nice summit. But then, as before, there was a lack of popular input. ("A Pivotal Moment," Ian Black, *Guardian*, February 28, 2002)

However, the constitutional convention raised fears about a further encroachment on the UK's sovereignty, resulting even in calls for a referendum about the UK's membership in the Union ("Tories Turn up Heat on EU Constitution," *Guardian* March 30, 2004). These populist sentiments have remained visible in the public and might be vindicated by future referenda on the UK's relationship with the EU. After the rejection of the constitution in France, the *Guardian* eloquently describes the unconsolidated nature of the EU and links it to the treaty's failure:

> The enlarged EU is still groping towards a coherent but capacious identity that consigns not just Franco-German conflicts to the past but historic east-west divisions too. The rejected constitution had its weaknesses. But it was a serious attempt to secure these goals. It marginalised some of the worst centralising political impulses of the past; but it made practical improvements too. ("Britain and Europe," *Guardian*, June 5, 2005)

The *Daily Mail* picks up on the constitution late, with most of the articles on this topic published in 2003 and 2004. In this short time, meanwhile, the paper puts an astonishing amount of pressure on the issue of popular ratification of the constitution, without reporting substantively on the contents of the document as such. While the *Guardian* permits equal space for the contents as well as for the ratification (17 percent each), the *Daily Mail*'s negative coverage of resistance to the EU Constitution is the biggest topical category, with 23.5 percent, followed by the referendum issue with 23 percent. Tony Blair's involvement and support of such a document is viewed highly critically by the paper, and at times protest against the EU constitution becomes indistinguishable from dissent with the prime minister—a sentiment confirmed by declining popular approval polls:

> Terrifyingly, the Government is today well on the way to surrendering all these aspects of nationhood. Within two years yes, just two years the new constitution could be ratified by all members of the EU. What a nightmare. Before the next election and if he can get away with it without a referendum, Mr. Blair could sign away British sovereignty, liberty and democracy. ("A Blueprint for Tyranny," *Daily Mail*, May 8, 2003)

In an unprecedented move, the *Daily Mail* gave its readers a chance to vote on the need for a popular referendum on the ratification of the document. This was a highly publicized event and suggested more of a protest vote against the purportedly undemocratic way of domestic policy making than against the EU constitutional draft itself ("90 Percent Demand a Say on Europe," Sam Greenhill, *Daily Mail*, June 17, 2003). Not only experts on the issues such as Gisela Stuart, MP and one of the UK representatives in the convention, are reported to be critical of the document; even the queen is involved in the paper's campaign against the constitution ("Our Queen and the Constitution," *Daily Mail*, October 17, 2003). In addition to the disapproval of both the EU constitution as well as the Labor government, a general Euro-skeptic sentiment evolves in the *Daily Mail*'s coverage, eventually asking if the UK should not rather leave the Union at all:

> Never has such a barrage of lies and half-truths, contradictions and weasel words been thrown up during the life of this Government—and that's saying something. Oddly, though, there is one aspect of this in which Mr. Blair is being surprisingly honest. It is when he says that, in the end, this will be about whether or not we stay in the EU. ("Well, Maybe We Should Quit the EU," Simon Heffer, *Daily Mail*, April 24, 2004)

The *Mail* goes to great lengths to dissuade readers from Europeanist attitudes. In one example, demagogic myths about the constitution are actually presented as reality ("Myths and Realities of That Treaty," Chris Booker, *Daily Mail*, June 21, 2004), and in another, a creative projection of oppressive living conditions in a post-constitutional Europe is presented ("Europe: Who's Telling the Truth?," Simon Heffer, *Daily Mail*, May 14, 2003). Even after the constitutional failure in France and the cancellation of any prospective referendum on the issue in the UK, the EU is even portrayed as "the federal monster" (Chris Booker, *Daily Mail*, December 10, 2005).

Considering the overall press coverage about issues of national and European identity, as well as the four key instruments of post-Maastricht integration, the UK public is exposed to a high level of critical press about EU matters. Throughout the observed period, both papers reflect a defensive and at times protectionist and aggressive stance toward the Union and toward any attempts to only remotely interfere with British national identity, which places a burden on the development of a transnational civic identity, as can be seen in the decline of Eurobarometer values. While the *Guardian* displays a more balanced view of the impact of EU policies and tends to focus on the larger questions of balancing national sovereignty and European integration, the *Daily Mail* chooses particular issues, such as attempts to introduce metric systems or the harmonization of produce labeling, to construct the EU as a bureaucratic and illegitimate, undemocratic institution of the continental European states. Furthermore, it is noteworthy that toward the end of the observation period, the critique of the EU has become synonymous with the pro-EU politics of the Labor government under Tony Blair, together with the parallel development of deteriorating mass public opinion of the prime minister as well as the EU, indicating that the government's politics have less of an effect on (trans)national identification than the media. In sum, it can be deduced that the critical view of the Union, even in papers that are somewhat ideologically polarized, such as the *Guardian* and the *Daily Mail*, seem to instill in the British public a sense of protectionism of the national identity and criticism toward the EU, which is reflected in my interviews as well as in mass survey data. This particularly Euro-skeptic press discourse as part of the domestic reception of EU policies severely limits the chances for the emergence of a transnational identity.

Germany

The two print media analyzed here contrast well with respect to their target audience and their coverage of EU affairs. While both are considered broadsheets with substantial influence over the political discourse among the German leadership strata as well as the broader public, the *FAZ* generally displays a politically conservative, critical stance toward EU integration, whereas the *SZ* is said to be more left-leaning, progressive, and pro-European in its coverage. Both papers are nationally recognized, though they have their regional focus in Frankfurt, in the case of the *FAZ*, and in Munich for the *SZ*, so their structure makes them a good pair for comparison. The *SZ* has a higher market reach; as of 2005 almost 1.5 million people were reading its print or online edition, compared to the slightly slower figure of 1.1 million for the *FAZ*.

A look at the contents of these articles reveals how these topics have been perceived and changed their meanings for the public with regard to a transnational German identity over time. The articles treating issues of identity in both papers initially cover the constitutional implications of the Maastricht Treaty for Germany, as there was a challenge from anti-European groups and parties such as the right-wing "Republikaner" party to declare the treaty inconsistent with the German Basic Law. Such a strong Euro-skeptic sentiment had not previously been observed, therefore the reports about this incident mirror the various questions about Germany's involvement in a more strongly integrated Union:

> Stopping the Maastricht Treaty would mean an act of freedom: for us, for the community, for the accession candidates and for the rest of Europe. To deny Maastricht would also mean freedom from the arrogance of a power that without expertise and against the will of the people attempts further integration. ("Der Vertrag von Maastricht im Verfassungsstreit," Joseph Kaiser, *FAZ*, August, 4, 1993)[2]

The ratification of the treaty presented the practical problem of the larger question the role a unified Germany should acquire. Many articles dealing with Germany's "European identity" describe the search for orientation of this transformed country in the rapidly changing EU, pending between federation and a looser union of states ("Which Europe Do We Want?," Rudolf Seiters, *FAZ*, April 28, 1995). Statements about EU cultural policies, intended to foster common values and identity, appear regularly in both papers and declare the necessity of such policy measures ("The EU Commission Spends 0.04 Percent of Its Budget on Culture," *SZ*, May 8, 1998). In the coverage of policies, the *FAZ* seems to have a different focus, strongly linking EU identity development to economic integration, whereas in the *SZ*, political identity is to precipitate further economic measures:

> The EU is bound together by economic prosperity, political stability and structures of interest negotiations. In addition to these basics, the concept of European solidarity impacts policy and institutions and the identity of Europeans. ("Europa vor der Vollendung," Werner Weidenfels, *FAZ*, July 3, 1998)[3]
>
> A common identity able to evoke solidarity and reciprocity such as that between East and West Germany is missing. Despite forty years of integration 'Europe' is a construct, no single state perceiving itself as a community of fate. ("Der Währungsunion muss die politische Union vorausgehen. Josef Joffe, *SZ*, January 10, 1998)[4]

Aside from a short-lived debate in 2000 surrounding the comments of German foreign minister Joschka Fischer concerning a possible future European federation ("Europe and Its Finality," *SZ*, December 16, 2000), the discussion about European identity changed after the decision to enlarge to Central and Eastern Europe and Turkey. In addition, the introduction of the euro and the constitutional convention evoked discussions about commonalities among Europeans. Most journalists and analysts, however, remained unclear about the direction or content of this identity. This comes as no surprise if one reviews the problematic relationship of

Germans with their own national identity and culture, and the additional identity confusion brought about by German unification:

> Outside academia, in real domestic policy making, identity and culture play no role because of the inability to define it, thus the debate about Germany's 'main culture' is a failure. Then again, this vagueness has its advantages. ("Kultur als Kampfbegriff," *SZ*, December 7, 2002)[5]

According to my topical classification, I categorized all articles according to their content. Of eight available categories, most of the *FAZ* pieces fell into the topical grouping "European identity and enlargement," with 21 percent of all articles dealing with the changing identity of the EU through enlargement. This indicates the strong emphasis of the *FAZ* on the widening aspect compared to the focus on deepening, but also marks the importance of Germany as deeply affected by the enlargement to the east. The second most utilized category is "EU and identity," in which 14 percent of all *FAZ* articles refer to issues surrounding the development of a common identity. In comparison, the *SZ* gives equal attention to these two categories, showing a balanced distribution of 23 percent for each. Third place in both papers is the category "German identity and the EU," which deals with the changing nature of the German—and in the *SZ*, also the Bavarian—identity as it relates to ongoing European integration. Particularly in the period 2003–2005, the war in Iraq and the constitutional debate provoked a variety of statements by conservative ecclesial and progressive public figures such as Habermas and Derrida, debating the value of a new vision for Europe ("After the War: Europe Reborn," Jürgen Habermas and Jacques Derrida, *FAZ*, May 31, 2005; "The Pope Wants to Convert Us," *SZ*, June 30, 2003), thus demonstrating the discourse-stimulating effect of such critical junctures.

A closer look at the articles surrounding the creation of the common market makes the contradictory nature of its implementation apparent. On the one hand, editorials and politicians voice their support for it, but on the other hand, insufficient knowledge and protectionist calls of the domestic economy are also prevalent:

> The Single Market is credited with the creation of 900,000 new jobs. However, commission president Santer criticized the insufficient implementation of common market laws through the member states. ("EU will Arbeitsmarktpolitik koordinieren," *FAZ*, December 13, 1996)[6]

> Trade barriers by states are still part of the common market. The directorate in Brussels responsible for the Single Market under the leadership of the Dutch commissioner Fritz Bolkestein is still busy, after ten years of

> the market's existence, with enabling the freedom of movement of people, goods, services and capital. ("Der EU Binnenmarkt bleibt ein mühsames Geschäft," *FAZ*, August 7, 2000)[7]

In contrast, the *SZ* views the common market more critically than the *FAZ*, which confirms the more leftist, pro-labor attitude of this newspaper. Many articles in the first years deal with the negative consequences of the free market area ("Mistakes That Make a Dream Impossible," *SZ*, January 27, 1994; "The Threat of Wage Competition," *SZ*, November 27, 1998). However, there is some recognizable similarity with the *FAZ*'s coverage in that the *SZ* criticizes not only the increased competition, but also the protectionism of the German government and economy. After almost ten years, the single market is still approached with apprehension, even if that means to be self-critical about German companies such as Volkswagen or Daimler who fought against Brussels' car market liberalization. Because these companies represent a big part of Germany's identity as an export nation, this case is of particular interest here:

> Europe's Single Market ends where the manager of the car companies wants it to end. These firms work with all available means to restrict the consumer's choice. ("Geschützte Konzerne," *SZ*, October 11, 2001)[8]

The differing priorities with regard to the implications of the free market for the readership are confirmed by the emphasis on the value-neutral subtheme categories. While for the *FAZ*, the pragmatic category "single market contents and competencies" is the most utilized one, with 37 percent of all articles found there, for the *SZ* the most important subtopic, with 39 percent of all market-related articles, relates to the "single market impact on Germany."

With respect to the euro, the *FAZ* portrays the currency slightly more positively than the *SZ*, with 32 percent of all articles reporting about problems with the euro, as compared to 35 percent in the *SZ*. Again, the former shows a more pragmatic policy orientation since most of its articles fall in the category dealing with the implementation of the euro itself (27 percent), whereas in the *SZ*, the category debating the utility of the euro and its challenges is prevalent at 31 percent. Both papers initially discuss the various consequences of the currency union and depict the momentous acceptance challenge for a country whose postwar identity is so closely connected to its economic and financial stability:

> The Euro will never attain the meaning for Germans that the Deutschmark had over the past decades. [...] Democracy, freedom, performance and

stability, all these notions were encompassed when Germany talked of 'its Deutschmark'. Now comes the Euro. It has passed its economic test but not yet the social-psychological one. ("Von der Mark zum Euro" *SZ*, May 12, 2001)[9]

Both papers similarly emphasize certain issues of the German political elite and the public with the plans for a currency union, such as the (missing) trust in the new currency, the lobbying for Frankfurt as seat for the European Central Bank, and, particularly in 1997 and 1998, the insistence on the stability pact ("Chancellor Kohl: I Won't Agree to 'Soft' Euro," *SZ*, August 18, 1997). More recently the question of the free movement of workers in the newly enlarged Union and its impact on the German economy has been frequently revisited. Previous to the public euro introduction in 2002, the advantages of a common currency had been praised and portrayed as a means of transnational identity building ("Europe Comes into Existence through Money, or It Won't Exist at All", *FAZ*, March 21, 2001). Both papers report on the positive and negative developments in anticipation of the changeover. Whereas one of the symbolic highlights covered was the awarding of the Karlspreis, Germany's highest European cultural award, to the euro, one of its biggest embarrassments was the linguistic choice of "teuro," meaning "expensive euro," as word of the year by the Society for German Language. And while the common currency has been watched more carefully following its launch because of its fluctuating exchange rate, in particular by the neoliberal-oriented *FAZ*, the euro is more positively reviewed by the *SZ* in view of the anticipated but never materialized problems during the currency changeover:

> The Germans use the new currency without problems, the prices rise slower than before and the Euro's value increased on the financial market. The result of the biggest currency change in the history is marked by the absence of a catastrophe. The time after the Deutschmark, awaited with sorrow, is of great normality. ("Das ungeliebte Geld" *SZ*, December 30, 2002)[10]

The *FAZ* remains more skeptical of the weakening of the stability pact through the Franco-German attempts to modify or evade it (based on their budgetary excesses), with a noticeable increase of critical reporting in 2002 and after. The paper connects these decisions with the teuro, the expensive euro:

> Here, the strong mistrust against the new currency is reinforced by the symbolic success of the Deutschmark for stability and international recognition [...] In addition, doubts about the bureaucracy in Brussels and the miserable economy and economic policy hurt the Euro's image. Thus, the Germans of all people violated the rules of the growth and stability pact

> this year. ("Das Wortspiel 'Teuro' praegt die Einstellung der Deutschen zum Euro," *FAZ*, December 31, 2002)[11]

Despite the literal ups and downs of the euro's value, both papers continuously stress its significance for the European project ("Strong Euro, Strong Europe," *SZ*, December 12, 2003; "There Is No Alternative," *FAZ*, August 12, 2004)—the same pragmatic acceptance mirrored by German polls regarding the currency in the previous chapter.

Compared to other policies initiated in the Maastricht Treaty, the introduction of the CFSP was of peripheral importance in the treaty itself, and accordingly the press took little notice of it in the years following the treaty (see the quantitative overview at the beginning of this chapter). Things drastically changed in 1996–1967 as the war in the former Yugoslavia dragged on and a common line among the major EU states was not to be found, resulting in debates about the relative importance of EU vis-à-vis U.S. approaches:

> The Maastricht Treaty, article J, states that a CFSP has been introduced. A case of wishful thinking. The unfortunate policy in ex-Yugoslavia has been proof of the volatility of the CFSP. ("Gemeinsame Außenpolitik," *SZ*, December 13, 1996)[12]

Similarly, the *FAZ* criticizes the national egoism of participating member states effecting little progress when unified action is needed—as in the case of the Balkan Wars. Such occurrence or lack of agreement over policy instruments is often the case in the intergovernmental second pillar:

> Even after Maastricht, the EU has not achieved an independent CFSP, as exemplified by the war drama in the Balkans. Again and again there was an attempt to harmonize different national interests to come to a common position. ("Die europäische Union auf dem Weg ins 21. Jahrhundert," *FAZ*, March 29, 1996)[13]

Interestingly, the *FAZ* as a more conservative press organ reiterates the necessity and support of a CFSP as integral part of the Union more strongly than the *SZ*, which displays skepticism about the objectives as well as the effectiveness of such a common foreign policy. In quantitative terms, both papers prioritize in its reporting articles dealing with the CFSP construction and effectiveness (19 (*FAZ*) and 23 (*SZ*) percent of all CSFP articles). But whereas the top three categories for the *FAZ* are the ones stating that this policy is a necessary, integral, and increasingly successful part of the EU, in the *SZ* the main emphasis is on the transatlantic tensions with NATO, and the U.S. and Germany's unwillingness to become a militarily relevant actor in the EU. In general, the attitude of the *FAZ* and the *SZ* toward establishing a functioning CFSP is congruent in its identity-based pessimism, as the two pieces below show:

> Of limited use is the coming together of Britain's and Germany's European policy—the former because it starts to become less ideological, the latter because it becomes more pragmatic in its approach to integration—if Europe's power potential is more determined by aspirations than by capability. ("Europa zwischen Wollen und Können," *FAZ*, March 25, 2002)[14]

> The EU is still searching for its defence identity. Its CFSP is not much more than a project. The European Council and the Commission argue about responsibility for it, so that the EU is far from unity. European troops that could be deployed 'out of area' in case of an acute terrorist threat are non-existent. ("Die Welt vom Bösen zu erloesen," Heinrich August Winkler, *SZ*, October 2, 2002)[15]

This ambiguity only increases with the U.S.-led invasion of Iraq in spring 2003 and the ensuing disunity over U.S. support and legality of this undertaking, with both papers critically assessing potential learning effects ("Did Europe Learn from the Iraq Crisis?," *FAZ*, December 13, 2003), similar to the attitude displayed by my German interviewees.

With reference to the project of the European constitution, coverage in the early 1990s is rare and depicted sporadically as an attempt to politically transform an economically forward-pushing Union. Some reports start to discuss the sense of such an enterprise at an early stage, questioning the ulterior motives behind such an effort:

> A European constitution is demanded—from opponents of European Integration to weaken these and from supporters in order to strengthen it. But do we really need a new constitution for Europe? And do we need it now? ("Braucht die EU eine neue Verfassung?," Klaus O. Nass, *FAZ*, July 24, 1994)[16]

Aside from the already heated discussions at the convention establishing the draft treaty, the lengthy post-convention negotiation process surrounding voting weights and institutional reform led to a further eroding of support among politicians and citizens, as portrayed in the newspapers. Statements like the ones below by Foreign Minister Fischer might easily be misinterpreted to convey more than was actually stated:

> Everyone can live with the constitution compromise of the European convent, even if no one is really satisfied with it. It is unacceptable to reject it. "We have the responsibility for creating a unified Europe," added Fischer.

("EU Verfassung nicht in Frage stellen," Heiko Krebs, *SZ*, August 27, 2003)[17]

After finally being approved by the EU heads of states at the IGC in June 2004, the constitution had suffered from hard-fought discussions driven by national interests. Overall, the negative coverage of the constitutional project in both papers is twice as high as the supportive treatment, with around 30 percent falling into the former and only 15 to 17 percent falling into the latter category. It is therefore not surprising that both papers similarly portray the end result rather as a means-centered piece, in particular with respect to transnational identity creation for the citizens:

> The treaty for a constitution for Europe is supposed to give the citizens of the EU a source of a new European identity. The text is not able to satisfy this self-set goal. Its authors miss for the most part the braveness and spirit necessary. On the contrary, they portray Europe self-admiringly as a community of values against the rest of the world. ("Wir Europäer," Armin von Bogdandy, *FAZ*, April 27, 2004)[18]

Yet, the German political elite purposefully coordinated the ratification in the Bundestag two days ahead of the French referendum so as to provide an added positive stimulus ("Bundestag Ratifies EU Constitution—German Yes to Europe a Signal for France," *FAZ*, May 26, 2005)—without success, as it turned out. Both papers then recognize the centrality of the constitutional project during an initial soul searching, aimed not only at finding reasons and pulpits, but also to come up with normative and practical ways out of the crisis—which eventually led to the slimmed-down reform treaty of Lisbon ("Die Zukunft Europas," *FAZ*, November 7, 2005).

In sum, both newspapers show a fairly similar quantitative as well as qualitative coverage of identity-related and more general European topics. In this case, the convergence of press views mirrors the elite-led approving consensus on European matters, thus creating a climate conducive to the development of a transnational identity. There exist small differences between both outlets in that the coverage of the *SZ* is more positively inclined about the chances for creating an identity through common policies such as the euro, while the *FAZ* dedicates more space to the overarching transnational effects of the single market or the CFSP. Particularly in the editorials, the *SZ* tends to be more idealistic in its calls for unification and reform, whereas the *FAZ* relies almost exclusively on fact-based assessments. Despite initial misgivings, both recognize the centrality of some sort of continuation of the European constitutional process, even after the constitution was pronounced dead. There is an extraordinary overlap in the coverage of both papers and an accompanying support for the policy variables, as expressed in Eurobarometer data, which has remained moderately stable over the years. Such press discourse, then, contributes to the public's transnational identification with the Union.

Ireland

With Ireland being a relatively small island nation, the media market seems transparent, relying foremost on local and regional newspapers. The two dailies utilized here, the *Irish Times* and the *Irish Independent*, have a circulation of around 100,000 each. They differ in that the *Irish Times* tends to be the elitist, conservative broadsheet, while the *Irish Independent* is moderately conservative and contains comparatively higher tabloid content.

Both papers recognize early on a fundamental problem with the way European integration plays out in Irish politics and public opinion. Ireland has been enthusiastic about economic integration from the beginning, but any attempts to politically strengthen the community, especially in fields of military defense, have been met with criticism—an issue reflected in the Eurobarometer data as well:

> The referendum on the Single European Act triggered a discussion which still continued today and which culminated in the Maastricht referendum—are the Irish willing also to accept political integration for the sake of economic integration? The focus of the conflict was Irish neutrality. ("German Study Finds Irish Fear Identity Loss in the EU," Joe Carroll, *Irish Times*, November 9, 1994)

A distinguishing feature of both papers during the 1990s consisted in the fact that the *Irish Times* seemed to reflect overall more comprehensively on Irish identity as being simultaneously part of Europe as well as having strong transatlantic ties, whereas the focus for the *Irish Independent* lay predominantly on Irish–Irish relations and the relationship with the UK—in itself a sign of the contested transnational Irish identity. In the secondary, content-based classification of all articles, I found that the ratio of articles dealing with Irish–Irish identities was about 15 percent higher in the *Irish Independent*. An excerpt from the *Times* exemplarily describes the question of Ireland's positioning vis-à-vis Europe and the United States as Americanization as much as Europeanization:

> We became accustomed during the Anglo centric period to define ourselves as peripheral in relation to Britain, and were tempted to extrapolate this

> state of being to Europe after 1973 [. . .] In that sense the Americanisation or Atlanticisation of Irish identity has been as important, as its Europeanization in reducing Irish Anglo centricity over the last 30 years. ("As Irish as It Is Possible to Be in This Circumstance," Paul Gillespie, *Irish Times*, March 15, 1997)

In the *Irish Independent*, a series of articles in 1996–1997 reflected on the separated identities on the Irish isle, with the unionist Northern Irish feeling a different sense of belonging than the rest of the Irish population. They report on former President Robinson's views on Europe and her advocacy of inclusiveness with regard to the Irish–Irish conflict ("President Calls for Irish Identity That Honours Unionists' Sense of Britishness," *Irish Independent*, October 2, 1996). Concurrent to these statements about the opening of Irish identity, the notions and fears about being a small state in a Union largely determined by bigger ones and about losing Irish identity as particularly expressed in the Gaelic language remain constant issues. At times the question of how compatible Ireland is with EU regulations and culture, or how Europeanized the island can become, emerges:

> Ireland is a strange beast. Though our politicians profess the value of our Europeanness at every twist and turn, we are in fact the least European of states in the European Union. In terms of competence in European languages, welfare rights, communications infrastructure and trade diversity, we are in truth the most backward. ("How European Are We?," *Irish Independent*, December 15, 1998)

In view of the enormous structural and developmental aid given to Ireland by the EU, the question of instrumental attachment to the Union becomes more pressing, but at the same time is viewed as difficult if based simply on reciprocal gratitude:

> Many people in Ireland seem to see Europe as outside us, a place to which we owe no allegiance, but which, for some unexplained reason, owes us financial support. The idea that we should join in developing a European identity in parallel with our Irish identity does not evoke much response here. Yet the huge net transfers we have received through the EU budget reflect our partners' sense of solidarity. ("Getting to the Heart of Our European Identity," Garret Fitzgerald, *Irish Times*, March 6, 1999)

A telling incident occurred in September 2000, when the Irish minister for the arts, Síle de Valera, remarked in a speech that Brussels directives and regulations would undermine Irish traditions, thereby linking cultural and civic identity issues. This singular event sparked an astounding media debate ("Crucial Debate Is on How We Run Our Country," *Irish Independent*, September 23, 2000), including a lively participation of readers not taken into account in the analysis because they don't represent the papers' opinion. This singular event testifies to the fact that issues pertaining to national culture are viewed as essential by both the press and its readers. This emphasis on cultural representation continued to figure throughout the enlargement period, particularly in view of the modernization the country goes through ("A National Identity Crisis Brought on by Our Rising Station in the World and the Blur of Life in the Fast Lane," *Irish Independent*, December 31, 2004), so that cultural identity is highlighted to show commonalities with the new member states:

> It is still mostly in terms of cultural self-assertion that we measure Irish success since we joined. It's the way we perceive our own history, the way we are seen from the outside and the way in which our history has now become a part of the European identity [. . .] There is a chance to begin anew now that the central and eastern European states are members. Cultural politics play a larger and more serious role in their societies. ("Sharing Cultures in the New, Enlarged Union," *Irish Times*, June 17, 2004)

The single market is seen in both newspapers as a theoretically agreeable and desirable measure from the onset, with both papers placing the value-neutral topic of the impact of Ireland under single-market inclusion in the top spot, with more than 35 percent of all market-related coverage dedicated to the gains and effects of the common market. On the other hand, while coverage of the market in the first half of the 1990s is not too extensive, there are apparent signs in both papers that it is more difficult to implement than expected with regard to the maintenance of jobs and social welfare:

> A survey of the experiences of Irish exporters this week showed that while 60 per cent experienced no problems in our major export markets, more than one-third had faced some form of technical obstacles [. . .] Surprisingly, exporters were irked by some consumers apparently being steered towards choosing a product of national origin over an equivalent imported item, an attitude put forward as it helps with import substitution and safeguards jobs. ("Self-Interest Is a Two-Way Street in EU," Victor Kuss, *Irish Times*, May 6, 1999)

In addition, the farming sector, in the past traditionally the strongest sector in the Irish economy, has been deeply affected and transformed in the thirty years of membership. This EU-initiated change in reduction in agricultural output, while accepted, is critically viewed by the *Independent* as loss of its rural identity ("Losing Step in a Tiger Economy," *Irish Independent*, December 28, 1999).

The *Irish Independent* in particular provides a more populist coverage of issues related to the single market than the *Irish Times*, which incorporates political background information. Content-wise, articles in both outlets primarily emphasize consumer rights:

> More than ever before, consumer interests are now taking top priority on the European political agenda. As we become a more affluent society which allows us to travel more and as electronic commerce allows us to shop anywhere in the Single Market, there is a greater need for European wide consumer protection. ("Getting to Know Your Rights at Home and Away," *Irish Independent*, March 6, 2000)

The *Irish Times*, in addition to the above-mentioned aspects of the common market, includes a number of articles that deal with the political implications of belonging to the EU free trade zone. This is referred to, for example, in the discussion surrounding the ratification of the Amsterdam Treaty in 1998, expressing the need to politicize the economic Union ("Put Human Face on EU by Voting Yes," John Bruton, *Irish Times*, May 7, 1998), but also portraying the consequences of the Irish boom for the future financing of the Union. Yet both outlets are in congruence regarding the designation of the Irish Internal Market Commissioner in 2004 in that they expected this move to benefit the strong Irish economy at the time ("McCreevy Is the Right Man for the Job, Says Taoiseach," *Irish Independent*, August 13, 2004).

With regard to the euro, the distinction between both newspapers becomes more pronounced. For one, the emphasis on the content is slightly different. In my content-based classification into subthemes, I found that while the *Irish Times* put coverage of the euro introduction first and the theoretical debate about the impact of the euro for Ireland in second place, with 28 and 24 percent, respectively, the focus in the *Irish Independent* is primarily on the debate about the currency's impact (29 percent), followed by the theme of problems with the currency more generally (20 percent). Secondly, for the *Irish Independent*, the euro introduction is not as important in the first half of the observation period, as is attested by the low number of articles reporting about it (see quantitative distribution table above). The *Irish Times*, however, as the main broadsheet on the island, pays more attention the topic from the beginning and devotes more coverage to it. So appears, for example, in 1994 a report on Ireland's ability to be part of the single currency, which testifies to early Irish ambitions to join the EMU:

> Mr Ahern, strongly rejected any suggestion that Ireland does not meet the rules laid down in the Maastricht treaty for those states wishing to make the final move to a single currency [...] The whole thrust of Irish economic policy in recent years has been to attempt to keep in line with the Maastricht rules. ("EU Green Light for Irish Public Finances," Cliff Taylor, *Irish Times*, September 7, 1994)

Four years later, the same issue is reiterated, but this time more critical about the chances for success of the euro project because of the existing elitist pro-European consensus covering up any possible dissent with giving up the national currency:

> The lack of any substantial political opposition to membership has meant that the issue has never really taken fire, despite the certainty that Britain will remain outside the first wave moving to monetary union. But with the Government insisting that we will enter, it is now time to consider how we might fare, once the champagne corks are popped on New Year's Eve. ("The Currency Countdown," *Irish Times*, March 1, 1998)

The *Irish Independent* as an overall "populist" newspaper covers rather the direct effects of the euro for the consumer and reader and less of the political implications, but in a 1998 statement it hints at the broader chances and risks associated with the currency, yet again questioning chances for popular consensus about EMU participation:

> The giant leap to creating monetary union across as many as 11 EU states will be taken. Political imperatives dictate that it must happen, even if many of the economic questions remain unanswered and the risks uncalculated. ("Euro: Year of Liberty?," *Irish Independent*, January 2, 1998)

The *Irish Times* is also particularly involved in reporting about the eurozone membership talks in 1998, displaying views that reflect both agreement with and a critical assessment of the project, as well as the status quo of preparations ("The Euro Is Born," *Irish Times*, May 4, 1998; "Worryingly High Levels of Ignorance in Republic on Euro," Patrick Smyth, *Irish Times*, September 18, 1998). In the years preceding the actual currency introduction, in which the euro floats relatively low against the dollar, the difference in attitude toward the euro in both papers becomes more distinct. While the *Irish Independent*, still critical of the euro, seeks also the advantages of the declined euro value, the *Irish Times* detaches itself from its previously shown supportive euro stance with reference to the citizens:

> The relative weakness of the euro against both the US dollar and sterling has become a welcome boost to the tourism sector. Visitor numbers from North America and Britain are set to hit new records this year. ("Euro's Fall Is Good for Tourism," *Irish Independent*, June 8, 1999)
>
> Given our strong fundamentals the "Irish Pound" is seriously undervalued while low interest rates encourage borrowing, deter saving and are a key factor driving Irish inflation. From an Irish perspective the euro gets a D or even a D-minus. ("Something Can Be Done about Euro Millstone," Rodney Thom, *Irish Times*, April 21, 2000)

Later, the *Irish Independent* emphasizes the euro's significance for ordinary citizens and customers, and repeatedly focuses on Irish–Irish relations as positively affected by the euro as a unifying element in a divided island despite the North's nonparticipation, in a rare example showing that EU-wide policy measures can have simultaneously national unificatory and transnational effects ("North Is Looking South," Richard Curran, *Irish Independent*, November, 11, 2002). As can be seen from the statements and tables above, the single currency is reviewed slightly critically by both papers, with around 10 percent more negative reporting on it than positive (although the bulk of it is balanced or neutral). With regard to content, the *Irish Times* contains deeper coverage of the political, long-term implications of the euro, such as rising inflation after 2003, while the *Irish Independent* portrays the euro in terms of Irish–Irish relations and how it affects the citizens as customers, and seems to exert a pro-euro attitude mirrored by high Eurobarometer ratings for the currency.

Probably the most contentious issue of all in Ireland is the development of the EU's CFSP and the impact it may have on the country's cherished neutrality. For both newspapers, this is the main issue, to which the *Irish Times* dedicated 28 percent and the *Irish Independent* 32 percent of all defense-related coverage. When looking at the content classification, a distinctive feature of the discussions in the British and German newspapers is missing; the Irish newspapers do not focus, like their counterparts, on the de facto performance of the Union's common defense, devoting less than 10 percent to this topic. Rather, the *Irish Times* excels in taking up the issue of ideational change early on and pointing out the divergent directions in which politicians and the larger public are headed:

> Ireland will have to be ready to end its traditional policy of military neutrality in 1996 if the European Union moves to a stage of full political union,

> the Tanaiste and Minister for Foreign Affairs, Mr Spring, said yesterday in a speech aimed at preparing public opinion for the change. ("Spring Warns on Role of Neutrality in EU," Joe Carroll, *Irish Times*, December 17, 1993)

The *Irish Independent*, on the other hand, as evident in the quantitative distribution table above, reports sparingly about early developments of the CFSP. Rather than questioning attempts to remove neutrality, the *Independent* informs about internal splits in the Irish representation of the European Parliament, reflecting domestic tensions and presenting a range of opinions about neutrality dividing the Irish political elite:

> Ireland's 15 MEPs split in all directions in yesterday's voting. MEPs [...] clashed openly over neutrality. Some MEPs feared that the passages dealing with the WEU and its future integration into the EU could compromise Irish military neutrality and leave Ireland bearing some of the financial cost of military actions. ("MEPs Split on Vote as FG and Labour Clash over Neutrality," *Irish Independent*, March 14, 1996)

Years later, the 1998 Amsterdam Treaty referendum and the discussion about the defense provision entailed in the treaty was a highly publicized event in both papers, with supporting and opposing views clashing over implications of a common EU foreign policy for Irish national identity as a neutral country. The end of this era is previewed and advocated by both papers similarly with reference to the facts that have been created by supranational integration, while public opinion drops, as evidenced by Eurobarometer:

> For pro-neutralists to claim that Irish neutrality can be restored to official policy is to join with the Government in a game of political make-believe. Ireland is not neutral, any more than China, Cuba or Zimbabwe. Against the fiction of both sides in the debate, there is nothing there to maintain, nothing left to preserve. The only viable option is to address the future character, not the fact, of a common defense in Europe. ("Policy of Neutrality No Longer Exists," Bill McSweeney, *Irish Times*, May 21, 1998)

This issue resurfaces with the referenda on the Nice Treaties in 2001–2002. Again, the factuality of defense integration remains the focal point of contention, with ensuing effects for Irish national identity and the popular referenda required for treaty ratification:

> In Irish public life there is a tension between the instrumental definition of neutrality policy held by the Government and the broader, more diffuse affirmation of the term as a synonym for national identity and core political values. That tension has come centre stage as the Government debates

how to present the Nice Treaty in a second referendum. ("Old Question of Who We Are Neutral Against Is Apt," Paul Gillespie, *Irish Independent*, June 22, 2002)

The *Irish Independent* in the latter half of the observation period concentrates on more-pronounced EU efforts to create a common European defense force, but provides more balanced coverage and even tacit support under the pretext that Ireland needs to fulfill its role as an EU member state. As in my interviews, the topic of (instrumental) reciprocity toward the EU reappears, in addition to the Irish interlocutor balancer role, especially in the run-up to the final constitutional negotiations during the Irish presidency:

> Irish public opinion provides some latitude and some encouragement to policy-makers. This is because Irish public opinion is more sympathetic to the role of the United States than most, takes a middle-of-the-road position on the development of a comprehensive CFSP, and is not particularly gung-ho about having an independent and ethical foreign policy. ("Polls Show Irish Could Bridge EU-US Divide," *Irish Independent*, June 29, 2004)

Overall, the perception of developing a defense capability that might infringe on traditional Irish neutrality is viewed in both papers fairly objectively and more progressively than the general population permits—Irish public opinion lagging behind the EU average and stagnating on this issue—giving proponents and opponents of further EU involvement space to voice their concerns about the future of Irish national identity as a traditionally nonaligned country in post–Cold War Europe. The fact remains, however, that in the papers, Ireland is portrayed as wishing to retain as much neutrality as possible and participating in common EU defense only to the extent necessary.

The EU constitution has been of importance for Ireland mainly after 2003, which is detectable from the majority of articles written in this period. In the few years following the Maastricht Treaty, there existed little enthusiasm for such a document, neither in Ireland nor in Europe more generally. This reality is attested to in one of the few early pieces in the *Irish Times* pointing to ever-present issues of Irish recognition:

> While some speakers felt that with the European elections approaching it was not an appropriate time to launch a blueprint for the future, others pointed out that there was still a need to rectify the defects in the Maastricht Treaty. MEPs from the smaller countries, such as Ireland

and Portugal, were opposed to what they felt were moves to downgrade the influence of their countries. ("European Parliament MEP Give Cool Reception for Report on EU Constitution," Frank Kilfeather, *Irish Times*, February 10, 1994)

In the course of the treaty negotiations, two themes were similarly dominant in both papers: the exclusion of a divine reference in the preamble, and the successful conclusion of the treaty negotiations under the Irish presidency in the second half of 2004. Whereas the first item evoked high emotions in the public, particularly the portrayal of a Catholic Irish identity as opposed to a secular European one, the second event was welcomed as a success not only for the Irish taoiseach, or chief of state, but also for the whole Irish nation. With regard to the exclusion of God in the preamble of the constitutional draft, both editorials state progressive opinions on the diminished role of the Church despite the protest of many readers who wrote letters in favor of it, thus placing this debate in a larger European context:

> The specter of a Godless Europe is haunting Ireland. The draft of the document has sent shockwaves across the religious communities which once held the power to shape the continent, but who are now relegated to the past tense of influence—the mere "inheritance of Europe." ("God Is Dead, at Least in the EU's New Constitution," *Irish Independent*, June 14, 2003)

> The text is not a historical document but a legal and justiciable contract [...] there is, however, a political agenda driving the demand for an acknowledgment of (a Christian) God in the EU Constitution. A dangerous willingness in some quarters to see the international dynamic of history now as a clash between the "civilised" Christian world and the "backward" Muslim world has the potential to poison Europe's own politics. ("God in the EU Constitution," *Irish Times*, October 23, 2003)

In contrast, the conclusion of the treaty negotiations under the Irish EU presidency has been viewed as significant bolster for the Irish government as well as for the Irish national role in the Union. This became apparent in the many articles in both papers that praise Ahern's successes during the negotiations, accompanied by a 5 percent increase in support for the treaty, according to Eurobarometer polls during that time.

> In shepherding the EU to a deal on its first constitution, Taoiseach Ahern has pulled off an audacious coup which will be remembered as a historic step forward for the continent. ("Triumphant Ahern Pulls off a High-Risk Strategy," *Irish Times* June 19, 2004)

The constitution, while being presented as a difficult document with respect to the many issues specifically important to the Irish, such as neutrality provisions and a divine reference, has been similarly extensively reported on and discussed in both media outlets. While the focus on the contents of the constitution has been higher than in the comparison cases of Germany and the UK, which discuss the viability of the document more generally, in the end a positive attitude toward it prevailed, which must in part be attributed to the determining role of the taoiseach during the Irish presidency's treaty negotiations. Such assertions, however, dissipated when the constitutional rejection elsewhere triggered a more pensive mode reflective of national prerogatives: "Using the word 'constitution' seemed to set up that, for Europe, unwinnable battle." ("Time to Slow Down and Listen When People Say No," *Irish Times*, June 8, 2004). The cumulative effect of rapid modernizing change, rising euro inflation, migration from new EU member states, and the constitutional debacle, however, weakened Irish resolve to promote European transnationalism, or at a minimum raised some deeper questions about Irish involvement in the construction of the EU ("It's Not a Sin to Be Skeptical about a European Utopia," *Irish Independent*, June 8, 2005), with dramatic repercussions in the following years, as the initial rejection of the Lisbon Treaty has shown.

In sum, both Irish newspapers offer slightly different messages about Irish identity to their readership. The *Irish Times* as an elitist outlet remains rather positive in its opinion of the single market and initially about the euro, but retracts and comes to view the currency as beset with many political and economical problems. The *Irish Independent*, in turn, offers a more positive coverage of the euro for consumers. With regard to the topics of CFSP, neutrality, and the constitutional project, both media outlets do not mirror the views of the Irish population so much as attempt to push a relatively progressive agenda supporting Irish inclusion in the CFSP and the acceptance of a secular constitution, hence advancing ideas supportive of a transnational civic identity among EU citizens. The disapproving reaction of the readership to these articles shows a disassociation of the papers with the citizens and the public opinion data on these issues, and delivers evidence of the constraints that media faces in the national political culture. Lastly, the constitutional debate became salient in Ireland as well, first because it touched on its neutrality, but also because Ireland wanted to show that it is a "good EU citizen." It is remarkable, then, that Ireland became one of the main stepping-stones in the ratification(s) of the Lisbon Treaty in 2008–2009, which can be traced back to a conflicting and continuously deteriorating domestic public sphere expressing fears regarding its impact on national politics and political culture, even after the country's leadership proved skillful in the closure of the initial constitutional debate during the Irish presidency.

Conclusion

Newspapers in all three countries observed display significant differences with respect to their foci on various topics that are of assumed importance for the readership, thereby influencing the public discourse and discussion of these issues. These debates are remarkably mirrored by the growth or decline in public opinion in Eurobarometer data, and are reflected in the interview responses as well. Consequently, this chapter illustrated how the domestic reception of EU policies is shaped through the creation of press discourse that is supportive or confounding in the formation of a transnational pan-European identity.

Although, for example, the UK's *Guardian* and *Daily Mail* are fundamentally different in their layout, content, and readership, they both reveal a Euro-skeptic attitude—the *Guardian* to a lesser extent than the *Daily Mail.* A distinguishing feature is the slightly different emphasis on specific issues in both papers, in that the *Guardian* focuses on political and identity-related issues, and the *Daily Mail* on themes that directly appeal to the citizens, such as the question of the euro introduction and the referendum about the European constitution. However, both show a higher than expected percentage of negative treatment. In each, British national identity is portrayed as coming under the pressure of the harmonizing effects of European integration, resulting in the need for the protection of the icons of British identity: the British pound, the monarchy, an Atlanticist foreign policy, etc. It comes as no surprise, therefore, that the public follows the lead of these communicators about the EU, in particular since the overall coverage, in tandem with public opinion of the EU, has become more negative over the past ten years.

In Germany, a much higher congruence persists in the reporting style of both newspapers, which creates a more stable environment for the construction of a civic European identity. They similarly depict the keyword-related issues with respect to quantity—there is only a difference of about 2 percent in positive, negative, and neutral coverage—as well as to content. It must be said, however, that the *FAZ* portrays neoliberal-oriented economic issues such as the single market and the euro slightly more positively, whereas the *SZ* views these economic topics more critically. The *SZ*, in turn, is a bit more welcoming in its coverage of the CFSP and issues relating to the broader topics of national identity and the external, international identity of the EU as a world power. Overall, the consensus of both newspapers on a relatively pro-European coverage, among other factors, contributes to the consistently high identification with the EU of large parts of the German population. Both papers, however, have become more critical of the effectiveness of a seemingly disunified Union, be it in the field of foreign policy making or constitutional negotiations. As in the past, Germans are portrayed as remaining dedicated to multilateral policy making, but also as increasingly disappointed about some of the configurations of common European policies. Coupled with the intense post-unificatory debate about Germany's "new" identity, this has led to a more sober and nationalist rendering of the EU, something that has also become visible in German public opinion data on their "European identity."

In the Irish case, the *Times* and the *Independent* display similar attitudes in their portrayal of EU-related issues. This is not surprising, since there exists no starkly contrasting ideological spectrum in domestic politics; therefore, the need for polarizing pronunciation of political topics is largely absent. The topics in Ireland are portrayed in a differentiated and often more positive light than in their bigger counterparts. In fact, the domestic-identity specifics of treaty referenda, neutrality, and the extent of EU involvement determine in large part the Irish media discourse about national identity and the EU. Both papers vary only slightly in their coverage in that the *Irish Times* is more analytical and the *Irish Independent* concentrates more on topics closer to the daily experiences of its readers. Of all three countries, the Irish print media examined here have remained more supportive of the EU over the observed time period; however, in issues of neutrality and constitutionalism, they reveal a more progressive agenda than current public opinion permits, thereby raising questions about the future bivariational relationship between the press and public. In addition, the recurring question of reciprocity toward the EU makes for a rather instrumental assessment of European identification, which may potentially delimit European transnationalism in Ireland.

Each case provided evidence that the print media portray and mirror the current political issues, and at various points even lead the public debates, and thereby create a political discourse conducive to or problematic for a civic transnational identity. Furthermore, each country, despite dealing with the same EU-related issues, emphasizes country-specific topics that remain nationalized, thereby constraining the extent of convergence toward an EU-wide communicatory space. To contextualize this analysis, the next chapter synthesizes all previous empirical ones to supply the reader with a valid account of the development of transnationalism in the analyzed member states and the EU as a whole.

Chapter 7

What Conclusion Can Be Drawn from This Study? A Results-Oriented Synopsis

About a decade ago, when I set out to explore the implications of post-Maastricht integration policies on transnational identity formation in Europe, I assumed that the key policies analyzed in this work had a profound impact on the citizenry in a neofunctional manner in that harmonization and the ensuing "identity spillover" would eventually lead to greater identity convergence. Empirical evidence, however, convinced me otherwise, and many political constellations in the EU as well as in global politics have drastically altered the picture: a new sobriety about the future of the bloc has taken place following the foreign policy disagreements over the handling of the Iraq crisis, the rejection of the EU constitution, and, more recently, the economic and financial woes exposing rifts among EU member states. The long-awaited ratification of the Lisbon Treaty and the resulting policy changes are signs of a recovery of the region, but at this point it is too early to tell how these latest developments will affect transnational identity formation. The following synopses of the empirical analyses focus on the period 1993 to 2005 and display a different stage in EU integration history with regard to public opinion and discourse, yet they foreshadow some of the later-appearing challenges. National preferences and constraints are clearly recognizable, and it is hoped that lessons can be learned from the post-Maastricht repercussions in the national public spheres. In this chapter, the current volatility of the integration process is taken into account for the research to prove useful in determining the future course of possible EU integration policies. The first section concentrates on the theoretical advances resulting from the three empirical studies, while the remainder reviews the originally posed hypotheses and synoptically applies the knowledge gained to the three case countries.

Theoretical Advances in This Study

The main theoretical tenets of this study and the formulated hypotheses have been built upon the insights of the constructivist school with respect to shaping states' and individuals' interests and identities. Among the constructivist main branches, the "soft constructivist" version allowing for utilitarian and normatively guided modes of agent behavior, together with a critical stance toward positivist empirics, provides the most appropriate explanatory social theory for this work. Among the many constructivist orientations, this sort of "middle ground" between positivist theorizing and interpretive subjectivity best captures the complexity of the subject matter, and it allows for an open yet generalizable outcome based on the interplay of identities of the participating actors (Checkel, 2001; Ruggie, 1998). In applying such reasoning to the case studies, the aim is to advance constructivist research on European integration as a sociopolitical process.

As laid out earlier, neofunctionalist integration theory has initially been included in my theoretical construct to account for the expected process of identity spillover based on ever-increasing functional pressures for integration and harmonization. The empirical evidence presented here, however, shows that the promises of this theory are too simplistic for a complex phenomenon such as collective identity construction, as it assumes a direct reorientation of allegiances toward the transnational level through subsequent power shifts from the national to a new, supranational level. The logic of this premise would expect that after the passing of the Maastricht and subsequent treaties and the implementation of far-reaching integration measures, such as the introduction of a common currency, together with the formation of a distinct political identity as was proposed by the Constitutional Treaty, an increased level of transnational identification with the EU would take hold. The analyses of the three case countries as well as the events of the past few years have shown that although the political elites in Brussels and the member-state governments moved ahead with the augmentation of EU policies and institutions, the proposed expansion in support and the subsequent formation of a strong transnational identification among the mass citizenry has not occurred in a significant or converging manner. While a slight quantitative increase of levels of support and in European attachment was observed throughout the twelve-year period in Eurobarometer data, these values do not expand linearly over time. Rather, they stabilize at existing midlevels, thus contradicting neofunctionalist predictions. In addition, citizens in the member states still hang on to nationally cherished ideas and traditions, as this domestic frame was dominant in all cases. In the largely qualitative country studies presented here, in particular in the UK and Ireland, the development of a common foreign policy was critically reviewed in the British interviews and media analyses, and outright opposed in Ireland. In Germany, the policy measures listed above were more positively received, though this reaction is based rather on the pro-European stance of Germans than on the policy itself, as will be explained below when dealing with the hypotheses of this work.

The underlying social constructivist ontology matters in the processes of identity acquisition since ideas and interests as main motivations form the basis for general changes in identification and, in the case of European integration, the expansion of allegiances and identities from national to transnational. Theoretically there is no substitution of other identities through the development of a transnational European identity; rather, an identity growth is postulated in modern social science that allows for multiple (transnational) identities to coexist simultaneously (Risse, 2003, 2010; Herrmann et al., 2004). However, at times citizens perceive and the print media portray these identity structures in absolute terms, viewing increased supranational policy creation as a threat to the individual and the collective national identity. Adding to this sociopolitical adaptation pressure, traditional territorial identities based on European nation-states are being transformed through EU enlargement processes, further contributing to identity transformation, but also causing identitive insecurity (see Chapter 8).

Another tenet of the constructivist school states that processes of social learning, mobilization, and socialization (re)shape collective identities (Kubalkova et al., 1998; Checkel, 2007), and some theorists, thinking about the "social construction of Europe," applied these concepts to the process of European integration (Christiansen et al., 2001). These changes are initiated by social agents, in this case EU institutions and policies, and received by the broader structure as constituted through the national public spheres made up of various domestic elites, civil society organizations, the general public, and the media. Depending on the mobilization of and manipulation in the media and public spheres, these policies result in different degrees of transnationalism in each country as they interact with national political cultures formed from domestic attitudes, values, identities, and interests. These distinct political orientations are acquired in the same manner as transnational feelings, so that both continuously influence each other, though without merging into one. In this bidirectional coalescence, the course of identity (re)construction is not fixed; that is, while constructivists assume a fluidity of identities in contrast to most essentialists, they do not prescribe the future direction or outcome of this transformative change. Such teleological indetermination opens the door for a twofold development of collective identities in the EU: one perspective would postulate the growth of transnational identities in the member states, brought about by EU governance reshaping the identity of citizens toward a composite yet pan-European orientation (leaving aside transnational feelings based on antagony towards the European project, which are harder to sustain because of a lack of content). The other perspective recognizes the possibility of a potential renationalization of collectivities in the EU as a reaction toward amplified integration and adaptation pressures. Hence, the constructivist theorem lends itself to explain the outcome of identity changes through EU integration, and I found both tendencies to be present, reflecting a codetermining balance of agency and structure. In fact, one could illustrate the continual development of the individual stances of the case studies as shown in Figure 7.1.

The case studies of Germany and Ireland exhibit a sort of "bounded" or limited transnationalism, which allows for forms of identity extension and tolerance toward citizens other than their own, to a certain degree. Yet it is restricted by national political culture and resembles a crude form of "EU nationalism" resting on shared civic values, but unable to evade cultural commonalities as binding components. In contrast, the UK experienced over the past two decades a form of renationalization,

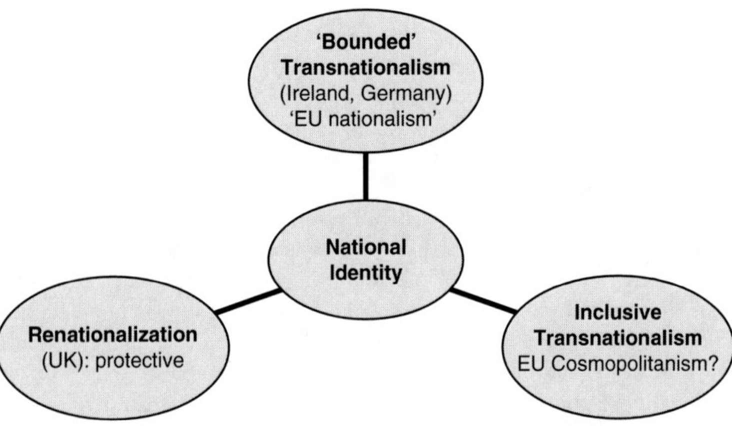

Figure 7.1 Collective Identities and EU Integration

which seeks to protect existing civic and cultural practices in the face of a culturally distant and politically overbearing continental model of regional integration. What is missing among the case studies, and likely in most EU member states, however, is an often propagated and normatively and institutionally advocated inclusive form of transnational identification. The resulting collective identity would be open to an ethnically and socially diverse population in the Euro-polity, in fact producing a "cosmopolitan" form of regionalism. The latter is continuously evoked in politics and academia, but cannot be detected in the studies conducted here and elsewhere. It may also simply be impossible to build up such an open yet regionally contained form of identification, as many aspects of collective identity construction, such as the communal agreement on common values or the differentiation from others, run counter to such an idealized, ambitious form of collective self-identification. Such "EU cosmopolitanism" challenges traditional notions of belonging, and aside from small, highly Europeanized pockets within each country—and the Union's administrative apparatus—this tolerant understanding of citizenship is still lacking in the larger public imagination. Furthermore, other structural processes reduce the likelihood of such developments as well, as will be pointed out in the next and last chapter.

With respect to the analyses employed in this work, each of the countries under examination underwent a different identity transformation during the observed period, depending on the compatibility of the integration measure with national political cultures. While these cases display a dissimilar outcome in identity-shifting terms, the basic constructivist assumption of identity change as a fluid process effected by social(ization) agents, such as the EU, national governments, or the media, remains valid.

The Four Hypotheses Revisited

A review of the hypothetical statements and research questions posed in the introductory chapter leads to a confirmation of the expected premises. To obtain an overview of the research process and its results, the individual hypotheses as well as the obtained outcomes are summarized below.

H1: For the majority of EU citizens, EU integration is not perceived as a threat to national identity.

It is important to reexamine this point because, as explained in the previous chapters, once people perceive European integration as threatening to their national culture and identity, they will reject EU policies and exhibit protective nationalistic attitudes. In addition, the objective of this hypothesis is to refute the generalization of the "post-Maastricht blues" stating that integration policies in the 1990s were uniformly perceived as hostile attacks on native identities. While increased interference in domestic policies might have evoked protective sentiments among particular segments of the population, the majority of citizens did not experience EU integration in such a way.

The last section of the Eurobarometer chapter provides the reader with the most frequently mentioned connotations concerning the EU, measured at four times during the observation period, from 1997 to 2004. In addition, the percentage values for responses that associated the EU with the risk of losing national identity were collected. For all of the EU-15 member states, the number of people fearing a loss of national identity fluctuated only slightly over the course of these years, between 11 and 14 percent. In Germany, the deviation from the average remained at a minuscule 2 percent, while in Ireland the percentage of concerned citizens grew parallel with the EU average cited above. Only the UK displays a well-above-average fear of losing identity, starting at 14 percent in 1997 and ending at 20 percent in 2004. Once again the UK seems to be the most Euro-skeptic of the three case countries, though it can be deduced from these findings that for the majority, European integration is not seen as a threat to national identity. Such thinking is also absent from the interviews as well, and for the most part from the newspaper discourse (with the exception of the UK). It is a rather small minority, usually located in specific fringe contexts, that finds the Union dangerous to the integrity of national culture and heritage, although the rise of this segment possibly signifies a worrisome trend with regard to the development of future public support for the Union more generally. Overall it is evident that European integration is not perceived outright as a threat to the majority of EU citizens, except for the outlier UK, which actually went through a process of renationalization.

H2: Post-Maastricht measures did not contribute significantly to identification with the EU compared to the pre-Maastricht era, as transnationalism through EU policy implementation interacts varyingly with national political cultures and domestic discourses, resulting in either "bounded" transnationalism or protective nationalism.

According to the Eurobarometer surveys and the interview samples, the majority of EU citizens admit to possessing a transnational identity to some extent, with a slight yet insignificant increase in the percentage of people feeling European over the observation period. In the three case countries, the values for Ireland and Germany are almost congruent with the EU average in that both countries display a majority of about

60 percent feeling European to some extent. The UK, however, has gone through a different development: there the ratings for European identity have decreased almost 10 percentage points to below 30 percent, which represents half of the EU average and contradicts a generalized evolution of a civic transnational identity.

National differences exist in the distribution of these allegiances, as in the interview samples little more than half of the British interviewees considered themselves European "to some extent," while in Germany and Ireland, more than two-thirds felt European. One question in my interview aimed particularly at the change of perception of the EU in the past decade indicating a change in orientation compared to the pre-Maastricht era. Two-thirds of Irish respondents saw an improvement of their view of the Union, while in the UK the most-mentioned response was that it stayed the same. Interestingly, in Germany, the views were almost evenly distributed among the respondents stating that their view has not changed, improved, or worsened, signifying a more critical stance among the population. The Irish and German cases displayed a majority of European-minded citizens, but not the British case, thus the results correspond to the limitations placed by national political cultures, as outlined in Chapter 3. While the above-stated hypothesis holds true, the degree of convergence on identification with the Union varies from country to country. For one, domestic reception agents as defined through national political culture and elites, public discourse, as well as socioeconomic conditions are relatively sticky, and attitude and identity changes in large collective entities occur only at a slow pace. However, some of the results in my analyses lend themselves to argue that a covariational relationship may exist in which the national characteristics become less distinct and slowly converge over time, as is visible, for instance, in the time-series graphs for the single market or the euro.

A look at the temporal graphs of the individual policy support values in the Eurobarometer chapter shows that there are limited signs of increased convergence among the three case countries and the EU average. In all four policy areas the variance in support may have decreased for some policies or case countries; however, outliers appear depending on the policy issue, and the inconsistency around 2005 shows that convergence is not uniformly taking shape. For the euro indicator, the UK as a non-EMU participant deviates from the value range assumed by most other countries, and in the case of the CFSP indicator, support from the UK and Ireland experiences a drop over the course of the observation period. In the British case, this plunge is related to the unsatisfactory performance of the foreign and security dimension, and in Ireland the uneven development is explained by the country's traditional neutrality clashing with the goals of European security integration in the Maastricht and the Constitutional Treaty—with ensuing consequences for the Lisbon Treaty ratification.

Another supporting but also novel argument is based on the results of the association question to the keywords "Europe" and "EU," as laid out in the chapter analyzing the interviews. When looking at the responses for these terms, one discovers that the culturally determined picture of Europe shows greater convergence than the notions connected to the EU, which is in line with current research about both facets. Four associations with "Europe" are most frequently mentioned in all three countries: cultural plurality, different countries, history/civilization, and geographical continent. For the keyword "EU," there is less apparent convergence: only in Germany and Ireland, two notions dominate ideas about the organization—unnecessary bureaucracy and economic integration/cooperation. The participants from the UK had different ideas about the EU altogether, emphasizing clashing political cultures and the euro as synonym for the bloc. These results prove that there exists a high level of convergence in thinking about Europe already, which contributes to the development of a culturally determined pan-European identity, but less so in thinking about the EU, in which the three case countries, in particular the UK, possess more diverging ideas. It makes sense that the convergence on "Europe" is further advanced, the term being a much older concept and reality, but it highlights the difficulties of the Union in attaining generalized levels of transnational awareness among the citizenry based on civic values and policy harmonization.

H3: (Print) media influences public opinion and thus reflects as well as constructs people's identification with the EU—to the extent that national culture and discourse allow it.

The print discourse analysis demonstrates the changing patterns of topic salience as expressed by frequency, as well as treatment as illustrated by topic coverage. In a dissimilar design, ideologically opposite papers were selected, and in Germany two widely read broadsheets were examined, while the UK provided a good contrast of an elitist newspaper with a tabloid, and in Ireland, two broadsheets were chosen that similarly provide in-depth analysis as well as some tabloid content. Congruence in the urgency and portrayal of themes prevalent in the media outlets with public opinion contributes to the validation of this hypothesis. As far as the interviews reflect public opinion, the similarity of issues mentioned in these with the current themes discussed and treated in the media was striking. At the time of conducting the participant survey, in the summer of 2004, the respondents and the papers in Germany stressed the role of the EU as a global civil and military power, while in both the British interview sample and in the corresponding media analysis, the euro and the Iraq crisis were similarly important issues. In Ireland, the notorious debate surrounding Irish neutrality was equally pronounced in the interviews and in the national media coverage. One can also detect this congruence in mass public opinion as registered by Eurobarometer. The comparison between prevalent EU-related topics in the press and the surveys shows a striking resemblance. In the UK polls, the themes of the euro impact together with negative connotations of a European government move up into the three most-mentioned preoccupations from 2001 on, just as they received increased attention in the print media landscape at that time. Similarly, in Germany and in Ireland, the notion of the EU as a symbol of peace reemerges in the early 2000s following the September 11, 2001, attacks into the top three connotations, while at the same time the topic of the Union as a world political and military power as it relates to the CFSP is hotly debated in those countries' media outlets. The qualitatively oriented analysis of the Eurobarometer survey aids in understanding this reciprocal process. The answers to the question about the meaning of the EU show how the connotations attached to the EU undergo changes and spread similarly into most countries. During the observation period, for example, the idea of the euro and the notion of peace entered in all EU member states' public perceptions in the same observation intervals. Therefore, one can deduce that these countries possess a minimum level of ideological convergence based on public spheres, which are in turn simultaneously framed and mirrored by mass media.

The quantitative and qualitative findings pertaining to this research statement have shown that national cultures and political discourse, as revealed in the historical-institutionalist country overview and the press analysis, are indeed important domestic factors determining the reception of EU integration policies and thereby the development of transnational European identities. Whereas in Germany and in Ireland, national domestic constellations are more susceptible to an identity extension as constructed through the press consensus of German papers, the press in Ireland is pushing the agenda of European integration, with the public lagging behind, while in the UK even slightly progressive newspapers such as the *Guardian* hesitate to publicly embrace EU policies, so that the print coverage there is overwhelmingly a reflection of the critical stance of the public toward the Union. These national estimations are mirrored by other research conducted in the field (Anderson and Weymouth, 1996; Risse, 2010). In this respect, the differentiated treatment of EU policies in the media is reflective of the public opinion as voiced individually in interviews and aggregated in the Eurobarometer surveys, while at the same time the media portrayal seems to be an expression of the culturally determined idiosyncratic policy preferences of each country.

H4: More EU citizens support a particularistic and possibly exclusionary conception of European identity versus a universalistic, inclusive one.

This particular hypothesis is inferred from the ones above and posits that citizens in the EU, as an effect of the integrating harmonization measures in Europe, are not developing an open, cosmopolitan understanding of transnational European identity. Rather, a particularistic notion of Europeanness prevails, built upon commonalities and differentiation toward perceived internal or external "others." It is interesting to note that while actual EU policies, especially cultural ones, aim at homogenization and the propagation of common features in Europe (cultural capitals, Europe Day, artistic and heritage promotion, etc.), the literature dealing with European identity regularly perceives of or calls for a more inclusive conception of European identity based on civic values and multicultural tolerance for diversity instead (Habermas, 2001; Kraus, 2008).

In contrast to many academic propositions, one can see that a skeptical stance toward diversity recognition and transnational identity development is supported by the results of my research. The main findings for this outcome stem from the interview section, in particular from answers retrieved about intra-EU solidarity, the distinctions between EU citizens and non-EU Europeans as well as between EU citizens and third-country nationals, and the views on European identity more generally. These suggest that while citizens in the three case countries are tolerant and accepting of other EU member nationals and perceive of non-EU Europeans as equally valuable (exhibiting a form of bounded transnationalism), they do make distinctions with regard to non-Europeans. It does not make much difference if the perceived "other" is distinctively non-European, such as in the case of the United States or China, or if the country is culturally seen as foreign yet arguably has European credentials, as, for instance, Turkey or the Balkan states. Even the new member states that were in the process of becoming EU members at the time of the interviews are viewed by a few as "outsiders." In their argumentation, most people expressed that the EU had a somewhat homogenizing effect on European countries, but cited a common culture and history as the preceding underlying factor determining belonging to Europe, pointing to internalized essentialist notions of statehood.

This particularism is not only visible in individual interview responses, but also reflected in the media coverage in Ireland and the UK. In both countries, the print media portray issues of identity retention in opposition to increased immigration, in the UK more so than in Ireland. In the former, articles covering immigration and asylum problems are quite pronounced. In Ireland, more attention is paid to the protection of national culture and language and the defense of Catholicism as the predominant cultural-religious feature; for example, in the debates about the inclusion of Gaelic into the EU language regime or about the constitution, where the Judeo-Christian heritage is evoked as a desired European element—even though few people still speak Gaelic and the Church has become rather marginalized there. Germany is the only country whose print media largely suppresses the theme of common cultural roots or ethnic "Leitkultur"—not surprising given the country's past—though the debate about Turkey's prospective membership provoked a heated debate about that country's Europeanness as well. So, while in all three countries a similar consciousness about the common cultural characteristics of Europe is prevalent, the findings here show that identity transformation through European integration is unable to evade the rather particularistic, exclusive ideational structure known and internalized from previous nation-state experiences, and that civic ideals of a pluralist and diverse Europe constitute thus far an unreachable ideal. In conjunction with immigration pressures, this has obvious policy consequences, as I will show in the next chapter.

Aside from that differentiating common reference point, special intra-European bonds characterize the relationships between certain EU members that on the one hand further delimit the cohesion of the whole continent, but on the other hand reinforce the argument that European identities are more particularistic than universal. For instance, the allegiance or expressed closeness lies in Irish media with other smaller states within the EU, such as Denmark, with which it also shares the referenda policies. The print media in the UK does not really align itself with any country within the EU; rather, it portrays the European continent as being entirely different and its distinct national identity in need of protection from outside forces of any sort, be it European federalists or non-European immigrants. In the German case, the media there does not specifically refer to any particular subset of countries that it feels it has more in common with than other ones within the Union, although it expresses a common purpose in the leadership position assumed by the Franco-German alliance and sensitivity toward EU enlargements to the east.

It is evident from these arguments that most transnational developments in the EU are of a particularistic and possibly exclusive nature, and that an expansion toward an inclusive, cosmopolitan form of European identity has not developed, although tolerance toward fellow EU nationals has increased. This process, however, poses a challenge for transnationalism insofar the common civic and cultural standards for participating in the European project tend to be differently weighted for citizens that might be viewed less "European" than others, or adversely manipulated by domestic politicians in search of populist support.

The insights gained from these hypotheses help in determining the potential and constraints for a gradual evolution of national and European identities with respect to EU integration measures and the national reception factors. In the following section, these determinants are applied to the individual countries to show how they play out on a domestic level, thus supplying a country-level synopsis of the research outcomes.

National Identities and Transnational Europeanism in the Three Case Countries

As detailed above, the compatibility of historically grown national identities and a culturally determined pan-European consciousness with the emerging transnationalism advanced through EU integration varies among all three case countries. This most dissimilar research design included three very different member states to capture a number of conditions and variations of identity construction. In addition to providing new insights into the multifarious directions of identitive transformations discussed above, it confirms research into the existence of nationalized European identities and the ambivalent impact of European integration upon these (Bruter, 2004).

In Ireland, national identification as traditionally determined mainly by Gaelic language and a solitary history of overcoming British oppression has been significantly modified over the course of EU membership. While Irish citizens retain a high level of national identity and pride, as consistently attested to by Eurobarometer surveys, the processes of integration and modernization initiated by EU structural policies have resulted in the gradual emergence of transnational identity extensions effected by economic growth and political recognition within the EU.

As is visible from the mass surveys conducted by the EU, the Irish population is largely supportive of European integration: on a case-by-case level, Ireland shows the highest approval ratings for the single market and the euro. The single market enabled it to break free from the overwhelming dependence on the British market, thereby made it possible to diversify its trade relationships. It is therefore not surprising that in the interview section, half of the respondents who knew about the common market supported it by mentioning that it improved trade relations and augmented consumer choices. In the same vein, the Irish press reviews the single market overwhelmingly positively. The strong support for the euro needs to be regarded as a path-dependent, permissive consensus to the course of European integration, and it is closely connected to the beneficial expectations and experiences of the common market. In the area of the CFSP, the Irish position is exceptional because of its traditionally neutral foreign policy stance, which is why in the time-series analyses the Irish support for such a common instrument stagnates on the bottom of the scale. Interestingly, the print media portray the CFSP as an inevitable necessity that Ireland needs to become involved in; however, the editorials range from recommendations to actively pursue this measure to public opinions defensively reflecting on the irreversible steps toward integration. In constitutional affairs, there is high support for this policy matter, but at the same time there is little knowledge in terms of what a common EU constitution would entail and what impact it may have on Ireland. The discourse in the papers is more antagonistic, with both papers presenting views supporting or opposing the document depending on the aspect covered, in particular with issues purportedly close to national identity, such as a reference to Europe's Christian heritage or the simple naming of the text. An astute observer of the more recent past will have noticed the repercussions of this ambiguity during the difficult ratification process of the Lisbon Treaty.

Aside from the high support for many individual policy instruments, identification with the EU as a political entity is evident within the Republic of Ireland. The quantitative surveys display a higher-than-average percentage of people feeling and taking pride in being European. This is similarly observed in the qualitative interviews there, which show a high affinity for the EU and Europe based largely on reciprocal gratitude for Irish material benefits and recognition. This conditional attachment to the EU constitutes though a potentially problematic form of a thinly "bounded" transnationalism, especially should the enabling conditions dissipate for some reason. Yet the tone in the press can be characterized as generally pro-European and it appears as if Ireland identifies at large with the Union, in part because Brussels is perceived as a leveler and enabler for smaller states in the region. However, questions of Irish–Irish relations still take significant space there, and a volatility based on instrumental gratitude may well become problematic under conditions of prolonged socioeconomic distress.

Germany's conflicted national identity, or, more precisely, lack thereof, contributed to the high compatibility of its post-national ideals with the goals of the EU. As much as the country was in need of physical rebuilding after World War II, it required reintegration into the political system and a reconstruction of its terminally damaged national identity. The Franco-German cooperation proved to be the stepping-stone for such developments. Naturally, its influence as a founding member of the EC was far reaching in the development of the community, as the EC was in the minds of the population, which was eager to reintegrate into the international community. Because of this mutual interrelationship and the country's rapidly achieved economic prosperity, it was able and willing to contribute significantly to the monetary and organizational capacity of the Union. With the reunification of the Eastern and the Western part, though, the country was faced with unprecedented financial, economic, and sociopolitical challenges. Since then, the reunified population has remained pro-European, but at the same time became more preoccupied with its own national identity and, as a consequence, developed a more assertive stance toward other member states and the Union.

Empirical evidence of this transformation can be found in the quantitative and qualitative results of my analyses. The Eurobarometer surveys confirm that support for the single market is not quite at the level of the EU average, but still parallels the positive temporal development of all other compared cases. The implementation of the common market was generally assumed to be an integral part of European unification, in particular for an export-oriented country centrally located within the Union, so that no noticeable popular rejections to this project occurred. This is reflected in the rather balanced media coverage of this topic in both papers in Germany. The euro, in comparison, was widely debated among the German public because it meant a replacement of the beloved deutsche mark, which was so important for postwar German national identity. The end of the strongest money in the region was unthought of before. Accordingly, the public opinion ratings for the single currency started on the lower end, well below average, but moved toward convergence with the other country cases to about 60 percent approval at the end of the observation period (which has been eroded somewhat since the Eurocrisis took hold in 2009). A small plurality of German respondents in the interviews also seemed supportive of the single currency, as was the media, although with a more critical stance toward the stability pact negotiations and its effective application in other potential eurozone members. As a medium of political reintegration and alternative to its harrowing historical detour, a common foreign policy as envisioned in the CFSP has consistently been advocated by a large majority of the German population. The overwhelming support in the mass surveys speaks of this high regard for a multilateral defense. In the interviews, however, I found that while many German citizens theoretically favor such a common project, they are less satisfied with the actual track record of this institution. The same sentiment persists in the domestic press, lending further evidence to the opinion formation power of the print media as generally assumed in communication theory.

Among the three case countries, Germany is the most supportive of the constitution, and its citizens, as expressed in the interviews as well as in the general population data, are also the most knowledgeable about it. The interviews and the media coverage about the constitution echo this dedication to the constitutional project despite its eventual failure, and signify a well-entrenched, dutiful sense of transnational identity expansion mixed with compensatory idealism of multilateral politics more generally.

Overall the German identity has remained consistently connected to the formation of a strong yet critical pan-European identity, which in Germany, more than in other countries, has actually been achieved through the (re)construction of the country's identity alongside the EU. This makes Germany a special case within my samples, because both collective identities are closely intertwined and even though after reunification a shift toward a unified national consciousness occurred, the EU is still informing German national identity and Germany's European identity. The country's "bounded" transnationalism materializes in its hesitancy to welcome new members and its pragmatic judgment of EU policies.

In contrast, the British experience has remained constant in its reluctant tolerance of and opposition to European integration. From its entry into the community in 1973, popular British national consciousness as explored in Eurobarometer surveys and relayed in the media landscape has consistently remained critical of any attempts to further deepen European policies beyond a merely economic free trade area. Historically, the country's identity, although regularly contested by the Scottish, Irish, and Welsh, has developed strongly over the past millennium and inflated during British rule of the colonial world in the nineteenth and first half of the twentieth century. At the time of accession, the UK's national character as perceived by its population had already been reduced in significance. The Union's policies, aimed at further integration and thus eroding sovereignty even more, are therefore received critically by large parts of the political elite, the media, and the masses. In addition, the degree of compatibility of the insular British national identity and a wider continental pan-European cultural identity is very low, further delimiting the foundational element of transnationalism there.

My findings illustrate the UK's difficult relationship and weak identification with the EU. According to Eurobarometer surveys, the percentage of people identifying with Europe has actually decreased by about 10 points over the observed twelve-year span. Similarly, the UK shows the lowest approval values for the four integration indicators, but simultaneously leads in the rankings for ignorance about the EU in general and its policies in particular. The latter point was striking in the interview findings, as out of all of the knowledge-based questions, the respondents in Britain fared the worst, even taking into account their comparable educational attainment with the Irish sample. The single market does not seem well appreciated, showing below-average support values, which contradicts lay views of the more economically liberal British orientation, but makes sense if one looks at the critical review of the common market in the British press, once again confirming the media hypothesis. Interestingly, the euro produces a high level of controversial debate among the interviewed individuals as well as in the press, although support for it remains far below the EU average (approximately 30 percent). This is another indication of a clear reluctance of British public opinion toward EU policies, but it also reflects the special case of British nonmembership in the single-currency scheme. With regard to the CFSP, the UK underwent a drastic transformation: initially after the Maastricht Treaty ratification, support for a common defense policy stood at 75 percent and almost reached the EU average. During the twelve-year observation period, it decreased 20 percent, showing a substantial drop during the Balkan war in 1995–1996, and then again during the Kosovo crisis of 1998–1999. This statistical unfolding is congruent with the actual responses of the interviewees and with the print media coverage analyzed. Although many of the respondents and the broadsheets initially favored a pooling of defense capabilities, they became disillusioned with the EU's impotence in the mid to late 1990s in the Balkans, and despite a short-lived improvement following the September 11, 2001, attacks, the British population rather referred to its traditional NATO and U.S. alliances, just as its positioning in the Iraq war, alongside the United States, depressed CFSP support. The quantitative results for the constitution are another fitting example of the impact of the media on public attitudes. The Eurobarometer values are once again on the bottom compared to the other case countries. And while many of my British respondents were unable to deliver information on the content of the document, the majority expressed disapproval of it. This mirrors the extremely unbalanced media debate about the constitution, even considering that the UK has no experience with a written constitution as of yet.

The UK demonstrates the emergence of a protective nationalism rather than a transnational European identity. The public sphere there abounds with indifference and disapproval of the EU, be it in the public opinion, the media landscape, or in the political arena, with the exception of the pro-European wing in the Labor party or minority parties more generally. Identification with the cultural-historical concept of (continental) Europe remained limited in the UK from the start, therefore the EU has no favorable background on which it can begin to occupy an identification space for itself, as it does at least to a certain degree in most other EU member states. One can conclude from these occurrences and the fact that the current government put a moratorium on any new integration measures that the UK will soon reach a turning point or crisis in which the question of EU involvement will have to be reconsidered by citizens, politicians, and the government alike. The country could decide to remain a member state under the condition of retaining limited integration measures and increased opt-outs, thereby further contributing to variable geometries of differentiated integration levels within the EU. The fact that the Lisbon Treaty is domestically contested in the governing coalition shows that there is little appetite for further integration existing under conditions of renationalization. In the unlikely case that the UK would decide to leave the Union—a provision included in said treaty—certainly a setback for the progress of European integration would occur, which would also severely damage the EU's quest for any sort of pan-European coverage. On the other hand, it could liberate the bloc to proceed with the willing members instead of having to fall back on the lowest common political denominator, a motion that has been built in already with voluntary "enhanced cooperation" measures. This in turn could increase identification with the EU since membership would become more contingent on national dedication to European unification rather than simply rational necessity or path dependency, although this scenario opens up a variety of other questions regarding similar Euro-skeptic states.

Based on empirical evidence, I conceptualized Irish transnational identity as a mainly "reciprocal" one, in which gratitude toward the EU for having been supported in terms of modernization and acknowledged as leveler is overwhelmingly present. I then contrasted this to the other forms of transnationalism such as those found in Germany—oscillating between idealism and newly set-in realism—and the British protective stance in response to EU integration pressures and the perceived increase in wasteful bureaucratization. One has to keep in mind that these results originate from work conducted at the mass level; the ubiquitous research conducted on elite socialization arrives at different, more pro-European outcomes across the board. And since this study concentrated on only three countries, a further exploration of identitive changes in all of the member states would be of interest for future research. Many transnational identities exist in the different domestic settings, thus an extension of this research project covering all member states would yield a more comprehensive view of the different national idiosyncrasies in political, cultural, and socioeconomic matters. In a similar vein, this research could be extended at a later point to include more recent developments, such as the impact of the economic recession or the ratification debacle of the constitutional draft and the rebuilding under the Lisbon Treaty.

For academic purposes, the implications of this research disclose the successes and the failures of EU integration in the contemporary era, but at the same time reveal the essential fragility and emptiness of the identitive content as well as the direction of transnational collective identities. On the one hand, one must be very careful not to overstate the capacity for collective political identities to be transformed, because they are an indispensible part of the individual's and group's overall characteristic constituency. While a pan-European cultural identity as a collective consciousness has been cultivated over a large period, a civic transnational identity expansion effected through European integration is still young, weak, and volatile. Identities are fuzzy, fluid, and multifaceted, so that any inquiry about them can only arrive at approximate conclusions. The empirical substantiation presented in this research serves as a reality check for social scientists and normative theorists who too easily advocate or generalize the existence of postmodern universalism as part of a civic European identity in contemporary European public life, or who come to overreaching conclusions from socialization research focused primarily on elites. The results presented here urge for more restraint and empirical testing into identity-related fields of social science. These findings show that while convergence in views on policies and transnationalism is possible to a certain extent, it is contingent upon the historically constructed structural frame in which it is domestically presented in media, through governments, and in public spheres more generally. In this case, feelings of a common European destiny or transnational identity extensions based on identification with the EU are clearly confined to the limits set by political-territorial borders of the Union and to the cultural boundaries of Europe.

These outcomes demonstrate that European integration advanced transnational identification with a nonterritorial, multinational political entity, even though its effort to tap into the cultural European identity remains limited and problematic. This in itself is a big success, although integration needs to be maintained with more attention paid to public opinion, the national mass media, and the limits posed by national cultures, as will be detailed in the following chapter. A worrisome finding of this work revealed the particularistic and possibly exclusive nature of common identity construction found in these cases, which leads critics to rightfully suspect the development of a European political character as little more than an EU-mandated federal nationalism or the building up of an exclusive "Fortress Europe." The future of a common identification with the EU will depend in large part on the EU's communication strategy on a national level, the protection of national cultures, and of course the effective delivery of prosperity and security through the EU's institutions, taking on the demographic and integrative challenges of an ever-more complex and larger Union. These measures alone, however, will not uniformly result in a pluralistic transnational polity; even if they succeed, it will likely be a particularistic integration model in danger of marginalizing perceived non-Europeans already residing in EU member states or inhabiting adjoining territories. In addition, there are other structural challenges to consider, such as population decline, immigration, and enlargement which may adversely impact a common European identification with the EU as well if not dealt with accordingly. The next and final chapter concentrates on the effects of these significant aspects on future transnational identification in Europe.

Chapter 8

Future Challenges for Transnational Identification in the EU

The politics of European integration have transformed in the past decades—markedly from the 1992 Maastricht Treaty ratification debate onward—from an elitist, technocratic process into a leaders-driven transnational mechanism with substantial public oversight and pressure by citizens and the mass media. The germination of (trans)national identities as presented in the preceding chapters is dependent upon a multitude of economic, political, and social factors playing out in member states as well as in the overarching construction of the Union, resulting in affective and utilitarian identifications roughly corresponding to the civic and cultural aspects of European transnational identities. Underlying trade, fiscal, and monetary conditions figure in the determination of instrumental support for the Union, but it is in the sociopolitical public spheres that emotive attachment to the transnational polity is deliberated and discursively developed. In addition to the agency-based policy measures determined by Brussels and the member state governments, a number of structural processes exist in which integration is embedded, such as immigration, demographic changes, and EU-intrinsic constitutive policies, such as enlargement or the treaties.

These are consistently underanalyzed in the field, yet potentially exert significant influence over the extent of transnational identification and hence the future of the integration process more generally. Having theorized and located identitive factors in the region, in this final chapter I argue that social cohesion may be harder to achieve as a result of the combination of limited transnational identification and structural, i.e., EU internal and external factors. Yet a minimal level of transnational identification and solidarity is required to facilitate and sustain policy integration—particularly so under less than ideal circumstances and a quickly changing international environment. In view of these considerations and the empirical results of this work, recommendations are provided below for retaining popular approval through improved EU communication, the proactive protection of national identities, and a concern for the final shape of the Union.

Aside from a constructivist ontology assuming an albeit limited malleability of collective identities undergoing regional harmonization, this book is based on a growing body of literature related to issues of collective identity in EU that has begun to emerge over the past few years (see Chapter 2). Particularly important for this work are the exploration of the constitutive civic and cultural aspects of a European identity and the way citizens, the media, and governments frame European integration discourse (Risse, 2010; Diez-Medrano, 2003), as these aspects and processes exert a significant impact on European citizens and their identitive positions. Various distinctions in the way people identify with Europe, such as demographic attributes and national political cultures, are important determinants and aid in the application to the challenges for identity formation as explored in this book. Transnational identities in the EU can, to some extent, be fostered by differentiation to what they are not—not the neoliberal "West," the communitarian "East," or the developing "South"—but without an intrinsic, cohesive ideational content they cannot sustainably persist or grow. In short, the paradox of EU-initiated transnationalism, which is transgressing national boundaries while simultaneously searching for unifying aspects, constitutes a multicausal phenomenon with no linear evolutionary constitution.

The coexistence, however, of various forms of socially and spatially conceived identities continues, with the transnational European one being in a more or less volatile relationship with autonomously existing national, regional, or local identities, and European integration impacting differently upon these. My research found that post-Maastricht integration measures such as the euro introduction, the common market completion, and the CFSP initiation had limited effects with regard to their resonance in the member states to the extent that the national political culture is deemed compatible with the goals of EU integration, leading some countries to develop what I called a "bounded" form of transnationalism and others to regress to protective nationalism. In the case of the constitutional debacle, the political climate actually deteriorated so as to generate wide-ranging debates about the EU's identity and future until the Lisbon Treaty came into effect. Whereas existing works concentrate on the detection of these important variables for a constitutive exploration of a European identity, my concluding objective here is to extend this view to include the impact of rather undetected long-term structural processes such as demographic shifts, immigration, continued enlargement waves, and integration indeterminacy, which will figure prominently in the future politicization of the Union.

In spite of the EU's official motto, "unity in diversity," suggesting an inclusive and cohesion-based approach to European integration, many cultural and other polity-building homogenizing policies (e.g., the euro introduction or the borderless Schengen agreement) aim at reproducing a unitary, particularistic form of common identification. In the process, not all member governments can or want to adhere to the dictum of an "ever closer Union," so that in reality a variable geometry of subsets of variously integrated countries within the EU is created. Accordingly, it becomes more difficult to attain social cohesion or transnational identification in such a decentered, disparate polity. In light of such developments, the aforementioned demographic and integration challenges will become even more pronounced as they further contest the commonality of an evolving region.

Common Structural Experiences of EU Member States

The demographic changes occurring in current EU member states exert an important yet underestimated influence on the configuration of transnational identities in the Union. In particular, the factors of aging and the resulting immigration pressures have profound implications for any future identification with the bloc. Such demographic trends will exhibit more dramatic repercussions than the rifts caused by post-enlargement intra-EU migratory waves. Because these societal shifts are long-term processes, they are not easily detected nor sufficiently theorized, but potentially undermine the augmentation of transnational identification and lead to an increased protective renationalization of public opinion in the member states in an attempt to distinguish "us" from "them" (Cedermann, 2001), or EU citizens from non-Europeans—although it may in this manner also strengthen a common exclusive identification against perceived "outsiders."

Even though the extent of the population decline is difficult to project and becomes more unspecific with an increased projection range, the demographic replacement rate in most EU countries today is below the necessary level, and the number of elderly persons in the EU in 2050 will be double that of today. In effect, the over-eighty population will triple (European Commission, 2005). This tendency exists in almost every member state, but is particularly pronounced in Italy and Germany, where the population is aging more rapidly than, for example, in France, the UK, or Ireland, which have a comparatively young population base in addition to more family-friendly social and workplace policies. Some analysts even perceive a "low-fertility belt" in Europe encompassing the native populations of the Mediterranean and Central and Eastern Europe (European Commission, 2005). Processes such as these cannot be changed easily, even if governments do adopt family-friendly policies. Hence the demographic setback provides for a major long-term challenge for European transnationalism based on an expanding cohort of more Euro-skeptic senior citizens, coinciding with fewer younger people able to maintain an optimistic outlook on the EU and the European social model more generally.

With regard to an aging population's impact on public support, there are several models trying to explain the phenomenon of decreasing support for the EU, either based on the life experiences gained by seniors, called the life-cycle effect (European Commission, 2000), or on the insufficient information about the Union available to the elderly population segment (Taggard, 2005). Thus, a graying European citizenry will make it harder for EU attachment and transnational identifications to develop in the overall population, independent of the actual policies pursued by national governments or the Union's institutions, this despite the fact that the generation that witnessed the war(s) and thus have good reasons to support peaceful relations with neighboring states is diminishing in numbers. On the other hand, Eurobarometer trends show a consistent, overwhelmingly EU-supportive majority of young people between the ages of sixteen and twenty-five, which means that a slowly emerging net difference in public support between the older-age cohorts and the younger ones showing a more pro-European stance could evolve, particularly as these generations will grow up more "Euro-socialized" in an already highly communalized polity. Yet a decreasing adolescent cohort, as is projected in many countries, coinciding with the increase of an older population will likely offset any advances in public support for the Union in the long run. Aside from attachment toward the EU, it seems far more certain that new kinds of "generation-based" cleavages will emerge with the demographic change occurring in Europe (Schmitter, 2000, p. 70), which in turn may positively (in the case of the environment) or negatively (in the case of welfare/social policies) affect transnational identities across Europe.

Another side effect of the maturation of Europe's population, if not counteracted by a more liberal immigration policy in conjunction with optimized integration policies of new arrivals, will be an economic slowdown caused by a dwindling labor force in member states. As a result, tensions surrounding issues of productivity and redistribution within an expanding EU are likely to occur, and a continued increase of the retirement age to evade demographic shock eventually reaches its limit as well, further contributing to an erosion of the European social model of welfare states. A Union in which member states compete more assertively for any kind of redistributive social, developmental, or structural funds might well lead to an increased renationalization of public spheres. In an illustration of this tendency, EU cohesion funds have for the first time ever overtaken agricultural ones as the biggest budget post in 2008, and thus the funding responsibility itself has become a somewhat contentious issue among the member states and negatively impacted public opinion in places such as Germany and the Netherlands. It is predicted that the demographic change will also influence EU policy making directly in that eurozone countries will be forced to abandon or at least loosen the common currency's Growth and Stability Pact as a result of increased budget deficits resulting from inflated pension funds (Eberstadt and Groth, 2007) or external recessionary pressures. During the global downturn of 2008–2009, tensions among EU governments and between them and the Commission flared up over the application of emergency state aid to large industries, and the most egregious intra-European dispute in recent history was caused by Greece's bailout through the Union's stabilization fund, challenging existing levels of transnational solidarity and trust. Coincidentally, 62 percent of Europeans seem to favor a harmonization of European social welfare systems, a step that could potentially mitigate redistributional issues in a disparate region comprising countries with a GDP per capita ranging from 37 percent (of the EU-27 average) in Bulgaria to 267 percent in Luxembourg (European Commission, Eurobarometer 251, 2007). This solution, however, which would massively interfere with domestic welfare regimes, affects related areas such as taxation and thus finds little support among member-state governments, as the recent, Germany-initiated proposals for closer coordination of socioeconomic and fiscal policies have shown. In the absence of a protective, harmonized welfare policy for EU citizens—which requires solidarity to begin with—the political pressures for national benefits will counteract a significant transnational extension of collective identities.

While few scholars perceive the graying of Europe's citizens as a positive trend under consideration of the added potential of an older, healthier, and more experienced labor force (Eberstadt and Groth, 2007), most analysts, myself included, view the accelerated aging process in member states as another ticking demographic "identity time bomb" if not adequately tackled through improved labor, public expenditure, and immigration policies aimed at increasing productivity and labor-force participation of a more diverse population.

A second, related demographic challenge, in part stemming from the graying of the population, pertains to the issue of immigration and the perceived economic and security threat resulting from it. Following the end of World War II, many countries in Western Europe invited migrant laborers or "guest workers" to help rebuild their destroyed infrastructures. A comparatively high number of immigrants from both inside and outside Europe, in particular from former colonies, moved to the European host countries in pursuit of employment and a better quality of life. Today, the non-European foreign population of the EU area is about 4 percent of the total and quickly rising. In 2007 alone, close to 2 million immigrants came to its territories; these populations contribute in the long run and exhibit higher growth rates than the "native" population, even after integration and nationalization (Eurostat, 2008). In addition to these residing third-country nationals, illegal immigration into the EU has increased in the past decade as well, and the most recent EU accession waves compounded the perceived migration problems within the Union, as the temporary labor movement restrictions by many older member states such as Germany prove. In cases where no movement barriers were erected, such as in the UK or Ireland, largely negative effects on the transnational identification resulted as these countries experienced massive immigration by new EU member-state citizens. In 2005, even during boom times, 80 percent of Irish citizens preferred immigration restrictions by the government (*Sunday Tribune*, 2005).

In many of these countries, the integration of foreign nationals has not been successful when measured by public opinion polls, educational attainment, or employment rates. In addition to ghettoization, the lack of tolerance for foreigners and recent intercultural conflicts all across Europe attest to this issue, as the xenophobic attacks in East Germany, the Danish cartoon crisis, or the murders of anti-Muslim Dutch citizens with the coinciding Islamophobic reactions by right-wing parties, and newly mushrooming "national defense leagues" have shown. Public opinion polls in member states consistently favor a more restrictive immigration policy under the added impact of intra-EU migration, and special citizen's consultations attest to the call of Europeans for a common EU immigration response (European Citizen's Consultation, 2007). Furthermore, the corresponding policies of most EU member states—with the exception of Spain and Italy, which implemented subsequent amnesties—are relatively restrictive even in view of the looming economic and social problems resulting from a dwindling native population. So far, cooperation on a common immigration policy has been rudimentary at best, with negotiations remaining at a consultative level in the Council and the commission's expressed policy emphasis on illegal immigration rather than on an extension of legal migration schemes across Europe arguably being constrained by national governments acting through the Council. With regard to the issue, the idea of circular migration—i.e., allowing limited labor migration that allows the member states to recruit according to labor market demands—is receiving increasing support (Deutsche Aussenpolitik, 2007). Others have pointed to selective immigration procedures, i.e., the recruitment of skilled laborer, as a solution for the problem (Alesina and Giavazzi, 2006), although such initiatives so far have been overly conditional and thus ineffective, as the German temporary labor program has shown. On an EU-level, a "blue card" scheme intends to attract qualified non-EU workers, though it encounters problems of national implementation as the Council passed it only in 2009, illustrated by the opt-outs of Ireland and the UK. In contrast to these difficult negotiations, the Union itself has taken on the issue of its periphery control with the establishment of the Frontex external border agency in 2005 and the negotiation of problematic repatriation agreements with third countries such as Libya, but not much has changed in terms of an implementation of a common EU immigration policy. During the French presidency in 2008, a European Pact on Immigration and Asylum was proposed, which contains only nonbinding principles related to the harmonization of immigration and asylum policies and the restriction of irregular immigration, with the promise of more to come in the next few years (Carrera and Guild, 2008). To sum up the problem: "European leaders have also allowed an increasingly securitized debate [...] while failing to recognize or to explain to the public the reality that Europe will increasingly need migration to counterbalance the problem of an ageing and declining population" (Cottey, 2007: 215).

Yet the demographic situation of the EU today actually calls for more migration to the member states if it is to avoid demographic marginalization and economic decline. It would go beyond the scope of this chapter to delve into the national immigration policies, particularly as the Union has gained co-competence to deal with these issues in the post–Amsterdam Treaty period. Even if such an influx should not occur in the near future, the issues of including already present foreign and non-EU nationals in the member states are likely to become tense, as evidenced in the last hypothesis, and thus the prospects for transnational identification and support will remain restricted. The latest confirmation of this matter consists in the attempts by some Western European member states to expulse Roma groups originating from new member states such as Romania and Bulgaria, citing security reasons. In addition, some EU member states, particularly the ones bordering the Mediterranean, attract a higher proportion of poor and often less-educated migrants from Africa, Asia, the Middle East and Latin America, which are harder to integrate into the host societies than more ethnically and culturally similar migrants from former colonies or proximate areas, further deteriorating the homogeneity of the EU's demographic makeup. This problem is augmented by the perceived need for these immigrants to acculturate, as desired by a majority of the EU's native population and recently evidenced by the divisiveness caused by a German central banker's provocative study of the detrimental impact of immigrants on the country.

Moreover, the influx of Muslim immigrants from Northern Africa, the Middle East, and the Balkan countries presents an additional dilemma: with the emergence of Jihadist terrorist cells in Europe, in particular in Spain, France, Germany, and the UK, the European public is questioning multicultural models of liberal coexistence within the EU, particularly as linkages between immigration and terrorism are frequently made in public spheres. Terrorist threats, which now can also originate from native-born or naturalized citizens as opposed to the previous domestic terrorism, only increase the likelihood for a stronger national rallying of collective identities over such challenges (Leiken, 2005)—advocating a common European response, which could indeed foster a common identification by excluding perceived harmful "foreign" elements. Returning to the previously argued teleological openness of identity construction, such excluding tendencies seem to prevail in the current integration process: "The increasing consensus on what is considered dangerous in Western Europe (terrorism, pollution, drugs consumption, urban crime, on one side, and Islamic fundamentalists, uncontrolled immigration from certain parts of the world, on the other) constitutes a substantial common ground for sharing perceptions of what we need to be protected from, not only as individuals but also as Europeans" (Garcia, 1993: 27). The ambiguous effects of this identity-forging, potentially xenophobic sentiment, found in this work as well, could prove far worse, inciting Euro-nationalism and compounding notions of a desirable "Fortress Europe" among the citizenry. In a thoroughly globalized world, such regression into nationalistic polemic neither presents a viable model for the future nor does it resonate with the normative and legal guidelines of the Union. Instead, European elites and the mass public are advised to embrace an active, integrative EU to make use of the potential of diversity rather than to lament the challenges presented by such transformations.

Newer research has detected additional migratory pressures through environmental degradation and man-made exhaustion of natural resources in other parts of the world. The changing climate and the depletion of, for example, West African fish stocks by, ironically, European fishing industries will further accelerate forced migratory streams from poor and environmentally affected countries to the more temperate and richer countries, such as the EU member states. It is projected that in the next few decades, between 50 million and 1 billion(!) environmental refugees will be displaced domestically or internationally (UNHCR, 2008). Even a small fraction of these populations ending up in the more moderately affected EU member states would severely impact the social fabric of already preoccupied European societies.

Governments in Europe attempt to come to terms with its need for immigration, because all major forecasts predict a decline in population, power, and labor force over the next decades, combined with the pressure of an increasing, mobile population at its border to the south and east. For the most part, public opinion lags behind these elite decisions—with ambiguous implications for transnational identity development, which could in the best case result in an EU-mandated inclusive transnational governance mode, more of the currently found "bounded transnationalism," or even deteriorate to protective or xenophobic nationalism.

EU-Related Integration Experiences of the EU Member States

Debates about immigration and related demographic changes raise questions about the potential of transforming European citizenship to foster public support and develop a more inclusive collective identity (Karolewski, 2006), either through advocating a more active, politicized conceptualization for current citizens or through an extension based on civic rather than ethnic criteria. However, the introduction of a European citizenship has not (yet) proven to contribute to stronger support for the European project, since it is based on the previous possession of citizenship in one of the member states. On a theoretical level, it has even been doubted that citizenship in a global age, under the erosion of the relationship between the citizens and the government, still constitutes a useful instrument to regulate belonging and identity (Sassen, 2006). Aside from such normative questions, implementation problems with the granting of citizenship persists in the Union in that only a comprehensive EU citizenship entailing social rights as well as other important entitlements such as free movement would be effective in fostering a European identity, in addition to the availability of voluntary adoption as such. Such a wide-ranging concept of citizenship is perceived as an intrusion into the naturalization and welfare regimes of the member states and is contentiously debated within the EU, particularly in the UK, Ireland, and the Scandinavian member states, and therefore will not be a likely instrument for attaining a common identification in the near future. Additional pressures for a change in how EU citizenship should be designed stem from the fact that with a projected increase in non-European immigration, larger segments of the member-state populations will be in need of a territory-based and less ethnicity-centered naturalization policy. The case examples of Germany, which eased its ethnically restricted naturalization law in 1999, and Ireland, which tightened its *jus soli* statute in 2005, demonstrate inconsistency in national approaches, which makes the formulation of an EU policy on that matter less likely.

Connected to the previous issue, the imperative of continuous enlargement of the Union further delimits efforts to strengthen a transnational identification among EU citizens. As pointed out earlier, the construction of identities is in part contingent upon the delineation of in-group members against outsiders, and under conditions of post-national construction such as exerted through the EU, such spatial recalibration enables both populism and its transcendence (Berezin and Schain, 2003). And while the enlargements to Central and East European states in 2004/2007, paradoxically, may be the result of a common "European" identity and responsibility after all, taking in new countries has become problematic in conservative policy circles and contentious among large parts of the European citizenry. With Brussels propagating enlargement as a necessary integration and stabilization tool, the unifying element of membership cannot solidify because the borders of the community are constantly redrawn and former outsiders have to be integrated to become insiders and accepted as such. In addition, accession of new states is seen by national-minded citizens as a further dilution of commonality, but it is potentially also perceived by supporters as a prevention of deeper policy integration (because of the competitive status of deepening and widening priorities as well as limited resources available for both). In practice, the last two enlargement waves, while still consisting of culturally European countries, have been received with hesitancy by member state citizens of the EU-15, and some commentators have commented on the previous EU constellation as a cohesive ideal format for integration (Papadopoulus, 2008). Following the enlargement activism of the past few years, support for future accessions to the bloc has significantly decreased from the previous decade, with currently almost as many Europeans for as against a further widening (45 percent and 42 percent, respectively) (European Commission 2006, Eurobarometer 255). Further evidence of this change of mind consists in the protest of citizens and police forces on top of the hesitant acceptance in the old Schengen states, particularly in Germany and Austria, to the extension of the custom-free area to Central and Eastern Europe in December 2007—with little recognition of the fear of and ambiguity about absorption into the Union by the new member-state citizens themselves.

Prospects for an EU enlargement to culturally and religiously dissimilar countries of the Balkans or Turkey are met by many current EU citizens with outright opposition (as evidenced in Eurobarometer surveys), because it becomes increasingly difficult to find culturally fixed identity references, an emotive precondition for the development of a transnational identity—at least as evident from the preceding chapters. The election victory of many center-right governments in Europe and party representatives in the last European Parliament elections 2009, for instance, is in part attributed to the skeptical stances toward the looming membership of Turkey, coupled with concerns about the problematic integration of culturally dissimilar immigrants and citizens already living in the Union. French president Sarkozy's push for the Mediterranean Union as an alternative to Turkish full membership adds to this conundrum, ignoring the potential benefits of Turkey's youthful demographics. Future enlargements will loosen the degree of territorial and cultural boundedness and homogeneity, and therefore make transnational identity expansion much harder to achieve. With each widening, the EU as a territorial and cultural identity space loses the cohesiveness necessary for a common identification. The Union's "unity in diversity" declaratory motto provides little guidance in dealing with the consequences of an ever-enlarging polity, which makes the inclusive concept irrelevant in the face of a population searching for more cohesive reference points.

In addition to the obvious consequences for public support and identification with the EU, problems of social cohesion and regional economic disparity increase with the accession of ever more member states, not to mention the strain on the decision-making procedures within the Union's institutions, be it in regard to the distribution of voting rights in the Council, legislative seats in the EP, or the fact that the Franco-German hegemony is increasingly being challenged by newcomers who, as former French president Chirac put it so (in)famously in the 2003 reaction to the Iraq invasion, should have "shut up" rather than voice their opinion. The widening wealth gap and competition between states, combined with the pressure to keep the Union's budget in control and differences in the political rights afforded to the new member states citizens (e.g., the restrictions in the freedom of movement or the visa obligations versus third countries such as the United States) produce an added detrimental effect on the homogeneity of the European public and thus dilute transnational allegiances. Connected to the assumption that enlargement preferences vary significantly and increasingly become constrained by the effects of previous ones, there exists an additional argument over "whether to prioritize EU deepening or widening" (Schimmelfennig, 2005: 135), with the current institutional design of the Union presenting another significant challenge to identification, as I will point out below.

One of the implications of the larger structural processes as they relate to public support and the development of a transnational pan-European identification is that the EU needs to resolve what in the literature is called the "finality issue." Many politicians in Brussels still portray EU integration in "Monnet style" as an open and undefined procedure in which the ongoing process of harmonization and political spillover extension is the main goal, or they avoid the discussion about a final geopolitical framework of the Union entirely. Yet, as Follesdal states, "scholars who study the extent of support for the 'political community' note that disagreements about its membership, borders and purposes may deprive the regime of diffuse support" (Follesdal, 2006: 164).

The finality of integration as an indeterminate process with respect to both the deepening of institutional policies and widening in member states increasingly produces a sense of insecurity among the population. And with EU policies advancing in many aspects of the domestic life of the citizens, the question of where the EU is headed as a transnational organization becomes more pressing. For instance, according to a recent special EB survey, a plurality of 37 percent of the EU-25 citizens sees the need of a "clear political project" for successful future enlargements (European Commission 2009, Eurobarometer 259). The argument that prospective member states such as Turkey would be accepted by the citizens of the older ones once they are prepared to enter the EU lacks empirical evidence, as the most recent Eurobarometer surveys show that while support for further enlargement is stronger in the new member states, Turkey and other applicant states continue to be rejected by the majority of EU citizens.

It appears that the ongoing balancing of the "ideal ratio between widening and deepening gives way to the more or less explicit fear that a more ambitious finalite geographique might prevent a more ambitious finality politique" (Marchetti, 2006: 5). It also neglects the voices that emphasize a geopolitically open, constitutionally conceived debate on the finality of EU integration efforts (Wiener, 2006). To answer both demands, the EU, under pressure from potent individuals, such as Sarkozy, in 2008 set up a "Wise Group" of the Union, established to discuss the impact of further enlargement waves and the challenges of the future, and to deliver a report by mid-2010 likely focused on the maintenance of social cohesion. Such undertaking always involves some soul searching as well, as a focus on the future necessitates taking inventory of the current constitution of the entity. In a fairly general manner, the group's tasks are to envision the long-term challenges and EU responses in the decades 2020–2030, including "strengthening and modernizing the European model of economic success and social responsibility [...] migration, sustainable development," as well as "ways of better reaching out to citizens and addressing their expectations and needs" (European Council, 2007: 3). Yet this initiative, as expressed in its wish to preserve the European social model and its focus on migration, etc., aims at producing more of a unitary common identity that implicitly rejects pluralistic conceptions of citizenship and belonging. A high-profile academic reflection on the outcome of this exercise equally evades the spelling out of any future configuration except an optimistic formulation that a sustainable EU "can be a power multiplier making its raison d'etre, the empowerment of others, individuals and nations, insiders and outsiders, born and not yet born" (Nicolaidis, 2010: 49). Normative theorists note that the openness of integration, coupled with the democratic deficit and expectations on policy performance, and a continuously strengthening public sphere may augment interest formation in Brussels by a variety of actors and thus democratize and popularize EU politics. Simultaneously, the direction of integration is sometimes described as "the perception of a free-floating collective will of the European people as a by-product of ongoing communication and contention regarding European governance" (Eder and Trenz, 2007: 49). In view of the manifold communication and implementation-problems a discussion has been started by politicians and academics about the necessity of differentiated forms of integration, be it in form of a core Europe, variable geometry, or the often resented establishment of a federation (Wood and Quaisser, 2008), though no further debate was ever developed to really search publicly or deliberately for a future model for the Union, let alone present a viable vision to the citizens. Some resist the idea of spelling out the frontiers of the Union, because this might hamper the ongoing concentration on policy outcomes or because the ideal of a supranational federation is perceived as resembling too strongly a state-like political system—something that is difficult to achieve under the volatile post-constitutional, economically distressed public atmosphere. In this regard, the Treaty of Lisbon as an aid in this search for a strategic plan for the future constitutes a minimalist vision for the EU since it concentrates on the means rather than the still-undefined goal, and is best characterized as a less objectionable leftover piecemeal of the failed Constitution. As we have seen throughout the history of European integration, the finality issue existed from the beginning accompanied the Union's evolution throughout, and has only recently been brought to the forefront in the conflict over the EU budget, the constitutional draft, enlargements, and the Eurocrisis. In fact, the constant support of a majority of Europeans for a constitutional treaty of sorts might have less to do with enthusiasm about deeper integration as with the hope of finding a more clearly defined political and legal framework for the Union.

Having previewed some of the problematic constellations that affect the development of transnational identities in Europe, the last section spells out some policy prescriptions for an optimization of collective identities resulting from the empirical analyses and the above-mentioned structural conditions.

Implications and Recommendations

As pointed out before, there exist two streams of identity construction in contemporary political life: one that is based on the assumed common cultural identity of Europe, and one that in essence consists of a transnational identification with the EU as a political entity, thereby prioritizing civic ideas revolving around rights and duties. Based on the empirical evidence, I linked these two strands by positing that where there is a strong cultural-historical identification with Europe as civilization, a better chance of transnational identity formation exists. This conclusion is derived from the fact that the results have shown that the main integration policies of the 1990s have not automatically led to a neofunctionalist augmentation of civic identity among EU citizens. Rather, depending on the degree of compatibility of the cultural European identity with the national political culture, the augmented influence of the Union in the member states has led to varying degrees of identity constructions of the national and the nationalized European identities, in some cases (Ireland and Germany) toward a bounded transnationalism, and in few (the UK) toward a form of protective nationalism. The print media has been found to exert substantial influence on the direction and strength of these developments as part of the domestic reception in each country, thereby reinforcing the existence of the EU as an actor in contemporary European life. These basic findings are important because they relay information about factors that determine the future course of European integration. Precisely because the Union has found itself for the past few years in a critical period, a reflection on these determinants is more important than ever. The following implications are narrowly conceived as they derive from the results of the empirical analyses and the aforementioned sustainability challenges. They only partially touch on larger questions of accountability, democratic legitimacy, or socioeconomic balancing, as these well-known issues in the field have been widely written about, yet they focus on solutions that can be implemented and are in line with the augmented significance of discursive identity politics.

From a public policy perspective, one of the main implications of the empirical results is that the protection and value of national identities and cultures through the EU needs to be transmitted more strongly and effectively. Note that by "culture" I don't refer here to the domestic political cultures that are characterized by political value orientations mentioned elsewhere in this book, but to the ethnocentric traditions expressed in high and low cultural performances, symbols, and narratives. Such an identitive approach to cultural recognition would facilitate popular support for the Union and enable citizens to continuously feel secure in their national identity and culture, in turn allowing for a transnational expansion. As a transnational identity consists of cultural and civic aspects, the protection of the cultural base seems to be a prerequisite upon which the civic identity can be constructed. To a varying degree EU integration inevitably takes away part of the previous nationally existing autonomy, but according to my findings, that in itself is not seen as a problem by the citizens. The Maastricht Treaty legally affirmed cultural cooperation among cities and regions in Europe and declared that the Union shall respect the national identities of the member states, but aside from this general provision, which has been inserted in all later treaties, there is little to suggest that the EU takes precautionary measures to keep the cultural autonomy of each state or region alive. The previous constitutional text and current Lisbon Treaty refer in Article 2, section 3, to the protection of the national identities and to the preservation of *Europe's* cultural and linguistic diversity, but rhetoric and policy both should emphasize national, regional, and local cultural traditions and patrimonies as well so that EU cultural policies gain significance for citizens in their domestic environment, particularly as this area has been communalized for only twenty years now. There exist a number of transnational cultural initiatives under the commission's cultural division, but these are disjointed and mainly intended to augment and preserve Europe's *common* cultural heritage akin to the cultural politics of nation-states (Shore, 2000) and not to serve the protection and enhancement of local or regional cultural diversity—rather, "respecting the national and regional diversity" is all that can be hoped for. Such emphasis on common cultural features is also the result of the externally oriented protection of European culture industries, such as movies or literature, from other dominant influences like the United States or increasingly, the Far East—thus representing Europe's "cultural Maginot line" (Van Ham, 2010). A program conjointly administered by the national and regional governments that specifically focuses on the preservation of their cultural identities and that would be communicated efficiently through audiovisual and print media on a national level would signify to citizens that the EU is actively trying to promote intact subregional identities in Europe (similar to, but more prominent than the European Capitals of Culture-program). If citizens perceive the Union in support of their local, regional, or national identities, there will be less suspicion of an erosion of collective identities, and this in turn aids transnational identity development. Notably, until 2007, no Eurobarometer survey treated the topic of culture, yet close to half of the citizens reported that culture—however interpreted—was important to their life (European Commission, 2007, Special Eurobarometer 278). How to coordinate such programs with multilevel political instances and communicate information about EU-funded cultural programs more accessibly presents its own set of challenges, but there needs to be a preceding recognition of political necessity on the side of EU actors first.

In this respect, in today's information age the various mass media play an ever-increasing role in the dissemination of information and the shaping or framing of opinions. Naturally, these national institutions have their own market-led motivations in the coverage of EU affairs as laid out in the print analysis chapter, which can be detrimental to the EU's agenda of promoting a civic European identity through transnational actions and integration. However, until 2004 the communication strategy of the Union, if one existed, had been insufficient in terms of form and content. The creation of a commissioner-level post for institutional relations and communications strategy that year began to put an emphasis on the much-needed transparency and visibility of EU politics. While some media outlets and journalists already decried the novel communications strategy as a spin machine, there exists an obvious need for improved contact between the EU institutions and the national media. I concentrate here on the EU's potential for improvements in this area, since national media, as we have seen, provide a variety of sometimes ambiguous messages regarding European integration. The "communications" commissioner Margot Wallström produced an extensive information strategy summarized in a white paper on communication in 2006, suggesting that regional or national EU offices ought to translate the issues coming from Brussels onto a national stage, thereby giving them more importance and taking in national opinions and reactions in as well. And even despite the incremental increase in information delivery and press conferences, many communication deficits in the relationship between the institutions in Brussels and the national governments and media persist (Thiel, 2008). A localization strategy ought to be devised and implemented as soon as possible, and while some may question the legal basis for such a policy, improved public diplomacy could alleviate the much-criticized democratic deficit by providing more information and transparency over EU policy initiation. Arguably this could also have negative effects as it may lead to the uncovering of embarrassing EU practices or make the integration process more dependent on the volatility of public opinion. But Eurobarometer surveys consistently attest to a perceived complexity, disinterest, and ignorance of EU institutions and policies, so that a public informational mission aimed at the audiovisual and virtual mass media has the potential to contribute to a more positive image of the EU and thus the creation of transnational identities. In this sense, the Commission is taking a risk in improving means to not only provide more information but also to essentially further stimulate European public spheres, which could result in constraining Brussels. If the EU is really invested in the pursuit of more legitimizing communicative strategies, it ought to approach national mass-media editors more actively; recent ideas such as the creation of an EU television channel or EUTube channel on the website YouTube have only a small effect on reaching the masses as long as the newspapers and TV stations provide more access to the public (although this may be changing with the advance of digital media, see Trenz, 2009). The Union's communication strategy needs to become more efficient, and while the first step in institutional anchoring of these issues has been taken, the active localization of EU coverage through the Commission is of importance for a change in national media perception. Unfortunately, the efforts of Commissioner Wallström did not indicate that the mass media outlets are considered essential by Brussels as there were no plans to actively involve press journalists in the communication strategy of the Union even though a better inclusion of traditional media organs has been found essential by analysts (Euractiv, 2005). A report by the European Policy Institutes Network suggests improving the Union's communication with and in member states, for example, by creating information bulletins for the national media—an idea that has been taken up by the Commission in the publication of its first-ever communication priority document in 2009, which highlights the with regards to participation challenging EP elections of June that year. Following the dismal participation rate in those elections, the Parliament itself has begun to call for improved coverage of the EU, but aside from the above-mentioned issues surrounding journalistic independence, inter-institutional differences in communication priorities between the Commission, the Parliament, and other bodies remain.

In the aftermath of the constitutional rejection, Commissioner Wallström's "Plan D" called for more democracy, dialogue, and debate by increasing EU official visits to the member states, establishing roundtables, and even recommending the increased utilization of the internet for information dissemination, etc. But it failed to recognize traditional mainstream media such as TV and press explicitly. Toward the end of her tenure, she expressed the frustrations of her office and recommended that the next Commission scrap her post and replace it with a more broadly conceptualized "Citizen's Commissioner" instead (EU Observer, 2009). Accordingly, the second Barroso Commission now features a Commissioner for Justice, Fundamental Rights, and Citizenship, who focuses more on policy and less on communication. While this portfolio emphasis is essential in that the assurance of civil rights for minorities and the larger public in the EU has repercussions for transnationalism as well, it does little to improve the communicative deficit of the Union.

The outcomes of the empirical research seem to furthermore indicate that integration measures should ideally be additive and complementary in nature, instead of taking away existing national policy instruments. Such guiding prescriptions avoid disrupting nationally sensitive political cultures, even though admittedly, in practice this advice may be difficult to follow. I concluded in the interview section that integration measures that were generally additive, for example the single-market provisions or the complementary European citizenship, received more support than actions that potentially replace customary practices and policies, e.g., the replacement of national currencies or the fusion of national passport schemes or constitutions. Similarly, the press seems to have a more favorable coverage of complementary integration projects than of the ones that abolish national policies. It should be easy to see why additive or complementary policy measures evoke more positive reactions, since they leave the elements and symbols of national sovereignty intact and do not substantially impede on each state's sovereignty in the spirit of subsidiarity. Future integration projects could be developed and communicated along this recommendation, and particular policy areas seem to be more compatible with this idea than others. For example, trade agreements, environmental policy promotion, or the recent establishment of the diplomatic European External Action Service are then seen as less intrusive by citizens as long as they do not necessitate a substantial replacement of existing national policies or political institutions. More research along these lines could verify if that holds true for the majority of integration policies, particularly as the reality of policy prescription can result in negative repercussions for previous domestically regulated policies.

Conclusion: Improving Social Cohesion to Face an Uncertain Future

Part of the problem of the increasing scrutiny with which Europeans regard the EU lies in the augmented complexity and diversity as well as increasing political role of the Union for the member states. Aside from this ambiguous advancement, the aforementioned structural problems such as aging, immigration, diversification, and the question of integration capacity add additional pressures that may not centrally relate to the regulative policies of EU integration but nevertheless exert significant influence over the future course of regionalism. These may be more obvious in the case of nationalistic responses to immigration or less so in the effects of ageing on the European population, but together they represent a momentous challenge for public support of and identity construction in the EU. They act as potentially dramatic catalysts for societal and political change, particularly when these factors "are set in the context of weak job creation and slow growth, dramatic demographic shifts, and increasing worldwide tensions with the largest immigrant religious group, Europe's contemporary challenges of immigration and integration begin to look relatively unique in historical and comparative perspective" (Parsons and Smeeding, 2006: 20). In theory, these challenges could potentially be a source of common identification as well, particularly if the immigration and enlargement issues should be construed as a unifying object of disaffection and/or exceptionalism around which citizens bond together—as I observed in the last hypothesis. While it concentrated on indicators such as post-Maastricht integration measures, the salience of problematic demographic and structural issues may change the equation in the medium term. The Union's capacity to proceed proactively with these challenges and accordingly popularize its achievements will certainly affect transnational identity transformation as well as the building of utilitarian support.

Shortly after the EU's fiftieth "birthday"—the anniversary of the signing of the Rome Treaties in 1957—many analysts still tend to look primarily at the economic or institutional challenges of an ever more complex organization, but they don't realize that less noticeable societal externalities of European integration and structural processes, such as demographic changes caused by aging, enlargements, and immigration, which will further dilute homogeneity and produce novel cleavages, will cause citizens to question the ability of the Union to provide sustainable economic success, regional security, and a stable identity. To provide for a balanced integration process accompanied by favorable public support, the issues detailed above need to be treated with the same kind of attention and urgency received by similar politically and temporally abstract processes, such as global climate change—precisely so to avoid populist upheavals or protective nationalism.

With regard to the demographic changes in the countries of the EU, it seems that there are few alternatives to the predicted necessity of a rising immigration population. If member states are able to solve the problem of domestic weak fertility rates through national family-friendly policies or an EU-regulated, liberal immigration and (still nationally determined) integration policy that produce better results in European societies than they do now, then we can expect more cohesive and stable patterns of support for the Union. In other words, European governments, together with Brussels, have to steer the challenges by strengthening the best-practice coordination among member states and by communalizing more inclusive and less ethnocentric integration and citizenship policies rather than passively undergo structural disruptive changes, and they have to do so with the weight of public opinion, national cultures, and media in mind. While there are some notable efforts already taking place—for instance, the open method of coordination, which aims at the benchmarking and comparing of practices—unfortunately, short-term campaign thinking, national policy preferences, and populist posturing too often interfere with responsible long-term directing of common policy challenges.

Lastly, the nebulous finality issue, combined with the various prospects and scenarios for enlargements leading to differentiated blocs within the EU is likely to weaken "core Europe" and thus increase popular pressures for protection and recognition of the traditional Western, Franco-German leadership in the Union. The shift of attention to the former borderlands of the Warsaw Pact, the Balkans, or the Union of the Mediterranean (which may in the future become a center itself) coincides with an abating of the Union centered on Brussels and its surrounding states. The challenge of finding a balance between consolidation of policies and member states, and forward-moving integration cannot be circumvented by theorizing the EU solely as a "functional" community without any sort of envisioned final, constitutionalized status, and the often-heard bike metaphor suggesting a constant forward push to avoid a disruptive stop appears similarly inadequate. Citizens and elites still predominantly think in traditional, nation-state-oriented structures, and although there has been a hesitant acceptance of new forms of transnational governance such as the EU, in the face of its increasing interference in national politics and its expansion to ever more countries, it needs to supply some sort of teleological objective or framework. Nicolaidis recognizes the EU as "schizophrenic power" in its attempt to invoke state-like attributes while at the same time transcending these, because, as she notes, "statism is the EU's mother of all demons" (Nicolaidis, 2010). However, it appears that no European politician wants to spell out the geocultural or political objectives and limits of the Union, and if they do (such as former German foreign minister Fischer in his suggestion of a federal Europe), they become persona non grata in now-dominant conservative policy circles.

Two major events shaped the Union's ability to move forward with integration in the recent past: the long-awaited ratification of the Lisbon Treaty and the European Parliament elections. Both reflect the status quo of transnational identity formation in Europe, with some countries in strong support of the reform treaty, while others, such as Ireland and the UK, obstructively attempted to hold out on a firm commitment to Brussels. The Treaty of Lisbon has been amended to sustain continued influence of small states (such as the promise to Ireland to retain its commissioner) or appeal to hesitant governments or populations (the granted opt-out of the UK from the Charter of Fundamental Rights) to ensure final ratification. It contains provisions for a semipermanent EU Council president as well as a High Representative for Foreign and Security Affairs. These two positions could have helped alleviate the integration indeterminacy insofar they augment the formation of a more unified, quasi-federal structure among EU member states and Brussels. The creation and strengthening of these two leadership posts were advocated to provide more coordination among member states and more internal and external cohesiveness. In the end, two political functionaries with relatively little experience or recognition were chosen to avoid a change in the status quo, thus wasting an opportunity for developing legitimizing social and political stature. What is worse, the European public does not perceive of an added value of these positions so far, but rather view the horse-trading selection process by European leaders as a continuation of the backstage deals that were prominent in the past, but which have now come under intense public and media scrutiny. Ironically, the selection of these EU "leaders" showcased more of what kind of model the EU should not be rather than what the EU should develop into.

Similarly, the EP elections continue to struggle with low visibility as well as voter turnout and a tendency to attract protest votes over controversial national and EU policies, the latter proving once again that even institutionalized transnational elections cannot escape the primacy of national interests. In the past, the marginal turnout in European elections was perceived as a symbol of Euro-sclerosis, or simply, disinterest by European citizens, while the shift toward a center-right-dominated Parliament in the current legislative period indicates that citizens, if they vote at all, prefer a nationally sensitive leadership. The addition of a new right-wing, antifederalist party group in the Parliament reinforces the message of the problematic indeterminacy of future EU evolution, as they contest more than just the market- and value-liberal stance of European integration. The politicization of current integration policies may not automatically result in more pro-integrationist electoral outcomes; in fact, it could strengthen anti-European sentiment, but at least people will weigh in on and debate EU politics. More transparency and public involvement counteracts anti-European sentiments based on ignorance and protective nationalism. Such politicization of EU affairs contributes to the creation of a transnational civil society and identity in Europe.

In conclusion, it is clear from the empirical work presented in this book as well as from the implications raised in the final chapter that the future evolution of transnational identities in the EU is at a minimum predicated on the degree of compatibility of national political cultures with the goals of European integration. Thus, harmonizing EU policies have nationally preset limitations with respect to their identity-forging effects, and the Union's own modeling of state-like institutions and policies continues to remain in a tense relation with the transnational, integrative structure it is supposed to establish. At the same time, the internal and external structural factors mentioned above affect the cohesiveness of the European polity and will potentially further dilute any transnational identity developments, particularly in view of reactionary unifying immigration pressures from beyond Europe's shores and the internal lack of agreement and solidarity. Additional aspects such as recent enlargement waves, future contentious enlargement prospects, and the ensuing increase in diversity and national interests necessitate a more careful balancing of national identities and European integration to better comprehend how the current (re)configuration of the Union will influence public opinion in the years to come, and to adjust accordingly. As European integration must continue to respond to rapidly changing internal and global policy challenges, however, the time for such reflection periods is paid for with the stagnation in policy responsiveness and lower popular support for the Union. The "new" Union of twenty-seven members requires sufficient time to consolidate, and while the Lisbon treaty may aid in this respect by providing a more communalized decision-making procedure and an institutionalized leadership structure, future deepening of transnational policies and widening of membership circles need to be more carefully weighed based on the repercussions these measures have for European societies to respond appropriately to an ever more challenging future.

Appendix: Interview Protocol

1. Demographic information:
   - Age?
   - Male/Female?
   - Occupation?
   - Religion?
   - Highest degree earned in educational system?
   - Political affiliation (left/right/don't know/don't want to tell)?

Questions from the Eurobarometer survey:

2. In the near future, do you see yourself as (your nationality only, your nationality and European, European and national, European only)? Why?
3. Generally speaking, do you think that (your country's) membership in the European Union is a good thing, a bad thing, or neither good nor bad? Why?
4. Using a scale from 1 to 10, how much do you feel you know about the EU, its policies, its institution (1=know nothing at all; 10=know a great deal)?
5. About how often do you watch the news on television/read the news in the daily papers/listen to news broadcasts on the radio: Everyday, several times a week, once or twice a week, less often, never?

Open-Ended Questions:

6. What ideas or words do you associate with "Europe" and with "EU"?
7. How do you perceive EU membership for yourself; did it affect your life in any way?
8. Have you changed your opinion about membership within the past (ten) years? How and why?
9. If you think about developments in the EU, what do you think with regard to your country's political autonomy/sovereignty?

10. Have you ever heard about the "single market"? If yes, what does the single market mean to you?
11. What does the "euro" mean to you?
12. Have you ever heard about plans for a common foreign policy in the EU? What do you think about a common foreign policy for the EU?
13. Have you heard about the convention to establish an EU constitution? What do you think about a common constitution for the EU?
14. What would be your reaction to an EU decision that might be good for the whole of the EU but may be unfavorable for your own country, e.g., enlargement of the EU with loss of (structural) funds for your country?
15. Do you think you have more in common with other EU citizens than with non-EU citizens (for example, the Swiss, the Norwegians, or the Turks)?
16. Some people argue that there is something called a (transnational) "European" identity that is separate from national identity. Other people claim that there is no such thing, that Europeans feel only "British" or "Irish." What do you think; how do you view yourself?
17. Is there anything else you want to tell me or that you think I should know about your views of Europe and the EU?

Notes

4 How Do Citizens Perceive European Integration?

1. Original text: "Deutsch von meinen kulturellen Wurzeln her, aber Europa ist der gesellschaftspolitische Kontext in dem ich eingebunden bin und hinter dem ich eigentlich so stehe. Von dem her halte ich Europa fuer das erstrebenswertere Ziel. Das eine ist wo ich herkomme, das andere wo es hingehen soll."
2. Original text: "Deutschland ist zu klein um wichtig zu sein in der Welt, es ist eine Export-nation. Ausserdem ist es die Nation mit dem meisten Tourismus in Europa. Deutschland hat als geschichtliches Erbe eine Vorreiterrolle im friedlichen länderübergreifenden Miteinander zu haben."
3. Original text: "Europa als der Soll-Zustand, während die EU eher der Ist-Zustand ist."
4. Original text: "Nee, also ausser wenn ich grenzüberschreitend reise. das finde ich, ohne Grenzkontrollen und ohne Geldwechseln schon sehr gut."
5. "Ich war schon immer pro-Europa, aber diese Meinung ist verstärkt geworden. Gerade im Zusammenhang der weltpolitischen Entwicklung der letzten Jahre, sprich also Machtzuwachs der USA, finde ich es wichtig dass ein gestärktes Europa entsteht das mit Vernunft und Stärke zu sprechen weiss."
6. "Ich glaube sie ist ein bisschen schlechter geworden da es mir zu intensiv geworden ist. Das lockere ist da sinnvoller als wenn man zuviele Gemeinsamkeiten erzwingt. Ich glaube nicht, dass ich sehr nationalistisch bin aber, eher noch stolz auf meine Region, ich identifiziere mich damit wo ich lebe."
7. Original text: "Deutschland ist durch das Einbinden nicht mehr souverän. Das sehe ich aber als seinen positiven Aspekt. Dann können irgendwelche durchgeknallten Koepfe keine fragwürdigen Alleingänge machen, sondern müssen sich an einer übergeordneten Gemeinschaft orientieren. Dass man noch einen Standpunkt haben kann, hat Deutschland ja in der Irak-Debatte bewiesen."
8. Original text: "Zweiseitig. Einerseits hat der Binnenmarkt fuer wirtschaftliches Wachstum gesorgt durch den unproblematischeren Zugang zu Maerkten.

Andererseits, durch das europäische Wettbewerbsrecht hat der Staat weniger Handlungsmöglichkeiten, das ist manchmal ein wenig problematisch."

9. Original text: "Der Binnenmarkt ermöglicht ja den freien Warenhandel in der EU. Seit der Einführung des Euro kann man dadurch auch europaweit Preise vergleichen, und mit dem Internet ist der Kunde nun in einer gestärkten Position [. . .] Der Begriff erinnert mich auch an die freie Berufswahl innerhalb der EU."
10. Original text: "Ein Verlust der deutschen Identität, wirklich. Andererseits kann man nun Preise im Ausland besser vergleichen und hat mit den Menschen anderer Länder immer wieder ein Gesprächsthema."
11. Note that "teuro" refers to a play on words, in which the terms euro and "teuer," meaning expensive, are merged to the term "teuro"—expensive euro. Original text: "Euro ist ein Teuro, einwandfrei. Da können die Politiker noch so sagen, was sie wollen, zumindest fuer die normale Familie. Ja, negativ, denn mit der D-Mark hatte ich mehr in der Tasche wie mit dem Euro."
12. Original text: "Ich habe ein Problem damit da die Währung ja was typisches fuer ein Land gewesen ist, damit identifiziert man sich natürlich. Dadurch geht Individalität verloren."
13. Original text: "Finde ich grundsätzlich eine gute Sache. Ist ja auch relative stabil. Ich kann mir gut vorstellen, dass er eine Alternative zum Dollar werden wird."
14. Original text: "Ja, das einzig sinnvolle Konzept—siehe Irakkrieg. Hier wurden nationale Interessen über die europäischen gestellt, was den Verlust des Europäischen Einflusses bedeutete. Daneben sollten die Nationen auch ihre eigene Aussenpolitik gestalten können."
15. Original text: "Die europäische Aussenpolitik hat meiner Meinung nach in den letzten Jahren versagt. Die Europaer konnten sich nicht gegen die USA nicht durchsetzen und waren unfaehig, innerhalb der EU eine konsequente Aussenpolitik zu formieren. Zudem fehlt neben Konsenz auch die Durchsetzungsfaehigkeit, es bleibt ein Papiertiger."
16. Original text: "Eine vernünftige europäische Verfassung, in der auch die Menschenrechte und Bürgerrechte festgelegt werden und eine Art Mindestsozialstatus definiert wird, das würde mit Sicherheit das Ansehen der EU Institutionen steigern. Das bisherige Gezänke liefert allerdings eher ein trauriges Bild ab."
17. Original text: "Wenn wir nicht von unserem Standard zurückfallen, halte ich es fuer eine gute Sache. Und wenn Europa spaeter mal richtig zusammenwachsen wird, mit nur einer offiziellen Sprache, eigener Gesetzgebung, dann wird eine gemeinsame Verfassung eine sinnvolle Sache sein. Kann als Anweisung für weitere Kandidatenlaender von Nutzen sein, sozusagen als 'Spielregeln' oder so."
18. Original text: "Ich denke, die Leidensfähigkeit des deutschen Volkes ist da schon recht hoch. Und was mich betrifft, ich muss das akzeptieren da das Gemeinwohl doch über das des Einzelnen geht. Ist ok, wenn es einigermassen nachvollziehbare Gründe dafür gibt. Ist die Frage, ob Europa schon gefestigt genug ist um eine rasche Osterweiterung sinnvoll umsetzen zu koennen."

19. Original text: "Ich denke, vierzehn Jahre nach der Wiedervereinigung hat Deutschland mehr Probleme im eigenen Land und muss seine Interessen einfach mehr einfordern. Es wird Zeit, dass Europa was für Deutschland tut und nicht nur umgekehrt."
20. Original text: "Das hält sich die Waage. Einmal sind wir dran, dann sind die Engländer dran, dann die Franzosen. Jeder muss dann mal gucken. Nicht immer kann jeder nur gewinnen und da muss man kompromissbereit sein."
21. Original text: "Würde ich nicht sagen, nein. Man sieht es ja krass jetzt, mit Deutschen und Italienern. Ist von der Mentalität grundverschieden und da dürften die Deutschen und die Schweizer eher was gemeinsam haben. Das kann man nicht mit politischen Grenzen bestimmen." (Note: In 2003, an Italo-German affront occurred that reflected idiosyncratic stereotypes.)
22. Original text: "Nicht wirklich. Ich glaube dass gerade, wenn man die Türken in Deutschland anschaut, dass diese genauso oder vielleicht sogar europäischer sind als im Vergleich ein Nachbarland. Ich glaube die EU macht da nicht den Unterschied, es gibt aufgeklärte Geister auch ausserhalb der EU."
23. Original text: "Nee, ich fuehle mich nicht als Europäer, sondern als Deutsche. Ich kann mich nicht mit Europa so stark identifizieren. Ich fuehle mich in Spanien als Ausländer, da ich die Sprache kaum kann. In Frankreich ist das anders, da ich die Sprache gut kann [...] Ich glaube auch nicht, dass ein Spanier mich nicht als Ausländer betrachten wuerde. Man fuehlt sich immer noch seinem Land zugehoerig."
24. Original text: "Die Identität, die wir haben, hoert nicht mit deutschen oder europäischen Grenzen auf, sondern eher mit den Grenzen der Medien oder den Grenzen die die globale Konsumgüterindustrie setzt. Levi's, Coca Cola, Microsoft und Madonna sind in Deutschland, in Europa und der ganzen Welt präsent."
25. Original text: "Ich denke die nächste Generation, unsere Kinder, wachsen damit schon viel mehr auf. Die kennen gar keine D-Mark mehr und die Grenzen von früher, da wird sowas eher entstehen. Aber ich denke es ist o.k. wenn jeder seine nationale und lokale Identität behaelt."

5 Large-Scale Survey Analyses through Eurobarometer

1. The question is as follows: "In the near future, do you see yourself as (Nationality) only/(Nationality) and European/European and (Nationality)/ European only/Don't know?" Data in this chapter was taken either directly from the Eurobarometer website of the European Commission, http://europa.eu.int/comm/public_opinion/index_en.htm, or from the online data storage facility at the German Social Sciences Infrastructure Services (GESIS), http://www.gesis.org/en/index.htm.

6 Newspaper Discourse and Public Spheres

1. Multiple cross-listings of keywords are possible and are counted individually, so that one article could have been counted several times and classified differently depending on its tone. In a second analysis, I divided each of the five combination categories into subcategories according to their content; e.g., in the case of the category "EU + identity," I subdivided these articles into those dealing with "national identity," "cultural policies," "impact of EU policies upon collective identity," etc.
2. Original text: "Das Vertragswerk von Maastricht zu verwerfen wäre ein Akt der Befreiung: für uns, für die Gemeinschaft, für die Beitrittskandidaten und für das übrige Europa. Briten und Dänen haben sich ja schon von einigem befreit. Die Verwerfung von Maastricht wäre die Befreiung von einem Akt der Arroganz der Macht, die unsachverständig und gegen den Willen des Volkes eine Integration meinte fortschreiben zu können."
3. Original text: "Die Europäische Union verbindet wirtschaftlichen Aufschwung, politische Stabilität mit Strukturen des Interessenausgleichs. Zum Grundgedanken dieser Schicksalsgemeinschaft gehoert das Konzept europäischer Solidarität, das heute in vielen Facetten der Politik und der Institutionen der EU verankert ist und die Identität der Europäer prägt."
4. Original text: "Es fehlt eine geinsame Identität, die ein Gefühl der Verpflichtung erzeugt—so wie zwischen den alten und neuen Bundesländern. Trotz vierzig Jahren Integration ist 'Europa' ein Konstrukt, kein gemeinsamer Staat, der sich als Schicksalsgemeinschaft versteht."
5. Original text: "In der realen, jenseits der Akademien stattfindenden Innenpolitik spielen Identität und Kultur wegen dieser Nichtdefinierbarkeit keine Rolle; die von der Union angestoßene Debatte über deutsche "Leitkultur" ist kläglich gescheitert. Gewiß hat diese Verschwommenheit auch ihre Vorzüge."
6. Original text: "Dem Binnenmarkt sei in den vergangenen Jahren die Schaffung von bis zu 900 000 zusätzlichen Arbeitsplätzen zu verdanken. Der Kommissionspräsident (Santer) bemängelte Verzoegerungen bei der Übertragung der Binnenmarktgesetze durch die Mitgliedsstaaten."
7. Original text: "Dem Binnenmarkt sei in den vergangenen Jahren die Schaffung von bis zu 900 000 zusätzlichen Arbeitsplätzen zu verdanken. Der Kommissionspräsident (Santer) bemängelte Verzoegerungen bei der Übertragung der Binnenmarktgesetze durch die Mitgliedsstaaten."
8. Original text: "Europas Binnenmarkt endet dort, wo es die Manager der Automobilkonzerne für opportun halten. Die Branche arbeitet mit allen Tricks und Kniffen, um den Kaeufern ihre Wahlmöglichkeiten einzuschränken."
9. Original text: "Er wird für die Volksseele auch niemals die Bedeutung erlangen, die die D-Mark als Zahlungsmittel des Wirtschaftwunders erhalten und über Jahrzehnte bewahrt hat. Das wäre nicht weiter tragisch, sondern ein Stück begrüssenswerte Normalität—wenn sich die Bürger Europas stattdessen auf

andere Symbole verständigen koennten, die Staat, Wirtschaft und Gesellschaft zusammenhalten. Demokratie, Freiheit, Leistung, Sicherheit, Gemeinschaft, all diese Begriffe klangen irgendwie mit, wenn."

10. Original text: "Die Deutschen gehen selbstverständlich mit den neuen Scheinen um, die Preise stiegen langsamer als zuvor, und am Devisenmarkt gewann der Euro sogar. Die Bilanz der größten Währungsumstellung der Geschichte entbehrt jeder Katastrophe. Die marklose Zeit, sorgenvoll erwartet, ist von grandioser Normalität."
11. Original text: "Zum hierzulande besonders starken Mißbehagen an der neuen Währung trägt auch bei, daß die D-Mark als Symbol für wirtschaftlichen Wiederaufstieg und internationale Anerkennung geradezu Kult-Status genoß [...] Zudem färbt wohl auch das Unbehagen über die bürgerferne Bürokratie in Brüssel und die allgemeine Misere von Wirtschaft und Wirtschaftspolitik auf den Euro ab. So haben gerade die Deutschen in diesem Jahr die Regeln des Stabilitäts—und Wachstumspakts verletzt."
12. Original text: "Hiermit wird eine Gemeinsame Außen—und Sicherheitspolitik eingeführt, heisst es in Artikel J des Vertrages von Maastricht. Ein frommer Wunsch. Wie labil die Gemeinsame Aussen—und Sicherheitspolitik (GASP) der EU bislang war, hat die verunglückte Politik im ehemaligen Jugoslawien bewiesen."
13. Original text: "Die EU hat auch "nach Maastricht" keine wirklich eigenständige Außen—und Sicherheitspolitik entwickelt, wie das Kriegsdrama auf dem Balkan zur Genüge gezeigt hat. Mühsam wurde immer wieder versucht, unterschiedliche nationale Standpunkte auf einen Nenner zu bringen."
14. Original text: "Es nützt zum Beispiel wenig, wenn die britische und die deutsche Europa-Politik einander näherkommen—die eine Seite, weil sie dabei ist, ideologische Scheuklappen abzulegen, die andere, weil sie pragmatischer an die Integrationspolitik herangeht—aber das Weltmachtpotential Europas mehr von Wollen als von Können bestimmt wird. Wenn Europa Weltmacht sein will, muß sie sich mit allen Währungen der Macht in ausreichender Menge ausstatten."
15. Original text: Die EU ist immer noch auf der Suche nach ihrer verteidigungspolitischen Identität. Ihre Gemeinsame Außen—und Sicherheitspolitik ist bisher kaum mehr als ein Projekt. Der Europäische Rat und die Kommission konkurrieren um die Zuständigkeit auf diesem Gebiet, so dass die EU weit davon entfernt ist, mit einer Stimme zu sprechen. Eine europäische Eingreiftruppe, die im Falle einer akuten terroristischen Bedrohung auch "out of area" tätig werden kann, gibt es nicht."
16. Original text: "Eine Europaeische Verfassung wird gefordert—von Gegnern der Europaeischen Integration, um diese zu schwaechen, und von Anhaengern, um sie zu kraeftigen. Aber brauchen wir wirklich eine neue Verfassung fuer Europa? Und brauchen wir sie jetzt?"
17. Original text: "Mit dem Verfassungs-Kompromiss des Europäischen Konvents könne jeder leben, auch wenn keiner damit wirklich zufrieden sei. Ihn abzulehen sei "unakzeptabel". "Wir sind gemeinsam in der Verantwortung, das gemeinsame Europa zu schaffen", fügte Fischer hinzu."

18. Original text: "Der "Vertrag über eine Verfassung für Europa" soll den Bürgern der EU zur Quelle einer neuen, europäischen Identität werden. Diesem selbstgesetzten Anspruch wird der Text kaum gerecht. Den Verfassern fehlt es über weite Strecken an Mut, Geist und Feder. Andererseits stilisieren sie Europa selbstgefällig zu einer Wertegemeinschaft—gegen den Rest der Welt."

Bibliography

Abdelal, Rawi, Yoshiko Herrera, Alastair Johnston, and Rose McDermott. *Measuring Identity: A Guide for Social Scientists.* New York: Cambridge University Press, 2009.

Alesina, Alberto, and Francesco Giavazzi. *The Future of Europe: Reform or Decline.* Cambridge: MIT Press, 2006.

Anderson, Benedict. *Imagined Communities: Reflections on the Origin and Spread of Nationalism.* London: Verso, 1991.

Anderson, Jeffrey. *German Unification and the Union of Europe: The Domestic Politics of Integration Policy.* New York: Cambridge University Press, 1999.

Anderson, Peter, and Tony Weymouth. *Insulting the Public? The British Press and the European Union.* New York: Longman, 1999.

Ardagh, John. *Ireland and the Irish: Portrait of a Changing Society.* New York: Penguin Books, 1997.

Baker, David, and David Seawright. *Britain for and against Europe.* New York: Oxford University Press, 1998.

Banchoff, Thomas. "German identity and European integration," *European Journal of International Relations* 5(3) (2002): 259–289.

Baumann, Zygmunt. *The Individualized Society.* London: Polity Press, 2001.

Beiner, Ronald. *Theorizing Nationalism.* New York: SUNY Press, 1999.

Bloom, William. "Identity Negotiation: Where Two Roads Meet," *Journal of Personality and Social Psychology* 53(2) (1987): 1038–1053.

Bloom, William. *Personal Identity, National Identity, and International Relations.* New York: Cambridge University Press, 1990.

Breakwell, Glynis, and Evanthia Lyons, eds. *Changing European Identities: Social psychological Analyses of Social Change.* Oxford: Butterworth-Heinemann, 1996.

Breuilly, John. *Nationalism and the State.* Chicago: University of Chicago Press, 1994.

Brubaker, Rogers. *Nationalism Reframed: Nationhood and the National Question in the New Europe.* Cambridge: Cambridge University Press, 1996.

Brubaker, Rogers, and Frederick Cooper. "Beyond 'Identity.'" *Theory and Society* 29(1) (2000): 1–47.

Bruland, Peter, and Michael Horowitz. "Research Report on the Use of Identity Concepts in Comparative Politics," Harvard Identity Project, Harvard University, 2003. http://www.wcfia.harvard.edu/sites/default/files/identity_ComparativeReport.pdf.

Bruter, Michael. "Winning Hearts and Minds for Europe: The Impact of News and Symbols on Civic and Cultural European Identity," *Comparative Political Studies* 36(10) (2003): 1148–1179.

———. "On What Citizens Mean by Feeling 'European': Perception of News, Symbols, and Borderless-ness," *Journal of Ethnic and Migration Studies* 30(1) (2004): 21–40.

———. *Citizens of Europe? The Emergence of a Mass European Identity*. New York: Palgrave, 2005.

Bryder, Tom. "A Contribution from Political Psychology." In *European Commission: Forward Studies Unit*, edited by Janson Thomas. *Reflections on European Identity* (1999).

Burgess, Peter. "What's So European about the European Union? Legitimacy between Institution and Identity." *European Journal of Social Theory* 5(4) (2002): 467–481.

Calhoun, Craig. *Nations Matter: Culture, History, and the Cosmopolitan Dream*. New York: Routledge, 2007.

Caporaso, James. *The European Union: Dilemmas of Regional Integration*. Boulder: Westview, 2000.

Carey, Sean. "Undivided Loyalties: Is National Identity an Obstacle to European Integration?" *European Union Politics* 3(4) (2002): 387–413.

Carrera, Sergio, and Elsbeth Guild. *The French Presidency's European Pact on Immigration and Asylum: Intergovernmentalism vs. Europeanisation? Security vs. Rights?* CEPS Policy Brief (2008). http://shop.ceps.eu/BookDetail.php?item_id=1706.

Cederman, Lars-Erik. "Nationalism and Bounded Integration: What It Would Take to Construct a European Demos," In *European Journal of International Relations* 7(2) (2001): 139–174.

Cerutti, Furio, and Enno Rudolph. *A Soul for Europe*. Sterling, VA: Peeters Leuven, 2001.

Checkel, Jeffrey. *International Institutions and Socialization in Europe*. New York: Cambridge University Press, 2007.

———. "Why Comply? Social Learning and European Identity Change." *International Organization* 55(3) (2001): 553–588.

———. *Norms, Institutions, and National Identity in Contemporary Europe*. Arena working paper, WP 98/16, 1998.

Checkel, Jeffrey, and Peter Katzenstein, eds. *European Identity*. New York: Oxford University Press (2009).

Christiansen, Thomas, Knud Erik Jorgensen, and Antje Wiener, eds. *The Social Construction of Europe*. Thousand Oaks: Sage, 2001.

Chryssochoou, Dimitri. *Theorizing European Integration*. New York: Sage, 2001.

Connor, Walker. *Ethnonationalism: The Quest for Understanding*. New Jersey: Princeton University Press, 1994.

Conversi, Daniele, ed. *Ethnonationalism in the Contemporary World*. New York: Routledge, 2002.

Cottey, Andrew. *Security in the New Europe*. New York: Palgrave, 2007.

Csergo, Zsusa, and James Goldgeier. "Nationalist Strategies and European Integration." *Perspectives on Politics* 2(1) (2004): 21–39.

Davidson-Schmich, Louise. *Becoming Party Politicians.* Notre Dame: University of Notre Dame Press, 2007.

Davies, Norman. *Europe: A History.* New York: Oxford University Press, 1998.

De Bardeleben, Joan, and Achim Hurrelmann, eds. *Democratic Dilemmas of Multilevel Governance: Legitimacy, Representation, and Accountability in the European Union.* New York: Palgrave, 2007.

DeVreese, Claes. "Europe in the News: A Cross-National Comparative Study of the News Coverage of Key EU Events." *European Union Politics* 2(3) (October 2001): 283–307.

Delanty, Gerard. *Inventing Europe: Idea, Identity, Reality.* New York: St. Martin's Press, 1995.

Delgado-Moreira, Juan. "Cultural Citizenship and the Creation of European Identity." *Electronic Journal of Sociology* (March 29, 2005). www.sociology.org/content/vol002.003/delgado.html.

Dinan, Desmond. *Ever Closer Union?* Boulder: Lynne-Rienner, 1999.

Duff, Andrew, John Pinder, and Roy Pryce. *Maastricht and Beyond.* New York: Routledge, 1994.

Dyson, Kenneth, and Klaus Goetz. *Germany, Europe, and the Politics of Constraint.* New York: Oxford University Press, 1999.

Díez-Medrano, Juan. *Framing Europe: Attitudes toward European Integration in Germany, Spain, and the United Kingdom.* Princeton, CA: Princeton University Press, 2003.

Díez-Medrano, Juan, and Paula Gutierrez. "Nested Identities: National and European Identity in Spain." *Ethnic and Racial Studies* 24(5) (2001): 753–778.

Dunkerley, David, Lesley Hodgson, Tony Spybey, Stanislaw Konopacki, and Andrew Thompson. *Changing Europe: Identities, Nations and Citizens.* New York: Routledge, 2002.

Drulak, Petr. "Introduction: The Return of Identity into European Politics." Working paper, www.euintegration.net, March 28, 2004.

Economist. "A Survey of Ireland." 2004.

———. "Fit at 50? A Special Report on the European Union." 2007.

Eberstadt, Nicholas, and Hans Groth. "Healthy Old Europe." *Foreign Affairs* (May/June 2007): 55–68.

Eder, Klaus, and Hans-Joerg Trenz. In *Debating the Democratic Legitimacy of the European Union,* Beate Kohler-Koch and Berthold Rittberger. New York: Rowman & Littlefield, 2007.

Eichenberg, Richard, and Russel Dalton. "The Welfare State and the Transformation of Citizen Support for European Integration, 1973–2002." Working paper, Center for West European Studies, University of Pittsburgh, 2003.

European Commission, Public Opinion Analysis Sector. Eurobarometer homepage: http://europa.eu.int/comm/public_opinion. Databases available (107, 306)

European Commission, Public Opinion Analysis Sector. "European Competitiveness Report 2001." June 25, 2005. http://europa.eu.int/comm/enterprise/enterprise_policy/competitiveness/doc/competitiveness_report_2001.

———. European Commission, Delegation in the USA, 2005. http://www.eurunion.org/partner/SocSecForumSumm.htm.

———. "How Europeans See Themselves." Luxembourg: Office for Official Publications of the European Communities (2000).

———. "Copenhagen Declaration on European Identity." *Bulletin of the European Communities* 12 (1973): 118–122.

———. "Demographic Change: The Regional Dimension." 2007. http://ec.europa.eu/employment_social/soc-prot/ageing/news/people_in_europe_en.pdf. European Council. "Conclusions of the December 2007 Meeting." http://www.consilium.europa.eu/ueDocs/cms_Data/docs/pressData/en/ec/97669.pdf.

Euractiv.com. Interview with founder Christophe Leclerqc on EU Communication. 2005. http://www.euractiv.com/Article?tcmuri=tcm:29–142254–16&type=Interview.

Eurostat. News Release 184/2008. http://epp.eurostat.ec.europa.eu/cache/ITY_PUBLIC/3–16122009-BP/EN/3–16122009-BP-EN.PDF.

Eurunion Delegation of the European Commission in the USA. 2005. http://www.eurunion.org/partner/SocSecForumSumm.html.

European Citizens' Consultations Report. 2007. http://www.european-citizens-consultations.eu.

EU Observer. "Wallstrom: EU Needs a Commissioner for Citizens." 2009. http://euobserver.com/9/28598.

Fairclough, Norman. *Analyzing Discourse: Textual Analysis for Social Research.* New York: Routledge, 2003.

Fitzgerald, Garret. *Reflections on the Irish State.* Portland, OR: Irish Academic Press, 2003.

Friedman, Thomas. *The World Is Flat.* New York: Farrar, Straus & Giroux, 2005.

Follesdal, Andreas. "EU Legitimacy and Normative Political Theory." In *Palgrave Advances in European Union Studies,* edited by M. Cini and A. Bourne. New York: Palgrave, 2006.

Gabel, Matthew. "Public Support for European Integration: An Empirical Test of Five Theories." *The Journal of Politics* 60(2) (1998): 333–354.

Gaskell, George, and Martin Bauer. *Qualitative Interviewing with text, Image, and Sound.* Thousand Oaks, CA: Sage, 2000.

Gellner, Ernst. *Nations and Nationalism.* Oxford: Blackwell, 1983.

Giddens, Anthony. *Runaway World: How Globalization Is Reshaping Our Lives.* London: Profile Books, 2002.

Gilland, Karen. "The Party Politics of Euroscepticism in Ireland." Paper presented at the Joint Session for the European Consortium of Political Research, Turin, Italy, 2002.

Gillespie, Paul, and Brigid Laffan. "European Identity: Theory and Empirics." In *Palgrave Advances in European Union Studies,* edited by Michelle Cini and Angela Bourne. New York: Palgrave, 2006.

Graumann, Karl. "Soziale Identitäten." In *Kultur, Identität, Europa: Über die Schwierigkeiten und Möglichkeiten einer Konstruktion*, edited by Segers Viehoff, 59–74. Frankfurt/Main: Suhrkamp, 1999.

Goff, Patricia, and Kevin Dunn, eds. *Identity and Global Politics.* New York: Palgrave, 2004.

Groothues, Fritz. "Imagine: A European Identity." 2003. www.opendemocracy.net.

Guibernau, Montserrat. *Nationalisms: The Nation-State and Nationalism in the Twentieth Century.* Cambridge: Polity Press, 1996.

Habermas, Jürgen. *Post-National Constellation.* Cambridge: Polity Press/MIT, 2001.

Hall, Rodney Bruce. *National Collective Identity.* New York: Columbia University Press, 1998.

Hall, Stuart, and Paul DuGay. *Questions of Cultural Identity.* New York: Sage, 1996.

Handwerker, Penn. *Quick Ethnography.* New York: Rowman & Littlefield, 2001.

Harenberg Staatslexikon. *Grossbritannien.* Dortmund, Germany: Harenberg, 2000.

Hardt-Mautner, Gerlinde. "How Does One Become a Good European? The British Press and European Integration." *Discourse and Society* 6(2) (1995): 177–205.

Hayes, Carleton. *The Historical Evolution of Modern Nationalism.* New York: Macmillan, 1955.

Held, David. *A Globalizing World: Culture, Economics, Politics.* New York: Routledge, 2000.

Herrmann, Richard, Thomas Risse, and Marilynn Brewer. *Transnational Identities: Becoming European in the EU.* Lanham: Rowman & Littlefield, 2004.

Heurlin, Bertel, ed. *Germany in Europe in the Nineties.* New York: St. Martin's Press, 1996.

Hix, Simon, and Klaus Goetz, eds. *Europeanized Politics? European Integration and National Political Systems.* Portland, OR: Frank Kass, 2001.

Hobsbawm, Erik. *Race, Nation, Class: Ambiguous Identities.* London: Verso, 1991.

Hogg, Michael, and Dominic Abrams. *Social Identifications.* New York: Routledge, 1988.

Holmes, Martin. *The Eurosceptical Reader* 2. New York: Palgrave, 2002.

Horowitz, Donald. "The Primordialists." In *Ethnonationalism in the Contemporary World*, edited by Daniele Conversi, 72–82. New York: Routledge, 2002.

Hurrelmann, Achim. "Should There Be a Transnational Theory of European Integration?" Paper presented at the European Union Studies Association, Los Angeles, 2009.

Hurrelmann, Achim, Hartmut Wessler, and Stefan Leibfried. *Public Deliberation and Public Culture*, New York: Palgrave, 2008.

Hooghe, Lisbeth, and Gary Marks. "Europe's Blues: Theoretical Soul-Searching after the Rejection of the European Constitution." *Political Science and Politics* 39 (2006): 247–50.

Imig, Doug, and Sidney Tarrow, eds. *Contentious Europeans: Protest and Politics in an Emerging Polity*. Lanham: Rowman & Littlefield, 2001.

Ingraham, Jeson. "The European Union and Relationships within Ireland." 1998. Conflict Archive on the Internet, Web Archive, http://cain.ulst.ac.uk/issues/europe/euireland.htm.

Ignazi, Piero. *Extreme Right Parties in Western Europe*. New York: Oxford University Press, 2003.

Jolly, Seth Kincaid. "Mediating European Integration in the 1990s: National Identity and Economics in France and Ireland." Working paper. Berea: Centre College, 1998.

Jupille, Joseph, James Caporaso, and Jeffrey Checkel. "Integrating Institutions: Rationalism, Constructivism and the Study of the European Union." *Comparative Political Studies*, 36 (2003): 7–40.

Kaelberer, Matthias. "The Euro and European Identity: Symbols, Power, and the Politics of European Monetary Union." *Review of International Studies* 30(2) (2004): 161–178.

Kaiser, Wilhelm, and Peter Starie. *Transnational European Union: Towards a Common Political Space*. New York: Routledge, 2005.

Karp, Regina. "Identities and Structural Change Since the End of the Cold War: Germany, Europe, and the Limits of Integration." *International Politics* 40(4) (2003): 527–558.

Karolewski, Pawel, and Victoria Kaina, eds. *European Identity: Theoretical Perspectives and Empirical Insights*. New Brunswick: Transaction Publishers, 2006.

Karlsson, Ingmar. "How to Define the European Identity Today and in the Future." In *Reflections on European Identity*, edited by Thomas Janson. European Commission, Forward Studies Unit, 1999.

Katzenstein, Peter, ed. *The Culture of National Security: Norms and Identity in World Politics*. New York: Columbia University Press, 1996.

Keohane, Robert, and Josepheds Nye. *Transnational Relations and World Politics*. Cambridge: Harvard University Press, 1971.

Kevin, Deidre. *Europe in the Media: A Comparison of Reporting, Representation, and Rhetoric in National Media Systems in Europe*. Mahaw: Lawrence Erlbaum, 2003.

Kitschelt, Herbert, and Wolfgang Streek, eds. *Germany: Beyond the Stable State*. Portland, OR: Frank Cass, 2004.

Kohli, Martin. "The Battlegrounds of European Identity." *European Societies* 12(2) (2000): 113–137.

Kraus, Peter. *A Union of Diversity*. New York: Cambridge University Press, 2008.

Krause, Jill, and Neil Renwick, eds. *Identities in International Relations*. New York: St. Martin's Press, 1996.

Kriesi, Hanspeter. *Nation and National Identity: The European Experience in Perspective*. Bern, Switzerland: Ruegger, 1999.

Lapid, Yosef, and Friedrich Kratochwil. *The Return of Culture and Identity in IR*. Boulder, CO: Lynne Rienner, 1996.

Laqueur, Walter. *Europe in Our Time*. New York: Penguin, 1992.

Lee, Nick, and Rolland Munro. *The Consumption of Mass*. Malden: Blackwell, 2001.

Leiken, Robert. "Europe's Angry Muslims." *Foreign Affairs* (July/August 2005). www.cfr.org.

Lepsius, Rainer. "Die Europäische Union: Ökonomisch-politische Integration und kulturelle Pluralität." In: *Kultur, Identität, Europa: Über die Schwierigkeiten und Moeglichkeiten einer Konstruktion*, edited by Segers Viehoff, 223–252. Frankfurt/Main: Suhrkamp, 1999.

Lesaar, Henrik Richard. "Semper Idem? The Relationship of European and National Identities." Paper presented at the "National vs. European Identity" conference in Prague, 2000. www.euintegration.net.

Liebert, Ulrike. "The Gendering of Euroscepticism: Public Discourses and Support to the EU in a Cross-National Comparison." Working paper for the Institute of European Studies, 1997.

Loth, Wilfried. "Identity and Statehood in the Process of European Integration." *Journal of European Integration*, 6(1) 2000: 22–43.

Maclean, Mairi, and Jean-Marc Trouille, eds. *France, Germany, and Britain*. New York: Palgrave, 2001.

Magnette, Paul, and Kalypso Nicolaïdis. "The European Convention: Bargaining in the Shadow of Rhetoric." *West European Politics* 27(3) (2004): 381–404.

Majone, Giandomenico. *The Referendum Threat, the Rationally Ignorant Voter, and the Political Culture of the EU*. Working online paper, April 2009. Reconstituting Democracy in Europe (RECON) Project. http://www.reconproject.eu.

Marchetti, Andreas. "Turkey and the Finality Geographiqué of the EU." *ZEI EU-Turkey Monitor*, Vol. 2, No. 2 (August 2006). http://www.zei.de/download/zei_tur/ZEI_EU-Turkey-Monitor_vol2no2.pdf.

Marks, Gary, and Liesbt Hooghe. "National Identity and Support for European Integration." Discussion paper SP IV 202. Berlin: Wissenschaftszentrum fuer Sozialforschung, 2003.

———. "Does Identity or Economic Rationality Drive Public Opinion on European Integration?" *Political Science Online* (July 2004). www.apsanet.org.

Marks, Gary, and Marko Steenbergen. *European Integration and Political Conflict*. New York: Cambridge University Press, 2004.

Mayer, Franz, and Jan Palmowski. "European Identities and the EU: The Ties That Bind the People Together." *Journal of Common Market Studies* 42(3) (2004): 573–598.

McCormick, John. *Understanding the European Union*. New York: Palgrave, 2002.

McLaren, Lauren. "Opposition to European Integration and Fear of Loss of National Identity: Debunking a Basic Assumption Regarding Hostility to the Integration Project." *European Journal of Political Research* 43 (2004): 895–911.

Michalski, Anna, and Jonas Tallberg. "Project on European Integration Indicators." Working paper, European Commission Forward Studies Unit, 1999.

Moravcsik, Andrew. *Choice for Europe: Social Purpose and State Power from Messina to Maastricht*. Ithaca, NY: Cornell University Press, 1998.

Moravcsik, Andrew. "Europe without Illusions." Paper presented at the Third Spaak Foundation-Harvard University Conference, Brussels, 2002.

Münch, Reinhard. *Nation and Citizenship in the Global Age*. New York: Palgrave, 2001.

Moxon-Browne, Edward, ed. *Who Are the Europeans Now?* Burlington: Ashgate, 2004.

Mushaben, Joyce. "Rethinking Citizenship and Identity Since the Fall of the Wall" *German Politics* 19(1) (2010): 72–88.

Nelson, Brent, James Guth, and Cameron Fraser. "Does Religion Matter? Christianity and Public Support for the European Union." *European Union Politics* 2(2) (2001): 191–217.

Neumann, Iver B. *Uses of the Other: The East in European Identity Formation*. Minneapolis: University of Minnesota Press, 1998.

Niedermayer, Oscar, and Richard Sinnott, eds. *Public Opinion and Internationalized Governance*. From the series *Beliefs in Government* 2. New York: Oxford University Press, 1995.

Oezkirimli, Umut. *Theories of Nationalism: A Critical Introduction*. New York: St. Martin's Press, 2000.

Panebianco, Stefania. "European Citizenship and European Identity: From the Treaty of Maastricht to Public Opinion Attitudes." Jean Monnet working paper No. 3/96 (1996).

Papadopolous, Constantine. "Why Nobody Loves Europe." *Europe's World* (March 2008).

Parsons, Craig, and Timothy Smeeding. *Immigration and the Transformation of Europe*. New York: Cambridge University Press, 2006.

Passerini, Luisa. *Images of Europe*. Florence: European University Institute, 2000.

Padgett, Stephen, William E. Paterson, and Gordon R. Smith. *Developments in German Politics*. Durham, NC: Duke University Press, 2003.

Paul, T.V., John Ikenberry, and John Hall. *The Nation-State in Question*. Princeton: Princeton University Press, 2003.

Perry, Robert, and John Robertson. *Comparative Analysis of Nations: Quantitative Approaches*. Boulder, CO: Westview, 2002.

Pichler, Florian. "Affection to and Exploitation of Europe." Sociological series paper. Vienna, Austria: Institute for Advanced Studies, 2005.

Preston, Peter. *Political/Cultural Identity: Citizens and Nations in a Global Era*. Thousand Oaks, CA: Sage, 1997.

Rawls, John. *Political Liberalism*. New York: Columbia University Press, 1993.

Reif, Karlheinz. "Cultural Convergence and Cultural Diversity as Factors in European Identity." In *European Identity and the Search for Legitimacy*, edited by Soledad Garcia. London: Pinter, 1993.

Reif, Karlheinz, and Ronald Inglehart. *Eurobarometer: The Dynamics of European Public Opinion*. New York: St. Martin's Press, 1991.

Renwick, Neil. "Re-Reading Europe's Identities." In *Identities in International Relations*, Jill Krause and Neil Renwick. New York: St. Martin's Press, 1996.

Risse, Thomas. *A Community of Europeans? Transnational Identities and Public Spheres*. Ithaca, NY: Cornell University Press, 2010.

Risse, Thomas. "The Euro between National and European Identity." *Journal of European Public Policy* 10(4) (2003): 487–505.

———. *Bringing Transnational Relations Back In*. New York: Cambridge University Press, 1995.

———. "A European Identity? Europeanization and the Evolution of Nation-State Identities." In *Transforming Europe: Europeanization and Domestic Change*, edited by Maria G. Cowles, James Caporaso, and Thomas Risse, 198–216. Ithaca, NY: Cornell University Press, 2001.

———. "An Emerging European Public Sphere? Theoretical Clarifications and Empirical Indicators." Paper for the European Union Studies Association Conference, Nashville, 2003.

Risse, Thomas, and Matthias Maier. *Europeanization, Collective Identities, and Public Discourses*. IDNET Thematic Network. Florence, Italy: Robert Schuman Center for Advanced Studies, 2003.

Rosamund, Ben. *Theories of European Integration*. New York: Palgrave, 2002.

Ross, George. *Jacques Delors and European Integration*. New York: Oxford University Press, 1995.

Ruiz-Jimenez, Antonia. "Representations of Europe and the Nation: How do Spaniards See Themselves as Nationals and Europeans?" Jean Monnet/Robert Schuman Working Paper Series, Miami: Miami EU Center, 2004.

Ruggie, John Gerard. "What Makes the World Hang Together?" *International Organization* 52(4) (1998): 855–885.

Rusconi, Gian Enrico. "The Difficulty in Building a European Identity." *The International Spectator* 23 (1) (1998): 23–26.

Sassen, Saskia. "The Repositioning of Citizenship and Alienage Emergent Subjects and Spaces for Politics." In *Migration, Citizenship, Ethnos*, Michal Bodemann and Goekce Yurdakul. New York: Palgrave, 2006.

Schain, Martin, and Mabel Berezin. *Europe without Borders: Remapping Identity, Citizenship, and Identity in a Transnational Age*. Baltimore: John Hopkins Press, 2003.

Schmitt, Herrmann, and Jacques Thomassen. "Dynamic Representation and European Integration." Working paper, Mannheimer Zentrum fuer europaeische Sozialforschung, Nr. 21, (2000).

Schimmelfennig, Frank. *The Politics of European Union Enlargement: Theoretical Approaches*. New York: Routledge, 2005.

Serfati, Simon, ed. *The European Finality Debate and Its National Dimensions*. Washington, DC: CSIS Press, 2003.

Shore, Cris. *Building Europe: The Cultural Politics of European Integration*. New York: Routledge, 2000.

Smith, Anthony. *Chosen Peoples: Sacred Sources of National Identity*. New York: Oxford University Press, 2003.

———. *Theories of Nationalism*. London: Duckworth, 1983.

———. *National Identity*. London: Penguin, 1991.

———. *Nations and Nationalism in a Global Era*. Cambridge: Polity Press, 1995.

———. "National Identity and the Idea of European Unity." In *International Affairs* 68(1) (1992): 55–76.

Snyder, Louis. *The New Nationalism*. Ithaca, NY: Cornell University Press, 1968.

Spencer and Wollman. *Nationalism: A Critical Introduction*. Thousand Oaks, CA: Sage, 2002.

Stern-Gillet, Suzanne, and Teresa Lunati, eds. *Historical, Socio-Political and Economic Perspectives on Europe*. Lewinston: Edwin Mellen Press, 2000.

Strath, Bo. *Europe and the Other and Europe as the Other*. Brussels: Presses Europeennes, 2000.

Stutzmann, Alexandre. "Europe's Fake ID." *Foreign Policy* 38(1) (2001): 94.

Sunday Tribune, "80 pc want tougher immigration rules", Aine Hegharty, May 10, 2005.

Swann, W.B. "Identity Negotiation: Where Two Roads Meet." *Journal of Personality and Social Psychology* 53 (1987): 1038–1053.

Taggart, Paul, and Aleks Szczeriak. "Supporting the Union? Euroscepticism and the Politics of Integration." In *Developments in the European Union* 2, Maria Green Cowles and Desmond Dinan. New York: Palgrave, 2004.

Tashakkori, Abbas, and Charles Teddlie. *Mixed Methodology*. Thousand Oaks, CA: Sage, 1998.

Tajfel, Henry. *Social Identity and Intergroup Relations*. New York: Cambridge University Press, 1982.

Thiel, Markus "Transnational Actors", In: *International Studies Association Compendium*, Robert Denemark (ed). Hoboken, NJ: Wiley/Blackwell, 2009.

Thiel, Markus. "Transnational Actors." In: Denemark, Robert (ed). *International Studies Compendium*. Hoboken, NJ: Blackwell-Wiley, 2009.

Thiel, Markus, and Roger Coate, eds. *Identity Politics in the Age of Globalization*. Boulder, CO: First Forum Press, 2010.

Thiel, Markus, and Lisa Prügl, eds. *Diversity in the European Union*. New York: Palgrave, 2009.

Tilly, Charles. *The Formation of National States in Western Europe*. Princeton: Princeton University Press, 1975.

Treaty on European Union. Consolidated version, 2006. http://eur-lex.europa.eu/LexUriServ/LexUriServ.do?uri=OJ:C:2006:321E:0001:0331:EN:PDF.

Trenz, Hans-Jörg. Conceptualising the European Public Sphere: The Europeanisation of political communication: conceptual clarifications and empirical measurements, in: In Cristiano, Bee & Emanuela, Bozzini (ed.), *Mapping the European Public Sphere*. New York: Ashgate, 2010, pp. 15–31.

Trenz, Hans-Jörg. *In Search of Popular Subjectness*, Arena Working Paper 7, 2009. http://www.arena.uio.no/publications/working-papers2009/papers/WP_07_09.pdf.

Trenz, Hans-Jörg. Digital Media and the Return of the Representative Public Sphere, *Javnost-The Public*, Vol. 16, 1, pp. 33-46.

United Nations High Commissioner for Refugees (UNHCR). *Climate Change and Displacement: The Time Is Now*. 2009. http://www.unhcr.org/496e052e2.html.

Van Ham, Peter. *European Integration and the Postmodern Condition*. New York: Routledge, 2001.

Van Ham, Peter. *Social Power in International Politics.* New York: Routledge, 2010.

Voltmer, Katrin, and Christiane Eilders. "The Media Agenda: The Marginalization and Domestication of Europe." In *Germany, Europe, and the Politics of Constraint,* Kenneth Dyson et al. New York: Oxford University Press, 2003.

Waever, Ole. "European Security Identities." *Journal of Common Market Studies* 34(1) (1996): 103–132.

Ward, David. *European Union Democratic Deficit and the Public Sphere: An Evaluation of EU Media Policy.* Washington, DC: IOS Press, 2002.

Weiler, Joseph H.H. "European Democracy and the Principle of Constitutional Tolerance: The Soul of Europe." In *A soul for Europe,* Enno Cerruti. Sterling, VA: Peeters Leuven, 2001.

Wessler, Hartmut, Bernd Peters, and Stefanie Sifft. *Transnationalization of Public Spheres.* New York: Palgrave, 2008.

Wendt, Alexander. *Social Theory of International Politics.* Cambridge: Cambridge University Press, 1999.

White, Timothy. "Nationalism vs. Liberalism in the Irish Context: From a Postcolonial Past to a Postmodern Future." *Eire-Ireland Journal of Irish Studies* (2002).

Wiener, Antje. "Constructivism and Sociological Institutionalism." In *Palgrave Advances in European Union Studies,* edited by Michelle Cini and Angela Bourne. New York: Palgrave, 2006.

Wintle, Michael. *Culture and Identity in Europe: Perceptions of Divergence and Unity in Past and Present.* Brookfield: Ashgate, 2002.

Witte, Bruno de. "Building Europe's Image and Identity." In *Europe from a Cultural Perspective,* Albert Rijksbaron. The Hague, Netherlands: Nijgh and Van Ditmar Universitair, 1987.

Yaffee, Robert, and Monnie McGee. *An Introduction to Time-Series Analysis and Forecasting, with Applications of SAS and SPSS.* New York: Academic Press, 2001.

Zaller, John. *The Nature and Origins of Mass Opinion.* New York: Cambridge University Press, 1992.

Index

Note: Page numbers in **bold** refer to in-depth treatment of the indexed topic.